POLITICAL PARTICIPATION
IN LATIN AMERICA

Volume I
Citizen and State

POLITICAL PARTICIPATION IN LATIN AMERICA

Volume I
Citizen and State

EDITED BY
**JOHN A. BOOTH AND
MITCHELL A. SELIGSON**

HM

HOLMES & MEIER PUBLISHERS, INC.
NEW YORK   LONDON

First published in the United States of America 1978 by
Holmes & Meier Publishers, Inc.
30 Irving Place
New York, New York 10003

Great Britain:
Holmes & Meier Publishers, Ltd.
Hillview House
1, Hallswelle Parade, Finchley Road
London NW11 ODL

Copyright © 1978 by Holmes & Meier Publishers, Inc.

LIBRARY OF CONGRESS CATALOGING IN PUBLICATION DATA
Main entry under title:

Citizen and State (Political Participation in Latin America; v. 1)
    Papers of a conference sponsored by the University of
Texas at San Antonio and held at the University's Lutcher
Conference Center, Nov. 12–13, 1976.
    Bibliography: p.
    Includes index.
    1. Political participation—Latin America—Congresses.
I. Booth, John A.   II. Seligson, Mitchell A.   III. University
of Texas at San Antonio. IV. Series.
JL967.A2P64 vol. 1   320.9′8′003   77-16666
ISBN 0-8419-0334-4
0-8419-0376-X pbk.

MANUFACTURED IN THE UNITED STATES OF AMERICA

Contents

Preface

The idea for this volume grew out of our own frustration with the lack of literature on political participation in Latin America. In the process of writing a joint paper on this subject, we found ourselves unable to recall more than a very limited number of books and articles which dealt directly with the topic. As a result we spent a number of weeks in the library attempting to strengthen our backgrounds in the literature. We both emerged with the same conclusion: little was to be found other than generalizations regarding the political involvement of Latin American masses. Seeing that considerable work needed to be done in the area, we dedicated ourselves to stimulating the effort. We eventually decided that the most appropriate way to do this would be to hold a conference on the subject and, with the early encouragement of Richard Newbold Adams and James M. Malloy, bent our efforts to that end.

The format of the resulting seminar—Faces of Participation in Latin America: A New Look at Citizen Action in Society—emerged slowly. Throughout 1974 we refined our thoughts on the direction of the conference and contacted many scholars doing work on this subject. One crucial decision at this point was that we would not confine the meeting to members of our own discipline (political science) but would open it to all branches of social science. This proved to be a fortuitous decision since some of the most exciting interchanges which emerged during and after the seminar came from the confrontation of different disciplines focusing on the same problem; the clashes of approach, methodology, and interpretation shed more light on the subject than we could possibly have hoped. Another major decision related to the selection of panelists. We wanted scholars who were actively engaged in research on political participation; we were not looking for warmed-over reports, but for genuinely new perspectives. As a consequence we cast our net broadly, contacting junior scholars only months away from their field work as well as noted senior scholars.

Beyond the question of conferee selection, another central concern in planning the conference was to provide a common basis for discussion. All too often we had attended academic meetings and panels where most of the panelists appeared to be uncertain of the central theme to be discussed. With each letter of invitation we enclosed an explanation of what we hoped to accomplish at the conference and included a thematic guideline around which we hoped the scholars would organize their papers. Once the final list of panelists was determined, we sent to each one a lengthy essay detailing the central areas of investigation and providing extensive bibliographic citation.

We hope that the present volume reflects our efforts in organizing the conference. The papers included have been written by some outstanding senior scholars as well as very promising junior scholars. More importantly, we feel that although the papers deal with a wide range of nations and many different forms of participation, taken together they form a unified whole; the papers speak *to* each other, rather than at each other as is frequently the case in edited volumes. The reader should not be surprised, however, to find strong disagreement among the views expressed. Many of the authors came to the conference with points of view in direct conflict with those held by others; many left the conference and revised their papers for inclusion in this volume with those views still intact, but more cognizant than before of opposing views. Ironically, both such differences of opinion and the overall cohesion of the volume derived from the fact that the whole enterprise was self-critical; authors have had to defend themselves against vigorous challenges thrown at them by the conferees, the discussants, and the editors themselves. We are convinced that all of the papers have been markedly improved by this process.

We have organized the volume into three sections. Part I, "The Theory of Political Participation," deals primarily with such conceptual issues as the definition of participation and its technical and normative significance for political systems. Part II, "The Citizen and Participation," examines citizen involvement in politics from the perspective of the individual, dealing with the great variety of modes, structures, levels, and constraints of participation in Latin American nations. The articles in Part III, "Participation and the State," treat the interaction between participating citizens and the formal governments of the region, devoting special attention to the policy impact of participation and to efforts by the state to manipulate citizen action.

We believe that students and scholars alike will find a bibliography a most welcome aid in pursuing further research on political participation. Thus we have combined all of the citations used in the contributions in the collected bibliography.

The success of the seminar on the Faces of Participation and the scholarly contribution which we hope this volume makes are fundamentally a product of the conferees themselves. In addition to those individuals whose papers appear here, the following scholars also presented papers: Richard Newbold Adams, Reynold Bloom, Susan C. Bourque, John T. Fishel, Bobby M. Gierisch, Thomas C. Greaves, Donna J. Guy, Howard Handelman, Henry A. Landsberger, Brian Loveman, Cynthia McClintock, Roberto Varela, and Kay B. Warren. Many of their papers will appear in a companion volume (Seligson and Booth, *Political Participation in Latin America*, volume 2: *Politics and the Poor*, forthcoming). Chairpersons and discussants for the various sessions were: Carlos Astiz, Wilber Chaffee, Torcuato S. Di Tella, Antonio Mitre,

Guy Poitras, Karl M. Schmitt, Antonio Ugalde, and Maria Luisa Urdaneta. Assistance at the conference was provided by Jody Goode, Roberto Hinojosa, and Beverly Schwartzman; our bibliography and manuscript preparation profited from the careful efforts of Mandy Braid and Ann Russell. We thank them all.

The meeting which took place on November 12 and 13, 1976, was held at the University of Texas at San Antonio's Lutcher Conference Center. The seminar was sponsored by UTSA.

Additional support for the seminar and the editing of the proceedings came from the Institute of Government Research of the University of Arizona, the Division of Social Sciences of the University of Texas at San Antonio, the Latin American Studies Association, and the Border States University Consortium on Latin America. Professor Di Tella's visit was made possible by the Distinguished Lectureship Program of the Latin American Center of the University of Arizona. We are deeply appreciative to all of these institutions for their support.

In all our collaborations we have followed the practice of alternating our names in the initial position to allow each of us equal recognition in citations. In this volume, its companion, and all our jointly written papers, we have each made a full and equal contribution to the finished product.

J. A. B.
San Antonio, Texas

M.A.S.
Tucson, Arizona
December 5, 1977

In memory of our parents
Allan and Grace Booth
Morris and Ethel Seligson

I
The Theory of Political Participation

Five conflicting images dominate the scholarly literature on political participation in Latin America. Booth and Seligson critically evaluate these images in light of recent research. They find that Latin American political participation is not characteristically violent. Neither are Latin Americans politically irrational. Increases in participation more often result from' government action than from forces beyond government control. Political activity is not severely limited, and levels of participation are similar to some First World nations. The wealthy do, to some extent, dominate participation and policymaking. The essay concludes by outlining a theory of political participation that integrates both individual and systemic perspectives.

1.
Images of
Political Participation
in Latin America

JOHN A. BOOTH and MITCHELL A. SELIGSON

Understanding the functioning of political systems requires accurate knowledge about the extent, scope, and nature of citizen political activity. Research in the United States (Woodward and Roper 1950; Berelson et al. 1954; Campbell et al. 1960; McClosky et al. 1960; Key 1966; Matthews and Prothro 1966) and in other industrialized nations has long focused on political participation. (For an extensive review and bibliography see Milbrath and Goel 1977.) Recently, the publication of several papers and monographs by a team headed by Sidney Verba and Norman Nie (Verba et al. 1971; Verba and Nie 1972; Verba et al. 1973; Kim et al. 1974) has promoted an increased interest in participation research. Unfortunately, however, even today political participation in Third World countries remains far too enigmatic, with research on Latin America being quite deficient.

A review of previous research and writings on political participation in Latin America reveals five confused and partly contradictory images: Scholars and other observers have characterized citizen activism as (1) predominantly

We wish to acknowledge with gratitude the comments of the panelists, discussants, and observers at the Seminar on the Faces of Participation in Latin America, San Antonio, Texas, November 12-13, 1976. That stimulating and critical discussion from a variety of disciplines and viewpoints contributed substantially to the development of this essay. We also gratefully acknowledge very helpful observations on an earlier draft of this essay by Thomas A. Baylis, Wilber A. Chaffee, Jr., Henry A. Dietz, Steven M. Neuse, and Karl M. Schmitt.

3

violent; (2) irrational; (3) increasingly widespread or mobilized; (4) extremely limited among the great majority of citizens; and (5) virtually monopolized by upper socioeconomic strata. We believe these images fall far short of accurately depicting citizen political action in the region. The nature of Latin American politics will remain obscure without careful scrutiny of the actions of citizens upon and within the state, and of the efforts of the state to manage, suppress, or respond to such actions. Because of these conflicting and incomplete images of Latin American citizen activism, we here report on the recent efforts of many scholars to shed some new light on the faces of participation.

One source of the confusion characteristic of much of the material published on Latin American political participation has been a tendency to approach the subject narrowly. Analysts traditionally have viewed citizen political activity as limited to electoral phenomena such as voting and party membership.[1] Thus defined, participation has been easily dismissed as insignificant in a region where authoritarian regimes suppress or manipulate both elections and parties. Such a narrow definition, we contend, has artificially constricted analysis, directing it away from many other kinds of activity of political importance. Latin Americanists are not alone in this respect, however. As several critics (Walker 1966; Berns 1968; Euben 1970; Pateman 1970; Salisbury 1975) have noted, a similarly restricted perspective has dominated most of the research on participation until a very few years ago.

But by no means have all scholarly efforts ignored or misunderstood political participation in Latin America. In fact, a number of studies have detailed citizen activism among various interest sectors. Analysis of Latin American politics by focusing on particular interest groups and social strata (Kling 1964, pp. 172-174; Ranis 1968a; Martz 1971) has produced comprehensive treatments of the military, organized labor, the middle classes, the Church, political parties, entrepreneurial elites, peasants, the urban poor, students, and large landholders. Such studies do reveal that the arena provided by electoral institutions is not the only, nor even the most important, realm of political action in Latin America. Nevertheless, such sectorial analysis has painted an incomplete picture of participation; intensively studying the parts has produced no clear account of the whole.

Some examples of research on political participation outside the electoral arena illustrate the importance of these contributions. Many studies have clearly demonstrated that Latin America's urban poor engage in numerous forms of political activism. Squatters organize themselves into community associations for planning invasions and for collective problem solving. And, what is more, poor communities pressure national and city officials for services—even in authoritarian political systems. (For example, see Ray 1969; Cornelius 1971; Portes 1971; 1972; Byars 1973, pp. 44-51; Roberts 1973; Dietz 1974; Handelman 1975a; and Moore 1977.) Organized workers have resorted both to such conventionally accepted behavior as lobbying public officials and to unconventional activities such as strikes and disruption in order to persuade policy makers to modify labor laws, minimum wage levels, and social security arrangements (for example, see Payne 1965; Wilkie 1970, pp. 182-189; Malloy 1977b). Anthropological community studies depict peasants often engaging in collective problem solving, organizational activity, and requesting governmental assistance with community problems (e.g., Adams 1959; Castillo 1964; Dobyns 1964; Doughty 1968; Richardson 1970; López Méndez 1974; McEwen 1975). The rural poor, supposedly condemned by poverty and tradition to political inaction, seem in many cases far from passive.

Such illustrations could continue at length, but to little further advantage. The major point stands out distinctly: looking beyond electoral phenomena will reveal a substantial amount of participation. However, the problem remains that research has not been systematic, but has generally dealt with political participation as a tangent to some other research enterprise. This problem calls for a more detailed and comprehensive study of political participation. The success of such an approach, however, requires conceptualizing political participation in a manner that can at once encompass the full richness and variety of citizen initiatives.

The authors have three principal objectives in this essay. First, we will suggest a definition of political participation so as to provide the basis for an analytical framework sufficiently broad to encompass most of the important forms of political participation. Second, we will evaluate critically the five aforementioned images of political participation in Latin America by reviewing the scholarly literature that advances each viewpoint and comparing it to the available empirical evidence. And third, we will suggest tentative guidelines for a general theory of political participation of utility for the Latin American case.

Defining Political Participation

Milbrath (1965, p. 1) has pointed out that a definition of politics and political participation must be narrow enough to avoid becoming "ubiquitous or universal," thereby losing its meaning. Of equal concern, however, is Verba and Nie's (1972, p. 2) caution that a definition not be too narrow. Since disputes over definitions usually wax fierce and lengthy and are seldom resolved,[2] we enter this passage between the Scylla of narrowness and the Charybdis of breadth with some trepidation.

Six issues commonly arise in discussions of the nature of political participation, issues which we might label as questions of action, support, efficacy, intentionality, governmental formalism, and conventionality.[3] The *action* question asks whether participation must consist of overt acts as opposed to perceptions, attitudes, or psychological orientations. The *support* question asks whether participation must be influential (that is, affect some policy choice) or may be merely supportive or ceremonial. The *efficacy* question concerns whether participation occurs even if the action fails to influence policy. The *intentionality* question asks whether political participation has occurred even if the actor did not conceive of his action as political. The *governmental formalism* question asks whether participation in politics can occur outside the realm of formal governmental institutions. The *conventionality* question asks whether to consider as participation only those actions that are legal, acceptable to elites, or channeled "within the system." After defining political participation, we will assess our definition by each of these points.

Our definition rests upon the notion of collective and public goods. While such a political economic treatment is not novel in the study of electoral behavior (Downs 1957; Tullock 1968; Czudnowski 1976), it is relatively new to the broader analysis of political participation in general, and especially in the field of Latin American politics (Chaffee 1976). *Collective goods* consist of goods that when supplied to one member of a collectivity cannot easily be denied to others of the same group. Collective goods are distinguished from private goods by the degree of control over their use which their supplier may exercise. While collective goods may not be easily denied to others once supplied to one, private goods may be so denied (Olson 1968, pp. 14-15).

Public goods, the focus of our definition, consist of a special type of collective goods provided by governments or by communities through governmental or community expenditure.[4] Streets, national security, and monetary systems provide classical examples of public goods. That is, they are supplied by governments and once in existence for one citizen may not be easily denied to others in a society. Analysts often overlook, however, that communities, too, (e.g., villages, neighborhoods) supply public goods, even though they may lack formal governments. Small towns and villages often provide themselves such public goods as roads, bridges, community centers, schools, and irrigation systems, through the collective expenditure of such resources as money, labor, and materials donated by residents.

Based on the above considerations, we define *political participation* as *behavior influencing or attempting to influence the distribution of public goods.* Thus, efforts by a citizen of a state or member of a community to affect the distribution of a public good constitute political participation. Our definition excludes attempts to influence the distribution of state-controlled private goods. Most such private goods consist of things like licenses or patents, etc., the consumption of which by an individual is normally controlled by their sale. To include state-controlled private goods within the scope of our definition would, we believe, excessively broaden the concept by applying the term political participation to a myriad of insignificant economic transactions. This distinction between public and private goods, and therefore between political participation and other behavior, bears further clarification. For example, the existence of a state-owned electrical utility or of a governmentally price-controlled commodity store in a region is a public good. This is so because their financing is collective and because *access* to such a service becomes nominally available for everyone once the basic facility is supplied. An effort to bring such a service into a region would, thus, constitute political participation. However, the actual electricity or the particular commodities thus made available consist of private goods whose consumption would require purchase by the consumer. Such a private economic transaction, by our definition, would not constitute political participation.

A few examples of the application of this definition in Latin American societies will more fully illustrate its implications. Roads are public goods because once they exist it is difficult to keep someone from using them, and because they are commonly supplied through either governmental or community expenditure. (The latter is more common in rural Latin America than in the United States.) Roads may be distributed in different ways: for example, there may be no roads at all, giving all citizens equal access—none. Under such circumstances, the efforts of citizens to build a road or to persuade the government to do so (to expand the supply of this important public good) would constitute political participation. A more common situation concerns the unequal distribution of roads. In Latin America one finds paved, all-weather roads concentrated around or between major metropolitan areas, while rural zones commonly have rutted and bumpy trails, which the rain often makes impassable. Efforts by rural residents to rectify such a problem (through petitioning public works ministries or municipalities, or by building or improving the roads themselves) exemplify an attempt to influence the distribution of public goods, the type of action that we consider political participation.

A second example, perhaps less obvious than the first, further demonstrates the scope of our definition of political participation. The stability of a regime in power is a public good to certain citizens of a society because stable governments can ensure particular economic, social, or political arrangements beneficial to certain sectors of the society. Therefore, attempting to bolster government stability or showing solidarity through attending progovernment rallies or voting in (even controlled) elections constitutes political participation. Similarly, such acts as casting an invalid ballot in such an election (a form of protest common to Latin America)[5] or engaging in an antiregime movement, rally, strike, or riot are also political participation. Such actions attempt (although they may not necessarily succeed) to influence the public good of regime stability through either active support or opposition.

We may now return to the aforementioned six issues to clarify further our definition of political participation as behavior influencing or attempting to influence the distribution of public goods. First, participation requires *action*— overt acts or behavior, not merely attitudes, beliefs, or cognitions. Consequently, an individual who favors a particular candidate but does not in any way make that support overt (e.g., through campaigning or voting) does not participate politically.

Second, *support* or ceremonial behavior intended to maintain a particular regime or constitutional system may help promote regime stability. One may regard the stability of a regime as a public good[6] (i.e., all citizens share in this stability equally). Thus, an effort to maintain a regime or a political system constitutes attempting to affect the distribution of a public good, just as if such an effort were directed toward some disputed policy. Thus, the adoption of a definition of participation based upon the notion of attempting to influence the distribution of public goods reduces the issue of influential versus supportive participation to a false dichotomy.

Unfortunately, in many areas of the world (but especially in Latin America, so frequently cited for examples of stable yet corrupt, inefficient, and unjust regimes) support activity may help maintain in power governments that seriously "misallocate" public goods. Nevertheless, our definition of political participation makes no reference to the ethical value of either the public goods or their allocation (i.e., it does not consider the equity or justice of the decision). Consequently, we consider support activity as political participation whether the regime supported is "good" or "bad."

The remaining four definitional issues are straightforward: As to the question of *efficacy*, we argue that whether an effort to influence the distribution of a particular public good succeeds is immaterial. What counts for our purposes is the effort itself. If one votes for a candidate but he loses, voting participation has nevertheless occurred. Concerning the *intention* of the participant, we disagree with those who would argue that an actor must perceive his actions as political for them to constitute political participation. Perhaps strike participation provides the most vivid illustration of why we take this position. In Latin America, the highly intrusive role of the state in employee-employer bargaining quite commonly transforms job actions into political issues. In many cases workers attempt to win their strike demands by forcing the state to become involved (see Payne 1965). Hence, success on the part of the workers both in involving the state and, in fact, in obtaining the legal right to strike are public goods. In many Latin American nations, governments have systematically denied certain sectors of the work force (especially rural labor) the right to strike. In other instances, even though a certain sector may have the legal right, their strike petitions (*pliegos*) have been consistently found to be technically imperfect, also resulting in denials (see Greaves and Albó, forthcoming; Loveman, forthcoming). Under such circumstances, a worker's joining a strike necessarily involves attempting to influence the distribution of a public good, regardless of whether he or she perceives the act as political or as purely economic. Although there is little systematic evidence on the point, we would argue that in Latin America the overwhelming majority of workers are clearly aware of the political nature of strike participation, even when the only motives for the strike are economic. Nevertheless, whether perceived as political, if the activity has implications for the distribution of public goods, we consider it political in nature.

As to whether political participation may occur in arenas of action other than *formal governmental institutions,* the answer is yes. While a large share of the public goods that occasion political participation do, indeed, fall under the aegis of formal governments, many other public goods exist outside the governmental arena in communities. And finally, concerning whether *conventionality* or legality is a necessary attribute of participation, our definition makes no distinction of this sort. Any means employed in an effort to affect the distribution of public goods is political participation, regardless of its acceptability to power holders or to cultural norms.

Our approach to political participation, we believe, holds two significant advantages. First, its breadth encompasses a substantial range of sociopolitical behaviors. Consequently, our definition facilitates more thorough and systematic attention to the varied political actions of the great mass of citizens in Latin America. We believe that the papers in this volume demonstrate that such a broadened conception of political participation permits researchers to examine many phenomena previously and erroneously deemphasized in research as politically insignificant.

The second advantage of our definition lies in the theoretical implications of linking such a broad range of citizen action to the distribution of public goods within social systems. Specifically, as Adams (forthcoming) points out, the utility of studying participation lies not just in understanding the participatory phenomena themselves, but in what they tell us about the society and polity within which they take place. Defining political participation in terms of influencing the distribution of public goods necessarily relates individual political acts (motivated by personal orientation and desire) to larger social, political, and economic processes and structures. Thus, such a perspective requires the careful analyst to examine not only the Latin American citizen and his/her actions and motives, but the reciprocal effects of the interaction between the state and the political participant.

Images of Political Participation in Latin America

More than a decade ago Kling (1964) and Flores Olea (1967) sounded calls to broaden and systematize research on political participation in Latin America. Despite their summons, the intervening years have brought little progress. Five partial and sometimes contradictory images still pervade the literature on Latin American politics. In this section of the essay we expand upon each of these images, referring to the literature from which they have developed. Then we turn our attention to more recent research, some of which is contained either in this or in our forthcoming companion volume, *Political Participation in Latin America,* volume 2: *Politics and the Poor,* in order to assess the validity of these images.

Violence. Probably the most widespread image is that violence, perhaps more than any other trait, characterizes political activity in Latin America. Needler has stated that "the prevalence of violence is, of course, one of the most characteristic features of politics in the area" (1968b, p. 43), and that revolutions provide the *only* means for democratic mass participation in decision making (1968b, p. 33). Observers of Latin America have entranced themselves with the image of violence, devoting millions of words to *golpes de estado* and guerrilla warfare, to peasant struggles and strikes, and to revolutions, riots, and violently repressive military rule.[7] The accretion of this vast literature has left many believing that citizens of the region are, if not incapable of peaceful and orderly political activity, at least largely indisposed toward it, preferring instead to seek their political objectives through force (Lambert 1967, p. 109; Huntington 1968, pp. 46-47, 134-135).

Is it true that Latin Americans are commonly prone to act violently in the political arena? Are they politically "schizoid," ordinarily uninvolved in any day-to-day, peaceful political action, but occasionally moved to sudden violence, as this image suggests (Seligson and Booth 1976)? There is little doubt that, in comparison to the more highly industrialized societies, Latin American nations rank high in systemic violence (based on data aggregated at the national level), an attribute shared with other rapidly modernizing societies (Feierabend and Feierabend 1966; Feierabend et al. 1969; Huntington 1968, p. 46). Nevertheless, this systemic violence should not mislead our search for evidence of less conflictual political participation. Much of the data that confirm systemic violence come largely from elite sectors' competition for control—coups d'etat, assassinations, etc.—and embroil most citizens as objects or victims rather than actors. Further, the fact that individuals do occasionally take violent political action does not preclude other political activity. Hence, while we recognize that political violence does indeed occur in Latin America, we urge caution lest the notorious and dramatic nature of violent behavior obscure the more pedestrian, nonviolent modes of behavior that may be highly important both for the individual and for the state. The evidence accumulated in this volume seriously undermines the notion that "the prevalence of violence" is "one of the most characteristic features of politics in the area"—at least as far as the actions of a vast majority of citizens are concerned.

The papers collected here marshal strong evidence that, attitudinally and behaviorally, Latin Americans favor nonviolent political participation. In their paper in this volume on the Venezuelan 1973 presidential election, Baloyra and Martz point out that despite Venezuelans' disenchantment with politicians and their role in the political system, the majority of citizens overwhelmingly favored the democratic regime instituted following the fall of Pérez Jiménez in 1958 and the consequent series of free elections. But even more interesting is the level of activity in political campaigning—almost half of all Venezuelans in the Baloyra and Martz national survey had engaged in at least one form of campaign activity (volunteer work for a campaign, electioneering, attendance at rallies, etc.), compared to only 26 percent in the United States (Verba and Nie 1972, p. 21). Some 23 percent of the Venezuelans had taken part in two or more such activities.

We have further evidence supporting our critique of the violence image from

Biles' survey of a broad range of political activities among Uruguayans. Residents of Montevideo and the other urban areas of Uruguay took part in four modes of nonviolent political participation: voting, political communication, communal activity, and campaigning-particularized contacting.[8] These findings from Uruguay substantially resemble Booth's (1975a, 1976) data on Costa Rica, one of Latin America's few remaining constitutional democracies. Booth found six modes of nonviolent activity: voting, partisan activism (similar to campaigning as reported by Biles), political communication,[9] contacting public officials, organizational activism, and community improvement activity.

Today a dramatic difference exists between Uruguay and Costa Rica. Shortly after Biles concluded his research, a military coup brought Uruguay under a regime that forcibly suppresses many of these forms of political participation. A similar event occurred soon afterward in Chile, another long-standing democracy. Although we now know much about the causes of military intervention (see Lowenthal 1976 and *Journal of Inter-American Studies and World Affairs* 1972 for the accumulated evidence), it is interesting to note here that before these activities were suppressed, Uruguayan and Chilean citizens took an active part in politics. Consequently what needs to be determined are the connections, if any, between these high levels of conventional participation by the Uruguayan and Chilean publics and the policies that eventually gave rise to unrest and eventually to military overthrow. While we can thus accept the view that Latin Americans do not always engage in conventional activities, we still do not understand the nexus between conventional and unconventional forms of political involvement.

Research by Seligson (1977c) in Costa Rica sheds some light on the relationship between conventional and unconventional participation. Numerous researchers, foremost among them Gamson (1968), Paige (1971) and Clarke (1973), suggest that the attitudes of trust and efficacy have a strong influence upon political participation. Among Costa Rican peasants, conventional political participation (e.g., organizational activism, voting, local government activism, and communal project participation) correlates quite strongly with high efficacy levels. On the other hand, unconventional participation (e.g., land invasions and strikes) associates with low trust in government (political cynicism). Moreover, more than 85 percent of those engaged in unconventional forms of participation also took part in conventional forms. Consequently we see that an individual frequently engages in both forms of political participation, suggesting that mistrust of government may play a critical role in motivating unconventional participation among Latin Americans who normally are quite active in conventional modes of behavior (see Huntington 1968, pp. 28–30).

Recent research has revealed a great deal more political participation among the poor in Latin America than previously believed. Loveman (forthcoming) and Bloom (1976) trace the history of extensive political involvement of rural labor in Chile. We know, however, that in the case of Chile repression by hostile landlords and unsympathetic governments often turned peaceful efforts at collective problem solving into violent strikes. Similarly, research by Seligson and Booth in Costa Rica (forthcoming-c) has shown that peasants engage in a wide range of political activities, but that extreme inequality in the distribution of land has sometimes forced normally peaceful peasants to embark upon violence-prone land invasions (see Seligson 1974; 1977a; 1977b; 1977c; forthcoming-a,b). Additional evidence of high levels of political participation among the poor in Latin America comes from Landsberger and Gierisch (forthcoming), who find unexpectedly high levels of some forms of activity among Mexican peasants.

Actions by governments which shake citizens' faith in the honesty, efficacy, and wisdom of the regime heighten cynicism regarding government and encourage unconventional behavior. Conclusions of this nature regarding the origins of unconventional participation in Latin America and its link to conventional participation strengthen our belief in the rationality of political action in the area, a subject discussed below.

The generality of the evidence cited thus far might be questioned, since we have referred only to the few democratic regimes in the region. In order to strengthen our position we now turn to data from countries ruled by authoritarian regimes, the dominant form of government in Latin America today. LeoGrande's article (this volume) on political participation demonstrates that Cubans take part in politics in a broad range of ways, especially since the recent institution of the People's Power program. While LeoGrande notes that "it is still too early to evaluate the effectiveness of its mechanisms for increasing elite accountability and popular input to local policy making," his study reveals substantial amounts of activity in neighborhood assemblies, nominations and elections for municipal officials, and contacting public officials.

Other evidence of nonviolent political activity in nondemocratic societies comes from studies such as Roberts' (1973) detailed observation of the contacting and communal activism of the residents of Guatemala City's poor suburbs, and Dietz's (1974; 1977a; 1977b) and Moore's (1977) work revealing similar activities among the urban squatters of Lima and Guayaquil, respectively. McClintock's (1976a; 1976b) studies of highland peasants in authoritarian Peru reveal considerable communal problem solving.

In conclusion, one certainly cannot gainsay the evidence of political violence in Latin America at the level of the national political system, nor of the studies of individual political violence in Colombia, Guatemala, and Mexico, which we have cited. However, the findings we have reported here show clearly that there is much more than just violent participation in Latin America. Much orderly and peaceful day-to-day political activity goes on. In fact, the sorts of conventional participation observed in the studies presented here and in our companion volume (Seligson and Booth, forthcoming-b) show that Latin Americans as individuals are neither characteristically politically passive nor violent. Thus, one must reject the common conclusion that Latin American political culture is pathologically violent. What appears to be more likely is that the politicoeconomic structures of Latin American states provide conditions that frequently encourage or require certain individuals and groups competing for personal rewards to use force in the political arena (Stokes 1952; Chaffee 1975; 1976).

Irrationality. The second image depicts Latin Americans, if and when they do involve themselves in politics, as irrational participants. A congeries of supposedly problematic cultural and socioeconomic traits allegedly bar the great mass of citizens from the pragmatic problem solving believed more common to other cultures. The prognosis for a future change from this distressing past and contemporary condition appears grim, according to Fitzgibbon (1971, p. 489): "To introduce rationality into the political picture will require additional political education and maturity on the part of the masses." Until such education takes place and the masses mature, one should assume, according to the irrationality image, that the following patterns will continue to bedevil the region:

> The certainty of the "true" solution and the quick description of the malady leads to a certain myopia which is visible in party politics, labor-business disputes, public versus private sector conflicts, and adds to a general malaise in inter-country disputes (Ranis 1971, p. 155).

Among the sources of the supposed political irrationality of Latin Americans most frequently cited by scholars, the following figure prominently: lack of understanding of their political role (Tannenbam 1974), lack of political sophistication (Johnson 1964, p. 4; Fitzgibbon 1971, p. 489), cultivation of the intellect (Ranis 1971, p. 155), emphasizing the "expressive rather than the instrumental" (Lipset 1967, p. 7), traditionalism (Kahl 1968; Inkeles and Smith 1974), deference to elites (Lipset 1967, pp. 7-8; Scott 1967), parochialism, disdain for pragmatism (Almond and Verba 1965; Lipset 1967; Williams 1973), *machismo* (Ramos 1962), superstition (Johnson 1964, p. 4), paternalism and patron-clientship (Powell 1970; Strickon and Greenfield 1972; Willems 1975), authoritarianism (Lipset 1967, pp. 7-9; Tallet 1969), and personalism (Scott 1959; 1965; Johnson 1964, p. 4; Willems 1975).

Are Latin Americans politically irrational? Do mass publics in the region fail to exhibit patterns of goal-oriented political behavior because of the effects of such sociocultural traits? At issue here is not whether such traits exist in Latin American political culture, but whether they inhibit people from pursuing their public goods related goals in a reasoned manner. Many recent studies have separately concluded that voting behavior in the United States and Europe follows basically rational patterns.[10] Do Latin Americans exhibit irrational political behavior while citizens of other cultures do not? We believe that the answer to these questions is no, especially after reviewing the evidence presented by several recent studies.

Booth (chapter 6), defining political rationality in terms of a means-to-ends model of political behavior, presents data from Costa Rica that show patterns of rational, rather than irrational behavior. The model tested assumes that individuals exhibit rational political behavior if they (1) have intensely felt political goals, (2) can identify a particular political institution as relevant for pursuing those goals, and (3) participate within that institution. For three separate arenas in which the distribution of public goods may be affected, national government, local government, and community politics, Booth reports participation was highest among those with both high levels of goals and the perception of institutional saliency. The study also shows that such rational patterns of behavior characterize not only socioeconomic elites (an argument commonly made), but Costa Rica's poor and illiterate rural dwellers as well.

Seligson (chapter 9), using a Costa Rican data set different from that analyzed by Booth, focuses on the peasant sector, finding evidence that reveals participant rationality. Peasants in the economically least developed regions of the country participate at levels significantly higher than those in more developed regions, when socioeconomic status variables are held constant. Seligson concludes that contrary to the theory advanced by the culture of poverty school (Lewis 1959; 1966) the poor are active participants. In fact, the very environment of poverty (i.e., underdevelopment) stimulates peasants in poorer regions to become more involved in local projects because the absence of government help forces them to rely upon their own resources (e.g., community labor) to create and distribute critically needed public goods.

The paper by Neuse (chapter 8) on 1952-1973 voting patterns of Chilean women indirectly treats the problem of participant rationality. After examining the trends in voter turnout and partisan choice among Chilean females, Neuse concludes that the patterns of support and activity demonstrate a rational response to actions by the political parties themselves. Rejecting the "tempting" argument that the preponderance of female votes for the Christian Democrats prior to 1970 reflected the "natural conservatism" of women, Neuse points out that the Christian Democrats had taken much greater pains than the Marxist parties to woo the female vote. The post-1970 rise in the lower-class female vote for the left he attributes to the strenuous efforts of Unidad Popular to mobilize lower sector women who had previously remained outside the political system. Overall, then, Neuse argues that shifts in female voting patterns in Chile across these two decades appear to reflect the decisions of women to pursue their personal goals through the political process because the parties persuaded women that they had become more useful for attaining these goals.

Chaffee (1975; forthcoming) theorizes that both participation and nonparticipation in politics in Latin America commonly respond to individuals' calculations of the potential relative costs and rewards of particular actions directed toward desired ends. Following a political economic line of reasoning, he argues that it is logical for an individual to expend some effort to influence the distribution of public goods if, but only if, the potential rewards to him/her in terms of private utilities (presumably either material, social, or psychic) exceed his/her potential losses in effort, time, cash, or psychic costs. Chaffee cites several examples from studies of both conventional and unorthodox participation in Latin America to support his contentions.

Certain other recently published studies reporting on Mexico and Peru at least partly support the conclusions of Booth, Chaffee, Neuse, and Seligson regarding participant rationality. Such findings from nondemocratic nations have particular interest here because of the plausible argument that the authoritarian settings found in much of Latin America might well inhibit or distort participatory processes sufficiently to bar rational political behavior. Dietz (1974; 1977a; 1977b), Cornelius (1974), and Cornelius and Dietz (1976) examine separately and comparatively the political participation of urban migrants and squatters in Lima and Mexico City. Their model of demand making describes, in essence, a somewhat more elaborate model of means-to-ends rational behavior than that tested by Booth (chapter 6). The multistep process they reveal isolates the following sequence: (1) perceiving needs (in essence, goal identification), (2) perceiving these needs as susceptible to government satisfaction, (3) perceiving a governmental channel for action (determining the saliency of an institution), and finally (4) making the effort to influence the distribution of public goods according to their desires—demand-making. Their findings confirm the considerable ingenuity with which the poor (despite the fact that the settings are authoritarian) pursue needed services, and demonstrate similar patterns of rational political behavior. Note that Mathiason (1972) in the democratic setting of urban Venezuela reports findings very similar to those reported by Cornelius and Dietz.

Portes' (1972) survey of numerous studies of the political behavior of urban slum dwellers in several cities (including Santiago, Lima, Barranquilla, Bogotá, and Guatemala City) led him to interpret slum behavior as conforming to rational action patterns of the means-to-ends type. Portes unequivocally comments that "the problems of peripheral slums and their causation are of an essentially structural nature. These problems have nothing to do with a unique 'way of being' or a deviant culture of irrationality" (1972, p. 286).

What may we conclude from these findings regarding the political rationality of Latin Americans? Several studies, conducted in both democratic and nondemocratic settings, report rational patterns of behavior, a finding directly contrary to the conventional image of participant irrationality. While the studies cited do not categorically prove that all Latin Americans behave rationally in all political arenas (a most unlikely proposition for any society) evidence abounds to suggest that rational behavior patterns are widespread if not predominant in the region, irrespective of regime type.

Thus, though Latin American culture may appear to some to contain "irrational" elements, political behavior in the region appears to be, at least in many cases, rational. Our findings neither deny nor confirm the possibility or the evidence to the effect that Latin Americans may be emotional, dogmatic, or personalistic (to repeat but a few of the litany of alleged sins), as far as their political culture goes. However, such attributes do not appear to cause political participation to deviate from basically rational patterns. We must add that an act that appears "rational" in the United States might be counterproductive— or even suicidal—in a Latin American political context, and *vice versa*. Future analysis should avoid the ethnocentrism of conceptualizing rationality in terms of Anglo-American or European culture or behavior.

Political mobilization. Social forces connected with economic moderni- zation and a revolution in communications have helped transform the Latin American masses from a state of relatively low political awareness and activity into much more politically conscious and active modern citizens. The twin themes of increasing social and political mobilization constitute the major trends of this third image of participation. Halper and Sterling admirably sum- marize the central idea of this body of thinking:

> As the modernization process advances, so does the ability of the lower strata to organize and express themselves. There has been an increasing tendency toward popular participation in the political system. (1972, p. xiii)

Among the processes described in the mobilization literature are the historical expansion of the politically active population from the tiny elite sectors of the colonial era to include the growing middle strata, the expansion of the electorate, the development of nationalism, the integration of increasing per- centages of the population into the participant sector, the growth of the number and size of organizations making demands upon the political system, and the increasing activism and political significance of the urban and rural lower classes.[11]

Research has shown that increasing political participation in national institutions has accompanied increasing levels of socioeconomic moderni- zation or development. Indeed, several studies in this volume (Neuse; Rosenberg and Malloy) and its forthcoming companion (see essays by Forman and Loveman in *Political Participation in Latin America,* volume 2: *Politics and the Poor*) have chronicled this process. But research on this subject often implies that the state cannot control the increasing political mobilization—the process seems an inexorable element of the modernization which has caught up most Third World governments (Lerner 1958; Huntington 1968). As one recent analysis points out:

> Socioeconomic changes have prompted the emergence or heightened the importance of peasants, urban workers, businessmen, bureaucrats, and stu- dents. . . . The emergence of these new groups has been accompanied by various and greater expectations on their part, and these expectations have placed formal governmental institutions in an extremely difficult position in that more is demanded of them than they can reasonably be expected to provide . . . all of which tends to foster a stagnant or immobile political situation. (Adie and Poitras 1974, p. 259)

To what degree does the greater participation in politics ascribed to political mobilization lie beyond the control of the state in its origin and development? Part of the answer to this question may be found in several papers in this book. Scaff and Williams (chapter 3) point out that elites commonly advance a fervent (if logically flawed) argument against widespread citizen participation in politics either out of fear of a putative mass authoritarianism, or on the basis of the bureaucratic-technical claim that masses are incompetent to make decisions. Scaff and Williams' reflections highlight the attempts of governments to manage political participation for self-serving ends.

Neuse's paper (chapter 8) traces the rise in female electoral participation in Chile between 1952 and 1973. During this period the major gains in voting turnout for women apparently stemmed directly from deliberate, competitive efforts of the Chilean political parties to promote female voting and to carry women's support. In the Chilean case, then, mobilization has occurred at the behest of competing political elites. The female vote was managed with varying degrees of success by three successive governments. Neuse reports that the Christian Democrats first brought women into the electorate and made quick progress in garnering their support. Later, the Allende coalition's (*Unidad Popular*) growing facility for mobilizing lower class women contributed to the very success that eventually led to the "marches of the empty pots" (*protestas de las ollas vacías*), a countermobilization by upper- and middle-class women immediately preceding the 1973 *coup d'etat*. Since the end of democratic rule in Chile, the military government has suppressed with great brutality most forms of political participation. These events suggest that much of the ebb and flow of electoral efforts to influence the distribution of public goods in Chile was somewhat less than an organic and inevitable process beyond the control of governing elites. Mobilization was stimulated, manipulated, and managed (although not always successfully) by elites, both within and outside the government.[12]

Rosenberg and Malloy (chapter 10) examine the evolution of popular participation and its impact in the area of social security policy throughout Latin America. Their paper clearly shows, in at least this policy arena, that governments control or co-opt demands for social security protection by specific groups as they enter the system. However, with time the aggregated interests of many recipient groups become less manageable for the state. A succession of groups enter under the social security umbrella as governments have made agreements with newly powerful interest sectors. But as Rosenberg and Malloy show, reforming Latin American social security systems tends to become extremely difficult for civil regimes once they incorporate many interest groups. Thus, these authors demonstrate that social security policy is one arena in which elite co-optation of rising popular demands (a manipulative device employed by the state in order to help control mass participation) may create a system that frustrates and even threatens elite control.

Three essays in this volume that focus on political participation in revolutionary societies argue that the coercive capacity of military regimes may give them greater control over the inception and manipulation of participation than that of civil regimes. LeoGrande's paper on Cuba (chapter 7) reveals the decisive role of the government in the recent institution of the People's Power (*Poder Popular*) program for local decision making. While it is still too soon to assess the amount of influence People's Power will have on the distribution of public goods in Cuba, one may rest assured that the Castro government will monitor its development carefully to make certain that the new participatory system is developing in accord with its goals (integration, socialization) for mass participation. Control of revolutionary mass participatory institutions by military regimes is also highlighted by the Peruvian case since 1968. The papers by Dietz and Palmer (chapter 11) and Woy (chapter 12) discuss the intensive efforts of the Peruvian revolutionary leadership to bypass old party institutions through the creation of massive new corporatist organizations to supplant the traditional parties. By 1975, however, two things happened: First, the new mechanisms for mass participation had become so successful that the military regime found it necessary to curtail sharply their functions. And second, severe economic reversals made the implementation of many policies impossible, sparking discontent and civil unrest.

In summary, although the evidence at hand is not definitive, it does lead to some tentative conclusions. While the widely observed tendency for increasing popular participation in national politics may at least partly derive from socio-economic processes beyond state control, Latin American governments and competing elites frequently have become involved in promoting such partici-pation themselves (see Palmer 1973; Bourque and Palmer 1975). Further-more, while it is true that the mobilization processes reported have often carried popular activism beyond manageable proportions in specific instances, strenuous repressive efforts by regimes willing to impose the high cost of such repression have often proven capable of controlling popular movements and pressure, at least for the short run (see Duff and McCamant 1976). Huntington and Nelson (1976, pp. 168-69) evaluate the trade-offs between participation and repression:

> Elite choices as to the relative priority of economic growth, socioeconomic equity, political stability, and other goals substantially affect the costs and benefits to groups and individuals of resorting to political participation as either a goal or a means ... [but,] political participation [of citizens] ... feeds back to and constrains the political choices of elites and groups. ... Participation becomes in-creasingly costly to suppress, at least among mobilized segments of the population.

Thus, while political mobilization has clearly occurred in Latin America, impressions of its inevitability and uncontrollability seem clearly overdrawn.

Limited mass participation. In apparent direct conflict with the mobili-zation image just mentioned, a fourth view regards participation among the great mass of citizens as very limited. A representative example of this perception of participation follows:

Political participation, the effort of individuals, groups, sectors, and social classes to influence decisions, is minimal. (Denton and Lawrence 1972, p. 28)

Edelmann (1969, p. 78) amplifies on this theme, presenting reasons underlying the alleged apathy:

> The large lower class has very little political power or influence. Most of the members are illiterate, a handicap that precludes an effective awareness of the ramifications of economic and political problems. . . . But even when given suffrage and possibly encouraged to exercise it, they often show very little interest. Their struggle for sheer existence leaves little time or concern for the privileges and duties of an articulate, politically conscious citizen.

Ranis (1971, p. 156) describes Latin America's "participant citizenry" as "still a somewhat abbreviated percentage of the total population." Overall, the picture emerges of a substantial majority of citizens who remain virtually inactive (much less active than their First World counterparts) as far as political affairs go, lacking the time, energy, skills, and interest necessary for participation.[13]

Is it true that mass political participation in Latin America is very low? What proportion of Latin Americans attempt to influence the distribution of public goods in their nations and communities in some way? The answer to these questions will likely surprise the many who cherish the image that political inactivity characterizes mass publics of the region. For the sake of unity we will report the available data on as many countries as possible, organized according to some of the principal modes of participation that have been identified. We recognize that comparing data from disparate studies is fraught with danger. Our analysis of the following statistics is conservative, therefore, and we restrict ourselves to general inferences.

Looking first at voting, we find that Latin Americans are active voters, where regimes permit elections. National election participation in the United States is around 55-60 percent (Campbell et al. 1964, p. 49; Sharkansky and Van Meter 1975, pp. 76-77), in Austria, near 95 percent, and in India, near 60 percent (Verba et al. 1971, p. 36). By comparison, about 80 percent of Costa Ricans and Uruguayans turn out to vote (Willems 1975, pp. 288-91; Biles, chapter 5; Seligson and Booth, forthcoming-c), and Venezuelans exhibit turnout rates over 90 percent (Baloyra and Martz, chapter 4). In the 1961-70 decade (Willems 1975, pp. 288-91), levels of voter turnout in Latin American nations varied from a low of 53 percent in the 1970 Colombian national election to a high of 94 percent in the Peruvian national election of 1963.[14] Voting levels in Latin America, then, are not unusually low in comparison to other nations, but in fact have a similar range.

Campaigning and partisan activism comprise a second mode of political activity. For comparison's sake, figures reported by Verba et al. (1971, p. 36) permit a rough estimate that an average of 20 percent of the voting age populations of Austria, Japan, India, and the United States engage in campaigning. Biles (chapter 5) reports that in 1970, 6 percent of urban Uruguayans belonged to a political club or party, and that some 13 percent had campaigned or contributed money to a candidate. Booth's (1976, p. 628) Costa Rican family heads professed even more activity in 1973, 27 percent reporting either current or past membership in a political party, and 16 percent attendance at party meetings and functions. In their paper in this volume, Baloyra and Martz reveal still greater activity in Venezuela—almost three-fourths of the electorate exposed themselves to campaign stimuli in the 1973 national election, while nearly half took a more active role in the campaign (professing interest in the campaign, volunteer work, electioneering, attending meetings, etc.). As with voting, the amounts of campaign activity in Latin America are comparable to those elsewhere.

A third mode of activity consists of contacting public officials. Verba et al. 1971) distinguish between contacting for communal ends and contacting officials for personal ends (personalized or particularized contacting). Overall, they report ranges for different elements of these types of contacting from 1-10 percent in Nigeria, the lowest level, up to 3-16 percent in Austria, the highest level. We believe the particularized versus communal contacting distinction may have certain problems (see note 17, below), and since few other Latin American studies have taken advantage of it, the following figures simply refer to contacting public officials in general. In the highly personalized system of Uruguayan politics, some 11 percent of the residents of Montevideo admitted having received some favor from a public official (Biles, chapter 5). A Costa Rican study (Booth 1976, p. 628) surveyed citizen-initiated contacts with several different types of public officials, and found levels ranging from a high of 13 percent for contacting the municipal executive (roughly analogous to a city manager) to a low of 3 percent for contacting the president of the republic. Dietz (1977a) found a third of his sample of Lima's urban poor had contacted government officials. Cornelius (1974, p. 1135) reports findings from several different studies in Latin America in which the percent making at least one citizen-initiated contact with a public official ranged from 6 percent to 42 percent in different sorts of lower class communities (peasants and the urban poor) in Mexico, Peru, Brazil, and Chile. Overall, then, the evidence suggests that Latin Americans contact public officials at rates equal to, and possibly greater than, those reported elsewhere.

In the area of communal activism—participation in collective problem solving efforts—Verba et al. (1971, p. 36) report levels of activity ranging from highs in Nigeria (near 30 percent) and the U.S. (slightly below Nigeria) to lows in Austria, India, and Japan (around 10 percent). Unfortunately, since this sort of activity within Latin American communities has been studied primarily by anthropologists through field studies, quantifiable information as to the percentages of persons engaging in such activity is rare, despite the plethora of evidence that the activity takes place. One useful example of such participant observation comes from Fishel's (forthcoming) study of the Peruvian district of Mancos, which details the numerous community improvements made through the collective efforts of the residents. Fishel goes beyond anthropological studies, however, by quantifying the number and type of projects over a long span of years. Nevertheless, a few studies have provided more detailed numerical data. Dietz and Moore (1977, p. 27) report that 73 percent of the residents of six of Lima's *pueblos jóvenes* (squatter neighborhoods) had collaborated with others in their communities in some sort of community work. Booth's 1973 national sample of Costa Rican family heads found that 56 percent had taken part in a community improvement effort, and that 16 percent belonged to some sort of community improvement group (Booth 1976, p. 628). Reporting only upon Costa Rican peasants, Seligson and Booth (forthcoming-c) found that 66 percent had engaged in some effort for community improvement. Once again, we find evidence of participation in Latin America that not only equals but exceeds that reported from other regions of the world.

Having now reviewed comparatively levels of activity on separate modes, we may conveniently summarize the findings by examining two studies that have attempted overall comparisons between Latin American nations and others. Biles' paper in this volume concludes that levels of political activity in urban Uruguay are almost as high as those in the United States and Great Britain, and higher than Italy's, as reported by Almond and Verba (1965). Biles states, "The vast majority of urban Uruguayans, then, participated at least occasionally in politics . . . [and] a majority participated on a regular basis." This hardly supports the image of consistently low mass participation. Booth (1975a, pp. 109-10; 1976, p. 629) compares levels of political participation in Costa Rica with those reported by Kim et al. (1974, pp. 105-32) for their five nation study. For mean levels of activity in voting, party membership, attendance at political meetings, community improvement actions, and contacting public officials, Costa Ricans take part only slightly less than Austrians, Americans, and Japanese, but slightly more than Indians and Nigerians. Once again, then, the differences between Latin America and elsewhere are surprisingly small when one considers the great currency attributed to the image of low mass political participation.

To conclude, substantial evidence exists that mass publics, and even the poorer citizens among them, engage considerably in politics. This appears to be true in the liberal constitutional regimes as well as in the authoritarian contexts, insofar as the latter do not suppress specific modes of participation. Thus, while there is no electoral campaign activism to speak of in authoritarian Peru, Nicaragua, or Ecuador, substantial amounts of contacting public officials and communal activism appear to be taking place. Ultimately, the expected dramatic difference between participation in several highly industrial nations and Latin America appears rather minor. We contend, therefore, that previous conceptions of political participation in Latin America have been so narrowly cast that they ignored many critical phenomena. The empirical evidence cited here divests of validity the image of low mass participation.

Participation monopolized by upper strata. Closely coupled with the preceding image of low mass participation is the final one—the domination of political activity by the upper socioeconomic strata. Masses in Latin America are regarded as politically passive, and the wealthier sectors are seen as politically dominant, extensively monopolizing participation. One observer clearly makes this point:

> Since political participation, like social participation, is limited to a relatively small minority of the population in Latin America, modern political elites can exercise a disproportionate degree of control relative to their numbers in the political process. (Von Lazar 1971, p. 49)

By implication, this line of thinking treats activity directed at influencing the distribution of public goods as so highly concentrated that only a select few exercise the vast majority of political influence, and that masses lack any significant influence.[15]

How accurate is the image of an upper strata monopoly of political participation? We may approach the answer to this query in terms of three separate issues. Such a participation monopoly could be said to exist (1) if no mass activity occurred at all; (2) if the rich were greatly more active than masses in politics; or (3) if masses exercised virtually no influence at all over the distribution of public goods. We know from our earlier discussion in this paper, as well as other studies,[16] that masses take an active role in politics in many Latin American countries. This is true not only for communal or organizational arenas of action, but also for contacting, party and campaign activism, and so forth. Thus, upper status sectors do not monopolize participation in this sense.

The second condition concerns disproportionate political participation by wealthier citizens. Is the political activism of the upper strata extraordinarily great in comparison to the lower strata? And if so, to what extent and in what arenas of activity? In this case, the answer to the first question is a qualified yes—elites are more active in many political arenas. Biles (chapter 5) provides evidence of such disproportion by showing a weak positive association between socioeconomic status (SES) indices and organizational membership in urban Uruguay. McClintock's (1976a, 1976b) data on the Peruvian countryside in 1969 and 1974 reveal weak to moderate positive associations between SES and political participation levels in a variety of occupational contexts, despite the relative homogeneity of the population samples. Costa Ricans at large exhibit low to moderate positive correlations between SES and five modes of activism—voting, partisan activity, political communication, organizational activism, and contacting public officials—even controlling for a broad range of demographic and attitudinal characteristics (Booth 1975; chapter 6).

Several studies focus upon the SES-participation link among rural dwellers. Among Costa Rican peasants, land ownership—an important index of social and economic standing in the countryside—contributes to a signifant increase in participation in organizations, community betterment efforts, and contacting local public officials (Seligson and Booth, forthcoming-c). Bourque and Warren (forthcoming) show that, among women in two rural Peruvian villages, heightened political activity comes about when women gain higher status through economic independence from men. Fishel's (1976) observation of another Peruvian highland village suggests far greater activism (especially in contacting public officials) among the political elite of the area than among the majority of citizens. All in all, then, there is substantial evidence to document that higher SES persons, whether the context is national or local, often engage more actively in politics than masses.

However, the available evidence does not universally connect high socio-economic status with high levels of political participation. In fact, many of the studies we have just cited contain evidence that in certain modes of participation SES either makes no difference, or that elites actually take less part than masses. For example, although Biles' Uruguayan study found one mode of participation (organizational membership) with an independent positive association with SES, voting and political communication revealed association below the level of statistical significance, and one, the contacting/campaigning mode, correlated *negatively* with SES. Thus in Uruguay, even when such other factors as political attitudes and information levels were held constant, higher status citizens were less likely to be campaigners/contactors than those of lower status.

Another example of an absence of status-participation association comes from Baloyra and Martz's (1976a) study of the Venezuelan presidential election of 1973. They found that voting had no correlation with SES, an uncommon finding (see Milbrath and Goel 1977, pp. 86-106; Salisbury 1975, p. 326) which they attribute to voting's mandatory nature and the intense mobilization of the presidential campaign. Yet a third example is provided by Landsberger and Gierisch (forthcoming), who report on a survey of political activities of residents of a Mexican *ejido* (communal farm) in the Laguna region. They find no statistically significant degree of association between objective status indices such as the amount of land held, education, and income and the Laguna area *ejidatarios'* levels of voting and political party activity. Thus, one must begin to entertain some reservations about the image of consistently higher political activism of Latin American socioeconomic elites.

Another area of political activity in which those of high SES are not disproportionately active concerns the distribution of public goods at the communal level. Efforts to improve one's community in Latin America typically reveal either no or a negative association with SES. For example, Dietz and Moore (1977, pp. 37-41) find no significant correlations between SES and community improvement efforts among Lima's poor squatters and migrants, and report that activists are systematically slightly poorer than inactive residents. Costa Ricans also tend to be more active in communal activities the lower status their jobs, their educations, and their incomes (Booth 1975a). This holds true for the entire population as well as for rural dwellers, whether the index of status is based on land ownership (Seligson and Booth, forthcoming-c) or contextual indicators of overall wealth in the community (Seligson, chapter 9). Furthermore, Costa Rican peasants take a more active role in communal betterment activities and in local school related organizations than do the country's more prosperous urbanites (Seligson and Booth, forthcoming-c).

Thus, we have assembled data from many studies in several different nations demonstrating no overall positive association between socioeconomic status and political activity. Rather, the relationship appears to vary depending upon the context and the mode of participation. Higher SES individuals evidently predominate in national level participation; the higher one's status, the more likely it becomes that he/she has vested interests the defense of which makes national politics important. Furthermore, higher SES individuals have the economic and educational resources to pursue their goals in complex and centralized national political systems.

However, the data presented also reveal that higher socioeconomic status citizens do not dominate all forms of political activism. System-specific attributes such as the extremely personalistic nature of Uruguayan politics or the tight integration of communal and national public goods within the Mexican *ejido* may produce uncharacteristically high levels of activism in national politics among nonelites. One area where lower SES persons commonly take more active political roles than elites is in communal improvement activism. The apparent reason for this is that the poorer an individual is in Latin America, the more likely he/she is to live in a place that lacks many or all of the basic amenities of modern urbanized life—services that higher status people take for granted. The extreme centralization of service delivery within metropolitan centers and established neighborhoods, plus consistent evidence that central governments cannot or will not adequately supply the service needs of the poor, militate in favor of communal activism among the poor. Where national policies distribute public goods unevenly and offer scant prospect for local improvement, neighbors often turn to each other for the creation of public goods through communal efforts.

The central thrust of these findings undermines rather thoroughly the validity of Salisbury's (1975, p. 326) remark in his review of the political participation literature that higher status persons participate more than the poor, "no matter what the context or institutional setting." Upper socioeconomic status persons are usually more active than masses in the national political arena, but apparently less active than masses in the communal arena.

These findings suggest that the concept of *marginality* may have considerable analytical utility in predicting both the levels and types of political participation of Latin American citizens and their relationship to the institutions of national government. Latin America's poor, often referred to as *marginalizados* (left out) from the economic benefits of society, are also marginal in terms of their access to basic public services. *Barriadas* and *favelas* sprawl over hillsides with unpaved roadways that dissolve into mud in the rain. Their residents, the *favelados* or *pobladores,* commonly lack electricity, sewers, water, transportation, garbage collection, street lighting, health centers, and many other basic services. The conditions experienced by rural residents are, if anything, consistently more dismal than even those of the urban poor. The reason that such people (we might call them "service marginal") often turn to each other for assistance in the creation and supply of certain public goods is straightforward and highly rational—governments cannot or will not supply those goods. Among the more prosperous, to whom the national government commonly does provide basic public services, engaging in the national political system makes good sense. To the service marginal, however, helping each other not only is reasonable, it is a necessity in the absence of state resources and attention.

The final issue under the rubric of upper SES domination of political participation concerns the question of the relative degree of influence of those of high SES over public policy. While our definition of political participation explicitly rejects the idea that policy influence (i.e., success) is a sine qua non of participation (see above), the question of impact speaks directly to the substantive import of the whole question of participation. Even if masses do take part, some might argue, they seldom, if ever, succeed in influencing public policy in any meaningful way. And if only elites have policy influence, the argument continues, participation by the masses is meaningless and irrelevant. To what extent is this true in Latin America? Are citizens' efforts to influence the distribution of public goods largely ineffective?

Baylis, in his paper in this volume (chapter 2), argues that mass publics have at least some influence over the ultimate distribution of public goods in most political systems, even the more authoritarian ones. Although in Latin America, as elsewhere, mass participation is usually manipulated by elites, few political systems have the resources, organization, coercive strength and will necessary to exclude systematically all popular influence from policy making over the long run.

There is evidence that Latin American masses can exert at least some policy influence upon national governments in both democratic and authoritarian contexts. But the critical question remains—how much influence? For example, data from nations as diverse as Costa Rica and Bolivia demonstrate that even isolated rural communities extract small amounts of pork barrel appropriations from the national government (Booth et al. 1973; McEwen 1975). Rosenberg and Malloy (chapter 10) relate the success of pressure groups (especially those of the middle sectors) in the development of social security policy throughout Latin America, regardless of the regime context. This success has attained such proportions that efforts to reform the overblown, inequitable, and complex systems have met frustration in all but a few military regimes. The two papers in this volume on Peru (Woy; Dietz and Palmer) discuss how even the governmentally manipulated and dominated participatory institutions of SINAMOS began to attain an independent interest representation role. As a consequence, the Peruvian military has retrenched somewhat in its commitment to mass participation in order to lessen the restraints upon its authority and flexibility posed by this growing independence. And finally, although we would exaggerate to describe the demand making of urban squatters an unqualified success, the massive literature in this field documents many instances in which governmental decisions allocated enough scarce public resources to the squatter areas to placate their residents (e.g., Peattie 1968; Ray 1969; Fagen and Tuohy 1972; Roberts 1973; Dietz 1974; Cornelius 1975; Moore 1977). The evidence is incomplete, but suggests that the policy influence of the masses, observable although normally quite limited, varies from group to group and political system to political system.

Ultimately, then, one may conclude that while the masses in Latin America certainly do not rule, neither are they totally devoid of influence upon the distribution of public goods. Arenas for political participation abound in Latin America, as does evidence that individuals from throughout the socioeconomic spectrum attempt to influence the distribution of public goods in a variety of these arenas. The relationship between the citizen and the state appears varied and complex; a multitude of factors determine the probability that a particular actor will choose one form of activity over another, pursue his/her goals within the national system or turn to his/her neighbors, and succeed or fail in these efforts. To judge these factors, relationships, activities, and goals as not "meaningful" by U.S. or some other standards is thus most inappropriate; rather, they must be judged *contextually*. In the concluding section we will speculate further about the determinants of mass participation and mass policy influence.

Discussion

Summary. To recapitulate, we have shown that much of the conventional wisdom regarding political participation in Latin America lacks empirical validity. The use of a contextually sensitive definition (participation is action by citizens that influences or attempts to influence the distribution of public goods) has permitted us to examine a range of important modes of citizen involvement that goes beyond the traditional focus on electoral phenomena (e.g., elections, parties, campaigns) to include other national system activities, as well as participation within communities, organizations, and local governments.

The assembled evidence has undermined the validity of the widely held image of low or infrequent mass political participation in Latin America. Political participation in many arenas and of many kinds appears quite widespread. In fact, the data reveal that differences in observed levels of participation between Latin American countries on the one hand, and other Third World and First World countries on the other, are quite small. Mass political participation in Latin America takes many forms, some of them violent, but many others peaceful, involving orderly, day-to-day actions through which individuals pursue their personal goals in ways that might influence the distribution of public goods. Furthermore, these actions appear neither irrational nor random, as a third image holds. Rather, Latin Americans pursue their personal ends through political actions when public or communal channels promise rewards.

We have noted an element of validity in the mobilization image; political participation in the national arena appears to have generally increased throughout the region, despite reversals caused by authoritarian regimes. Contrary to the conventional belief, however, both democratic and authoritarian Latin American governments and sometimes rival elites, rather than some vaguely defined but frequently inexorable forces of modernization, appear responsible for such increases. However, political elites' successes in stimulating participation often exceeds their ability to manage or manipulate this participation.

The final common assumption, that upper socioeconomic strata effectively dominate efforts to influence the distribution of public goods, needs considerable qualification. While masses do take part in politics at levels previously unexpected, upper socioeconomic strata still appear to dominate in (but not monopolize) national political arenas. The poor, however, may predominate in communal improvement activities and in arenas of governmental action that hold immediate importance for improving their life chances. Thus while masses do not exercise preponderant influence over decision making in any Latin American state (mass influence on policy thereby falling far short of that of socioeconomic or political elites), the capacity of ordinary citizens to influence the distribution of public goods exceeds previously imagined levels.

Toward a theory of political participation. But what, we must now ask, do these findings about Latin America tell us about the social and political structures within which citizens participate? In Richard N. Adams' words, "these things called 'participation' are reflections, imprints, residues, or signals about the nature of a much larger structure" (forthcoming). The forms, degree, and success with which Latin Americans influence or attempt to influence the distribution of public goods can tell us much about their political systems. Indeed, as Parry (1972, p. 4) points out, "There is a close connection between participation and the very idea of 'the political.' Politics itself implies action in common for certain purposes and hence it presupposes some degree of participation." We shall now attempt to seek some of the common ideas throughout our findings that illuminate larger social structures. These ideas may provide a basis for building toward a comprehensive explanation of political participation applicable to Latin America.

To understand the significance of political participation for social systems, one must consider the individual political actor. We will examine the individual participant from two perspectives, the motivation for taking part and the constraints upon participation. First of all, individuals apparently participate in politics for basically private motives. The evidence from the studies on participant rationality indicates that individual goals (desires, felt needs) motivate political action, and that the perception of appropriate channels for such participation determines the direction and form of such action. Motives for action appear to be private in large measure, even where the benefit from participation may be shared by many. That is, attempts to influence the distribution of a public good usually stem from the perceived likelihood that the good will be available to the individual for his/her private benefit. For example, a worker might join a general strike in the hope that the government will raise the minimum wage. Private motivation, of course, need not be purely economic: cultural and psychological motives (sense of duty, affection, patriotism) as well as social goals (affiliation, friendship) can also provide the private incentive for attempting to influence the distribution of public goods. One may vote out of a sense of allegiance to electoral institutions, or join a community improvement project, not because a community center will produce material rewards, but because of the camaraderie afforded by attending meetings.[17]

Second, there are, as Adams (forthcoming) points out, "dynamic and constantly varying constraints" upon individuals in the pursuit of their private interests, similarly variable, through political participation. Three classes of constraints—resource, psychological, and contextual—will illustrate this point.[18] Individuals have different and variable *resources* that determine their capacities for participation. Wealth, social roles, time, occupational status, education, intelligence, contacts, and organizational skills, among others, can bear directly upon one's participatory ability. A second type of constraint is *psychological* or *cognitive*. Individuals act within the boundaries of their perceptions, knowledge, and beliefs. Many psychological attributes have been linked to political participation, including cynicism, efficacy, political interest, political knowledge or information, anomie, and civic duty. A theory of participation must consider indigenous variants of these and other psychological phenomena. The third class of constraint could be called *contextual* or *environmental*. The socioeconomic and political conditions imposed by the nature of individuals' nation, neighborhood, productive system, level of development, availability of resources, and services restrain or encourage participation.[19] A comprehensive theory of political participation in Latin America must account for such factors. It should also, however, go beyond the mere identification of the correlates of participation to integrate such factors into a larger explanatory scheme that links the individual to his/her sociopolitical context.

The sociopolitical context of participation, therefore, provides the second level of analysis that a comprehensive theory must encompass. One important insight provided by the research reviewed above consists of the identification of various arenas of participation. Citizens take part not only in the national polity, but in local political and communal arenas as well. We mention these spheres of action not simply because of their analytical convenience, but because the research reviewed above demonstrates the existence of distinct sources of public goods that define these arenas. Latin American governments make policies that distribute many kinds of public goods, but both local governments and communities control other public goods and these must not be overlooked.

These participatory arenas do not exist isolated from each other, but are linked through the systems of allocation of political, social, and economic values of individual societies. The citizen takes part in one arena or another according to his/her particular goals, selecting the ways and institutions in which he/she engages, according to perceptions of their relevance and utility. Thus, for example, the construction of a rural school commonly provokes activity within the community related to the building project, but often also draws citizens into the national political arena for authorization and funding of a teacher. Similarly, residents of an urban neighborhood may organize communally to confront a traffic problem, then enter the local government arena to obtain a traffic signal at a dangerous intersection. Overall, we believe that such patterns of participation in different arenas by different individuals and classes will reveal much about the power structures that control the distribution of access to many valued resources within Latin American societies. For example, one common pattern of participation finds peasants confining much of their participation to the communal arena. This occurs because national political institutions often do not afford campesinos access to services or influence nearly so openly as to urban upper and middle sectors. A comprehensive theory of political participation should examine such patterns for the insight they provide regarding social structure.

The preceding thoughts about the individual's choice of an arena for participation lead us to delve more deeply into the relationship between the citizen and the state from the perspective of the citizen. Citizens, individually and collectively, attempt to influence the distribution of public goods in Latin America, and sometimes they succeed. The studies we have cited indicate that such influence occurs when citizens have sufficient power that they may either control elite decision making (a rare event), or when their power is sufficient that the state must at least placate either their potential or actual demands or co-opt them (a somewhat more common occurrence). It appears likely that the degree of influence over public policy (how often and how much decisions about public goods are actually affected) by citizens will vary in direct proportion to their power vis-à-vis the state. One index of the influence of different social sectors may well be the degree to which they engage in national arenas versus communal arenas of action.

For example, Argentina and Mexico's labor unions and Bolivia's armed peasant leagues have figured prominently in national politics and have received numerous benefits as a result. The Bolivian peasantry provides an illustrative case of the extraction of national arena resources for local problem solving and entry into local politics because of the power derived from campesino organizations (*sindicatos*). The sindicatos' organization and mobilization efforts have "politicized the campesinos and provided them with means for challenging local power structures" (McEwen 1975, p. 414). These organizations have been "aware of the relevance of state and national politics, especially as a source of help in the form of schools, electricity, etc. They have pressed their desires . . . by manipulation of the party structure and other entrees into central authority" (Malloy 1970a, p. 214). Conversely, the less a sector or group's power, the more likely it will be excluded from the national arena and seek communal solutions to its basic needs. Thus, for example, Guatemalan and Mexican Indians, largely excluded from taking part in the national political system and from receiving its benefits, consequently turn toward one another for problem solving. Even in Bolivia, where campesino organization has brought many payoffs from the national system, the less-organized peasant communities rely more heavily upon communal problem solving than national assistance (McEwen 1975, pp. 415-16). A theory of political participation should examine in detail the sources and conditions of citizen influence upon the state.

And finally, a theory of political activism must also examine the link between the participating citizen and the state from the perspective of the state itself. First, governments and ruling elites can, often conveniently for them, ignore much of the participation that takes place in the communal arena. In fact, the very nature of communal activism, as we have pointed out, may well derive from the successful exclusion of communal participants from access to national arenas of action. Forman's (forthcoming) contention that communal activism forestalls revolution among the peasantry points out the advantage of communal activity to elites—it reduces the necessity to share with masses the profits from the production of public and state-controlled private goods.

However, ignoring participation by mass publics is not the only posture assumed by states in Latin America. A second is the attempt to mobilize mass publics. States mobilize their citizens for various reasons—usually connected with efforts to expand or consolidate the power of incumbent elites over contenders, to expand the economic or military capacity of the state itself, or to increase the internal stability and security of the system. Among the forms of mobilization commonplace in Latin America have been the expansion of electorates and the creation of mobilizing institutions under government control (SINAMOS, labor confederations, community development associations, etc.). Such efforts have characterized nonrevolutionary and revolutionary, civilian as well as military governments. However, revolutionary regimes pursuing social reforms (such as Cuba and Peru) resort to mobilization of formerly excluded sectors to consolidate power, while both such revolutionary and counterrevolutionary regimes (e.g., Guatemala, Chile, Brazil) have demobilized (repressed) previously active sectors.

This brings up the third posture, that Latin American states attempt to control or manage participation, whether it be spontaneous or mobilized by the state itself. Just as the influence of citizens over public goods decisions derives from their power with respect to the state, so the ability of the state to control mass participation depends upon its power. Latin American governments that engage in liberal interest politics often find themselves over-powered, so to speak, by the numerous obligations they have incurred to different sectors (see Smith 1974). As a consequence, sectors of the state are frequently "parcelled out" to various interest groups, producing corporatist structures of interest representation (Malloy 1977a). Latin American military rulers, on the other hand, have often cruelly demonstrated that armed force, especially with external backing, provides the additional power for the control or repression of citizens' efforts to influence public goods distribution (Duff and McCamant 1976; Adams 1970).

Ultimately, then, a theory of political participation will need to examine the conditions and characteristics of states and national elites which affect their capacities to manage mass participation. This theory must be integrated with an analysis of the sources and determinants of the political activity of citizens, based not upon categories derived by observing other systems, but upon the particular characteristics of specific Latin American contexts and cultures. With such an approach, the study of political participation can tell us much about Latin American politics. As Adams (forthcoming) notes:

> Participation, it seems, must be seen not as a thing that people do with respect to governments, but rather as a structural, dialectic condition of complex societies. What it calls for is study of the efforts of all parties that are trying to exert power, to influence decision-making of other parties, actors, and sectors. Participation is merely another way of looking at power.

Notes

1. For example, for political parties see: Taylor (1954); Fitzgibbon (1957); Alexander (1964; 1969); Martz (1964; 1972); Tugwell (1965); Horowitz (1965); Williams (1967); Ranis (1968b); Burnett (1970); Petras (1970); Davies (1971); McDonald (1971; 1972); Mabry (1973); Ciria (1974); Chalmers (1974-75); North (1975); Wellhofer (1975).

For elections see: Lott (1957); Taylor (1960b); Borricaud (1964); Gil and Parrish (1965); Martz (1967); Soares (1967); Parrish et al. (1967); Schmitt (1969); López Pintor (1969); Sinding (1972); Harkness and Pinzón de Lewin (1975); Isuani and Cervini (1975); Prothro and Chaparro (1975); Valenzuela (1977).

2. For example, Milbrath's first choice of a definition was "behavior which affects or is intended to affect the decisional outcomes of government" (1965, p. 1). Though potentially a broad approach, Milbrath's application of the definition produced a hierarchical and unidimensional concept of participation that confined itself almost exclusively to electoral phenomena. Reacting to this, Verba and Nie took a broader approach. While their definition of participation, "those activities by private citizens that are more or less directly aimed at influencing the selection of governmental personnel and/or the actions they take," (1972, p. 2) did not differ greatly from Milbrath's, their operationalization did. The research project by Verba, Nie, and associates greatly expanded the use of the term. Their findings (Verba et al. 1971; Verba and Nie 1972; Verba et al. 1973; Kim et al. 1974) produced numerous new insights into the structure of participation and have rejuvenated an interest in the subject in general. In response to Verba and Nie's findings and critique of Milbrath's original definition, Milbrath and Goel revamped Milbrath's original formulation; participation became "those actions of private citizens by which they seek to influence or support government and politics" (1977, p. 2). It is ironic to note, thus, that while Milbrath's redefinition incorporated the Verba-Nie findings, it also went far beyond Verba and Nie's approach to include "support" participation, which Verba and Nie had explicitly rejected (1972, pp. 2-3).

3. For example, Verba and Nie (1972, pp. 2-3) elucidate their definition along several of these dimensions, accepting the criteria of action, conventionality, and governmental formalism, while rejecting support participation. Huntington and Nelson's (1976, pp. 4-7) definition requires action and governmental formalism, but rejects conventionality and the need for efficacy. As operationalized, Milbrath's (1965) approach included the criteria of action, governmental

formalism and conventionality, but rejected requirements of efficacy and intentionality. Refining this definition a decade later, Milbrath and Goel's (1977) approach remains basically the same, save that they explicitly include unconventional modes of participation within their definition. Parry's (1972, pp. 4-5) thoughtful essay insists on action and implicitly rejects governmental formalism through its flexible conceptualization of politics and public policy.

Certain of the contributors to this and its forthcoming companion volume (Seligson and Booth, forthcoming-b) differ with the editors on some of these issues. For example, Woy (chapter 12) follows Weiner's (1971) approach, which would appear to require efficacy (success) for an act to constitute participation and would reject at least some support activity. Scaff and Williams (chapter 3) emphasize a preference for discourse on issues as a basic requisite of politics, thus rejecting the notion that violent efforts to influence public goods distribution constitute participation.

4.   Our definition of public goods derives from Olson (1968, pp. 13-15) and Chaffee (1976, p. 56; forthcoming). We differ from Chaffee by expanding the notion of public goods to include those provided by communities, as well as formal governments.

5.   Abstention from suffrage constitutes a form of protest in nations such as Mexico, where officials consider high turnout to indicate support for the system. Abstention has also been used by the Peronists in Argentina to protest the exclusion of Peronist candidates. Unfortunately, "nonactions," like the "nondecisions" of Bachrach and Baratz (1963), commonly provide great difficulty for analysis because they are hard to identify and to measure. An interesting attempt to analyze this sort of activity is reported by Baloyra and Martz (1976a) who perform a statistical analysis on the reported casting of null ballots in the 1973 Venezuela presidential election.

6.   The reader should bear in mind that we use the term "good" in the economic sense, not in the ethicomoral sense. Thus, the stability of a regime is a good in the sense that it has value (either negative or positive). Chaffee (1976) alludes to this distinction when he refers to public goods regarded as undesirable by certain groups, as far as such groups are concerned, as "public bads."

7.   For example, see such works as Stokes (1952); Friedrich (1962; 1970); Johnson (1964); Lieuwen (1961; 1964); Urbanski (1966); Nun (1967); Blasier (1967); Needler (1968a; 1968b); Bailey (1967); Nash (1967); Bwy (1968); Payne (1968); Yglesias (1969); Von Lazar and Kaufman (1969); Anderson (1971); Bell (1971); Moreno and Mitrani (1971); Horowitz (1972); Suárez (1972); Romanucci-Ross (1973); Booth (1974); Kohl and Litt (1974); Russell et al. (1974); Schmidt (1974); Seligson (1974); Handelman (1975b).

8.   One difference between Biles' findings and those of Verba and Nie for the U.S., Austria, Nigeria, and India consists of the combination of the so-called personalized contacting mode with the campaigning mode in Uruguay. Biles speculates that this difference derives from Uruguay's intense and long-standing patterns of patronage politics that have converted political clubs and parties into virtually ubiquitous brokers between the citizen demand-maker and the state.

9.   Both Biles (chapter 5) and Booth (1976) report a "political communication" mode of participation that consists of discussion of political affairs. Under the definition of participation we have suggested in this essay, such political communication probably would not meet the basic criterion of attempting to influence the distribution of public goods. It would most commonly represent a condition—that of the collection of information or formation of opinion regarding personal goals and public goods—necessary to but not sufficient for affecting the distribution of public goods.

10.   See Booth (chapter 6) for these citations.

11.   For example, see Johnson (1958); Silvert and Germani (1961); Pike (1963); Conchol (1965); di Tella (1965); Goldrich (1965); Hobsbawm (1967); Adams (1967a; 1967b; 1970); Lambert (1967); Kahl (1968); Malloy (1970b); Bell (1971); Cornelius (1971); Fitzgibbon (1971); Germani (1972); Schmitter (1972); Smith (1974); Portes (1973a; 1973b); Inkeles and Smith (1974); Willems (1975, pp. 280-370).

12.   Similar processes for both Chilean and Brazilian peasants are described in Forman (1976) and Loveman (forthcoming). See also Henderson's (1976) description of the Colombian

government's post-*Violencia* efforts to encourage peasant participation in the campesino league ANUC and in the coffee grower's association.

13. Further statements which document the final two images (mass passivity and elite domination of participation) are too numerous to mention exhaustively, but a few more citations will serve to buttress the evidence. Milton Vanger (1969, p. 90) states: "One of the central insights of those who have analyzed peasant revolutions elsewhere is the political unawareness of the lower classes." Martin Needler describes peasants as very inactive (1968a, p. 59) and also states that "the political activity of the slum dweller is at present minimal" (1968a, p. 64). Denton, speaking of Costa Rica, has said: "For the majority of working-class members, participation is restricted almost exclusively to the formal act of voting" (1971, p. 82). Other examples may be found in Bonilla (1964, p. 194), Adie and Poitras (1974, pp. 48-49), Von Lazar and Kaufman (1969, pp.1-12), Edelmann (1969), Ray (1969, pp. 74-83), Bourne (1970, pp. 4-12), Prebisch (1971, p. 217), and Dealy (1974, p. 91).

14. While in many Latin American nations (e.g., Venezuela, Mexico, Costa Rica) voting is mandatory, this is also true in many European nations as well.

15. See note 13 above for citations.

16. See also, for example, McClintock's material on Peruvian peasants (1976a; 1976b) and the articles in the forthcoming companion volume to this collection: Seligson and Booth on Costa Rican peasants, Greaves and Albó on Bolivian miners, Landsberger and Gierisch on Mexican peasants, Handelman on Mexican union members, and Bourque and Warren on Peruvian peasant women.

17. The apparent primacy of private motivation raises a question about the distinction Verba and Nie draw between contacting public officials for personal as opposed to social objectives (1972, pp. 64-69). We disagree that the difference between personalized or particularized contacting and social contacting lies in "the scope of the outcome," by which Verba and Nie seem to suggest that the interests are either selfish (personalized) or altruistic (social). Rather, we believe the distinction lies in the nature of the goods toward which participation is aimed. The distinction is really between the nature of private and public goods. The contacts Verba and Nie describe as referring "specifically to the individual himself or to those immediately around him, such as his family" (1972, p. 66) have as their object *private* goods produced by the state (e.g., patronage jobs, exemption from military service). These are private goods, access to which may be easily controlled by the supplier. Contacts with social referents demand public goods: farm price supports, housing projects, public aid to parochial schools, etc. Public goods are provided by public expenditure, supplied to a group rather than a single individual, and may not be easily denied to any member of a group once supplied to one. The pursuit of public goods does not derive from a selfless effort on behalf of a collective benefit, but from the search for the private material reward each participant will derive from the use of the good (Olson, 1968, p. 22), or some private psychic reward attendant upon that pursuit. Such a distinction, if correct, would mean that "particularized" contacting is not truly political participation, since its object is the distribution not of public but of private goods.

18. We do not view this scheme of constraints as either exhaustive or definitive. There have been many others. For example, Matthews and Prothro (1966, p. 322) refer to historical events, socioeconomic attributes, community structure, attitudes and cognitions, and political system attributes. Milbrath (1965) and Milbrath and Goel (1977) identify stimuli, personal factors, social position, and environmental variables.

19. See Dietz (1974), Cornelius (1975), Booth et al. (1973), and Booth (1975a) for analyses of how the impact of residence in a particular community affects an individual's behavior.

*Baylis compares political participation in authoritarian, com-
munist, Third World, and Western capitalist settings. Each
system has its unique sets of rules and values that govern and
give participation its significance. Not limited to influencing the
choice of government personnel and policy, participation is
multifunctional and may serve very different purposes for governing elites and for ordinary citizens. Baylis then outlines four
types of participation and shows how participation and its
accompanying ideology provide important indicators of political change.*

2.
The Faces of Participation:
A Comparative Perspective

THOMAS A. BAYLIS

Few political phenomena can be said to be more protean than participation. If
one considers the forms political participation takes in authoritarian and democratic settings, advanced industrial and bare subsistence economies, or
capitalist and communist societies, it is quickly apparent that the term encompasses a great variety of activities and conveys many sharply divergent
meanings to participants, elites, and observers. Each society has its own
elaborate sets of explicit and tacit rules, values, and understandings that govern
political participation and give it its own gestalt for that society; and the
varieties of participation within a single society are nearly as diverse as those
between societies.

The empirical study of political participation by American political scientists, however, has generally reflected a narrower vision. Under the impact of
the voting studies and the self-celebratory bias that pervaded studies of
American politics until well into the 1960s, political scientists took a view of
participation highly colored by their own culture, and even within that culture
emphasizing the orthodox and approved forms of participation prescribed by
the doctrines of good democratic citizenship. The landmarks of this development will be familiar: the notion of a "hierarchy of participation" (Milbrath
1965, pp. 16-28), the model of the "civic culture" (Almond and Verba 1965),
and more recently, the notion of "modes of participation" based on empirical
clusterings of different participatory acts (Verba and Nie 1972).

It is probably especially significant that the Verba-Nie participation model,
intended from the outset for cross-national utilization, nevertheless also
emphasized a limited range of participatory activities chosen in accord with an

apparent ethnocentric bias. It is not surprising in this light that Verba, Nie, and their coauthors have tended to find the modal patterns of participation they discovered in the United States replicated in other societies. In many cases the types of participatory activities they chose to inquire about were probably less significant than those they overlooked. Where they did broaden their question-naire (the Netherlands, Yugoslavia), new modes or patterns of participation appeared (Verba et al. 1973; Verba and Shabad 1975). Other researchers using the Verba-Nie model made similar discoveries (see Booth 1977a, pp. 12-14; Biles, chapter 5; Dietz and Moore 1977).

Whatever its flaws, however, the Verba-Nie model has unquestionably per-formed an important catalytic function with regard to comparative partici-pation studies. Moreover, in some instances the Verba-Nie approach can usefully be brought together with a very different body of inquiry into participation (Verba and Shabad 1975). This literature attempts to relate democratic theory to the problem of political participation in contemporary settings, joining in particular a concern with the traditional forms of citizen participation to a "sociological" emphasis on participation at the place of work (see Pateman 1970; Bachrach 1966). Although much of this writing has been theoretical and speculative, it has acquired empirical underpinnings through the numerous studies of worker self-management in Yugoslavia (see, inter alia, Hunnius 1973; Broekmeyer 1970) and—as represented in the companion volume to this collection (Seligson and Booth, forthcoming-b)—studies of peasant and labor cooperatives in Latin America. Still another body of writing which deserves integration into a comprehensive and comparative portrait of participation is that dealing with political alienation, protest, and violence.

But it is not only that a greatly extended range of participatory behavior must be considered; we need to be more attentive to the diverse meanings of partici-pation in different settings. Participation studies have customarily sought to measure the quantity, distribution, and correlates of participatory acts among individuals; we need to look as well at the *context, functions, quality,* and *intensity* of participation. The cultural, ideological, and institutional setting within which participation occurs is of critical importance in determining its meaning both to the participant and the society. Moreover, however similar the forms of participation may be across societal boundaries, the functions they perform may be very different and go well beyond the influencing of decisions. By "quality" I refer to the subjective importance of participation to the participant himself; by "intensity" I mean the amount of time, effort, and emotional involvement invested by him.

My purpose in this paper is modest. I wish to begin by distinguishing between the perspectives on participation of political elites (or, more generally, of "the system") and those of the participant individuals, as a way of showing the variety of functions participation performs. Then I want to draw four sets of distinctions between types of participation, based upon my consideration of the forms participation takes in advanced capitalist, communist, and developing societies. My hope is that these distinctions can contribute to broadening our perspective on participation and particularly can help direct attention toward the questions of context, function, quality, and intensity mentioned above.

Elites naturally look upon participatory acts in terms of how effectively they serve elite goals. These goals may include the provision of public goods, as understood by the elites—e.g., legitimacy, stability, specific programs and policies, or (in the case of counter-elites) changes in policies and governments —and the securing of private goods for elite members—e.g., power, security in office, monetary and status rewards. Participation from the elite perspective is thus *multifunctional*. The ends it serves may include: socializing the individual into the value framework of the system; expressing support for or at least acquiescence in the position of the elites and/or their actions; communicating the sentiments and desires of the population to the elites and of the elites to the population; recruiting future political talent; mobilizing support for a given policy; exercising social control over potential and actual dissidents; diverting the dissatisfaction of citizens into manageable channels; or even carrying out quasi-governmental or quasi-administrative tasks (Baylis 1976b, p. 134-35).

From the perspective of the participant himself, participation may be a way of pursuing both collective and individual goods; it may be a means of influencing policy, but also of acquiring concrete monetary and occupational benefits, status rewards, social contacts, and other psychic and emotional gratifications. High rates of participation in authoritarian societies do not invariably imply coercion, but rather suggest the considerable range of rewards participation may bring apart from influence. The rational (or not so rational) calculation of costs and benefits the potential participant citizen may make need not include the possibility of genuinely influencing decisions at all (Seligson and Booth 1976, pp. 98-99; Booth and Seligson, chapter 1).

It is apparent that elite and citizen perceptions of the functions of participation will often not be congruent with one another. Of course, authoritarian governments and cynical citizens may each find participatory institutions useful for their own purposes, and the two may coexist with little conflict over a surprising period of time. In other situations, however, if exaggerated citizen expectations from participatory institutions are frustrated, the consequence may be political alienation manifested either in apathy or violence (e.g., Dietz and Palmer, chapter 11). Alternatively, the expectations and hopes invested in such institutions by elites may be disappointed by citizens whose view of them is more skeptical or more instrumental.

The social scientist studying political participation must be concerned with all these dimensions. But he is also obliged to ask still broader questions. What are the consequences of different patterns of participation for system stability and persistence? What is the impact, if any, of participation in bringing about, or retarding, basic social, economic, and political change? (See Huntington 1968.) And what is the relationship between the ideology prevalent in a particular society and the character of political participation in it? (See Zukin 1975.)

What the foregoing discussion makes evident is that, for our purposes at least, Verba and Nie's (1972, p. 2) definition of participation—"those activities by private citizens that are more or less directly aimed at influencing the election of governmental personnel and/or the actions they take"—is much too narrow. Participation can perform an enormous variety of functions, many of which have little to do with influencing governmental policy or the choice of personnel. Participation in authoritarian contexts is no less real or important because of its generally limited influence on decisions. Moreover, the psychological and emotional impact of participation may be just as powerful in the absence as in the presence of genuine influence.

This brings us to the first of the four distinctions I wish to draw and then to elaborate upon. It is between what Verba and Nie call "ceremonial" or "support" participation, on the one hand, and what we may term "influential" participation on the other. I will use the term "manipulated" participation for the first, although it suffers from pejorative overtones; "ceremonial" or "support" functions, however, are not the only ones noninfluential forms of participation perform. Manipulated participation is participation engineered or encouraged by a regime in pursuit of its own goals, while influential participation refers to activities having a genuine influence over the making of decisions. The distinction is not a new one; it corresponds roughly to the sociological pair of "felt" and "real" influence, although the emphasis I have chosen is on the functions of participation in the political system rather than for the individual (see Jowitt 975, pp. 79–80). The distinction is employed by Verba and Nie much in the way it has been by others: to dismiss most of the participatory activities carried out in authoritarian communist or Third World regimes by contrasting them unfavorably to Western forms of participation (1972, pp. 2-3). In fact, the distinction in practice is less clear-cut; four points in particular need to be stressed.

First, manipulated or support participation is not—because it is manipulated—therefore irrelevant and of no interest to political scientists; as we have observed, it may perform important and even crucial political functions. Second, *all* modern societies, whether dictatorial or democratic, have some forms of participation that admit a measure of genuine popular influence, and other forms that serve manipulative or supportive ends. Third, the two types of participation are closely related and often interdependent; for example, the same institution may serve influential and manipulative purposes simultaneously. An unusually instructive instance of this dual character might be found in the participatory structures imposed by the Peruvian military on its workers and peasants (Woy, chapter 12; Dietz and Palmer, chapter 11). Moreover, institutions created for manipulative reasons may over time acquire genuine influence, while once "real" participatory structures may atrophy and become shells for the ritualistic affirmation of decisions made elsewhere. Fourth—since influence is resistant to measure—the distinction between manipulative and influential participation may be apparent only to the beholder. A contemporary case in point is the phenomenon of group discussion and decision in mainland Chinese farms, factories, and schools. The conventional view of Sinologists that such discussions are of little weight or significance is opposed by commentators on the Left who view them as unprecedented examples of self-determination on the part of the Chinese masses (Townsend 1969; Hinton 1973).

The second distinction is between *citizen* participation and *worker* participation, and is based on the ideological setting within which participation occurs. Western democratic theory has emphasized the participation of the citizen as a continuing source of political legitimacy, and has seen the degree to which he can be persuaded to vote, inform himself, discuss candidates and issues, take part in campaigns, join political groups, and so on, as a measure of democratic success. The citizen, as the focal point of the theory and of political science research on participation, is defined according to his membership in a political-geographical unit. In spite of a loose historic (and, in French and German, linguistic) association between "citizen" and "bourgeois," citizen is generally understood as a *political* concept divorced from questions of social or economic standing (Dahrendorf 1967, pp. 63-77).

Marxism, on the other hand, concentrates its attention on the *worker* as a member of the class whose historical mission is to assume power from the bourgeoisie. In the orthodoxy of Eastern European Marxism-Leninism, working class rule is mediated during the transitional period from capitalism to communism by the rule of the class-conscious vanguard, the ruling Communist party. Nevertheless, even during this period the workers are expected to assume an ever greater range of social responsibilities, particularly in planning and management. The importance of worker participation understood as a form of political participation is enhanced by the centrality of the workplace in Marxist theory, where man creates his true self and which serves as a microcosm for social relations in the larger society. Western Marxists, unburdened by the bureaucratic and elitist elements of Leninism, tend to place still more emphasis on the primacy of workplace participation, often seeing it as the very essence of socialism, and denying that its full implementation need await the completion of a transitional period.

Existing communist states have generally been strongly influenced in their governmental structures and constitutions, if not in their political practice, by Western models; as a result, forms of "citizen participation" exist alongside those of worker participation, and sometimes blur indistinctly with them. This phenomenon is furthered by the tendency for communist states to expand the definition of "worker" so as to include collectivized peasants, white-collar employees, political functionaries, and members of the intelligentsia in it (Hough 1976, p. 10). In such circumstances proletarian and citizen legitimacy overlap and reinforce one another.

A similar dualism may well be found in Third World countries, although often with less overlapping. Political structures, especially in Latin America, often are based on Western models, while Marxian influence frequently finds its way into popular movements and peasant and labor organizations. Here the two sources of legitimacy may well be found in opposition to one another, the first more likely to be associated with conservative regimes, the second with radical regimes and oppositions. This opposition is, of course, among other things a reflection of political instability as expressed in the absence of a single consensual or authoritatively imposed ideological framework.

Is worker participation, one might inquire here, genuinely "political"? In the Marxian view, according to which the worker is the fundamental political and ideological unit, and the workplace is the locus of those basic relationships which define the society, the answer must be yes. A slightly different issue is raised by Western commenators who suggest worker participation as something of a substitute for broader citizen activities whose significance has dwindled in the face of the scale and bureaucratization of contemporary governments (Bachrach 1966; Pateman 1970). Often it is suggested that the organizations in which workers participate (or should participate) are "quasi-political" in their operations and effects. Yet there may be a significant distinction between the "collective goods" at stake in factory participation and the "public goods" at issue in societal participation. Worker participation might indeed turn out to be a *sublimation* of citizen politics, providing psychological satisfactions while actually solidifying oligarchical control over society-wide decisions.

Verba and Nie (1972, pp. 50-51) call attention to the dimension of *conflict,* which is the basis of our third distinction between different types of participation. Verba and Nie's assertion that voting and campaign activities are conflictual whereas "communal" and "contacting" activities are largely conflict-free can, I think, be justified only by the use of a narrow and mechanistic conception of conflict. To participate politically in Western pluralist settings, as I have argued elsewhere, almost invariably means to risk conflict, to put one's own interests and opinions forward in opposition to those of others (Baylis 1976a). Of course, "support" or manipulated participation is intended not to encourage conflict but, often, to suppress the potential for conflict; yet this motivation itself suggests the conflictual setting that most Western participation implies. Similarly, communal efforts on behalf of some project or set of goals, however much internal solidarity may be displayed, more often than not imply hostility toward or conflict with various "outsiders."

In the orthodox communist states, in spite of the dialectical character of Marxism, political leadership and "practical" ideology are directed toward social solidarity and an emphasis on the total social and psychological integration of society. Participation is meant first of all to reinforce social integration through its socializing and support-building functions. Principled conflict and faction-building are proscribed as of assistance only to the class enemy. The interest of East European writers in Marxian "conflict theory" has thus far not seriously eroded this view (Ludz 1973).

The attractions of participation without conflict are also powerful outside the communist bloc. Third World ideologies often claim a traditional basis of consensual and cooperative behavior, and reject both capitalist competitive economic models and the Marxian emphasis upon class conflict (e.g., Nyerere 1968, pp. 1-12). As a practical matter, fragile regimes may have good reason to fear the upsurge of ethnic, regional, linguistic, class, or other group rivalries, and seek to build participatory institutions that stress solidarity and mutual assistance. Such organizations may be presented as alternatives to parties or other older interest groups precisely because the latter are seen as excessively devoted to the conflict-laden pursuit of self-interest.

The difficulty is that it will almost invariably be necessary to place sharp restrictions on the autonomy, powers, and scope of participatory institutions if they are not to acquire conflictual characteristics—either internally or in their relationship to other groups and institutions. There is an apparent relationship here to the earlier distinction between manipulative and influential participation: the more the opportunity for genuine influence, the more conflictual participatory behavior seems likely to become.

The final distinction is between what we call simply—for want of more precise language—conventional and unorthodox foms of participation (Seligson and Booth 1976). The first, while not necessarily support or manipulated participation, remains within the received framework of accepted and acceptable political behavior. It is the sort of participation that has customarily received the greatest attention from political scientists. The specific activities falling under the conventional category will vary according to the ideology and political culture of a society; it is also evident that today's "unorthodox" activities may well become common and accepted tomorrow. Unorthodox participation, however, arises almost invariably from some level of disquiet with, if not alienation toward, the existing political system and the conventional participatory channels it offers; it will often emerge among a group that finds itself unable to use the conventional channels to any effect. Examples range from novel organizational forms to violence and demonstrations. Peasant self-help organizations, student riots, and guerrilla bands might all belong to this category. "Unorthodox" thus does not discriminate between reformist and revolutionary variations, or distinguish random unstructured protest, but its introduction here is meant simply to alert us to the danger of regarding as participation only that which is conventionally defined as such. Unorthodox forms also merit our attention as peculiarly important harbingers of political change.

A particularly interesting example of reformist, unorthodox participation is presented by the *jumin undo* of Japan, whose proliferation has accompanied the decline of partisan attachments and the apparent growth of alienation from the dominant political elites in that country.

> A typical *jumin undo* . . . is formed in a specific locale . . . and consists of volunteer activists from among its residents with an inevitably wide-ranging occupational, social, and economic spectrum who have never before associated or worked together. It attempts to generate public pressure, through boycott, demonstration, marches, public confrontation, sitdown strikes, and other forms

of activity upon one institution, organization, or agency or another deemed guilty of such public crimes as emission of pollutants; dereliction in enforcement or observance of environmental laws; charging of excessive prices; footdragging on effective environmental, housing, public health, sanitation, and anticorporate legislations; and so on (Tsurutani 1976, pp. 110-11).

There are somewhere between 1,400 and 3,000 such groups in Japan, and they have already had considerable success in electing local mayors and governors. Thus this form of participation is already well on its way to becoming "conventional" itself, although it remains apart and distinct from the national political system, which is said to be becoming still more bureaucratized and remote.

Unorthodox participation of a different type is illustrated by Greaves' and Albo's study (in Seligson and Booth, forthcoming-b) of the 1976 Bolivian tin miners' strike. What in democratic countries is a conventional way of expressing economic demands and a frequently accepted means of political protest was perceived by the Bolivian regime as a serious political challenge and was crushed with single-minded efficiency. It is worth noting that the regime also mobilized acts of conventional support participation in order to help isolate the strikers.

Conclusion

To this point this essay has avoided addressing directly the question of definition. In my discussion I have referred to a wide range of individual and group activities in the public realm. It seems to me an error to identify participation solely with attempts to exert political *influence* or to tie it irrevocably to the role assigned to the citizen in Western democratic theory. I have tried to suggest that a great deal of citizen political activity is neither particularly influential nor democratic, and yet is still important for understanding the political systems in which it takes place. The definition suggested by the editors of this volume—"activity influencing or designed to influence the distribution of public goods"—while having the virtue of going beyond an exclusive concern with *governmental* decisions, does not to my mind take adequate account of "private goods" and the other non-influential aspects of participation. What perhaps *does* distinguish participation is that in some sense it always pays rhetorical homage to influence and to democracy. That is, it is presented to the participant and is often accepted by him as a means of genuinely influencing, or at least becoming involved in, the authoritative decisions affecting his life and the lives of his fellow citizens. In authoritarian settings such a claim or belief is often mistaken or fraudulent; in Western democratic systems it may be equally misleading. One of the reasons for studying participation comparatively is to see how similar institutions and even similar ideological justifications for "participatory" activities can have very different functions and consequences; another reason is to uncover some of the myriad forms that attempts to assert and organize citizen influence may take.

What is common to both elites and masses in nearly all authoritarian and democratic regimes, communist and capitalist systems, and economically advanced and less developed countries, is their agreement that the ordinary citizen has a legitimate claim to influence or at least somehow take part in the public decisions affecting him. This apparent consensus on the fundamental justification for participation masks a great deal of hypocrisy and self-deception, of course, and often coexists with equally firm views on the need for the guidance of the citizen by technically and/or ideologically qualified elites. There is also substantial disagreement over the institutions and mechanisms that are most appropriate for giving effect to participation, and over the sorts of limitations and safeguards that need to be imposed upon it. Nevertheless, the fealty that all kinds of regimes swear to participation no doubt reflects their perceptions of the extent of popular aspirations for it. One may justifiably be skeptical over the intensity of the desire to participate in many cases, but one can hardly doubt its nearly universal existence. Because the desire exists—even in highly inegalitarian and tradition-bound settings—and because of the intimate relationship of participation to political change, it is a peculiarly important object of comparative study.

*Although the "primacy of politics" and "popular participation"
have an important place in the history of Western thought, both
have often been repudiated in recent studies of political development. Scaff and Williams restate and defend, with special
emphasis on Latin America, the arguments favoring political
forms of rule and extensive participation in the contemporary
developmental process. They argue that development depends
primarily on the organization of the polity, and that participation is the most effective mode of action for cultivating
political relationships.*

3.
Participation and the
Primacy of Politics
in Developmental Theory

LAWRENCE A. SCAFF and EDWARD J. WILLIAMS

"Popular participation" and the "primacy of politics" hold a hallowed place in
Western thought, yet neither has been totally accepted in theory and practice.
In one instance participation has been challenged on grounds of passion,
poverty, ignorance, fear, sin, or a frightening combination of these imperfections of human nature and condition. In another the spiritual, the social, or the
economic order has been posited as the primary dimension in the affairs of
mankind.

The postwar debate on development has added another chapter to this
chronicle by producing developmental theories and policies that deny the
normative and functional attributes of participation and the primacy of the
political order (Johnson 1964; Huntington 1968; Clark 1974). Participation is
counted a dysfunctional evil; in some cases the call is even for "departici-
pation" (Kasfir 1974). Politics is often thought to be beside the point. For
many contemporary developmental theorists economics and administration
instead are touted as the crucial developmental sciences and authoritarian
order the *summum bonum* of the political system.

Those who deny the normative and practical significance of participation
and politics have not yet carried the day. Many have begun to assail their
position (Key 1966; Thompson 1970; Pateman 1970; Barry 1970, pp. 13-46;
Hirschman 1971; Greenberg 1975; Berger 1976). It is the purpose of this
chapter to contribute to this critical response by presenting the argument for
political participation and the primacy of politics.

The Repudiation of Politics and Participation

Politics

Although the case against "politics" is found often enough in councils of government and the literature of political science, it will be useful to set forth briefly some of the relevant arguments. The rationale for repudiating politics extends from popular commentary to highly sophisticated claims about the epiphenomenal character of political factors, particularly when compared with their economic counterparts. The former typically fastens on the vulgarity of the entire messy performance acted out by a cast of selfish special interests, semisecret cabals, manipulators, and posturing *aficionados* engaged in a sleazy series of compromises, reciprocal back-scratchings, or outright corruption. It betrays deep-seated disaffection with both the inefficiency of the political process and the injustice and depravity of its results. In truth, popular dissatisfaction with politics is frequently a rather impatient and uncritical reaction to the imperfections of the human condition. It can be compared to the ambivalent self-hatred captured by J. D. B. Miller: "A reaction against politics is the rage of Caliban at seeing his face in the glass: politics is all too human" (quoted in Wiseman 1969, p. 2).

The more sophisticated repudiation of the political order is less vitriolic, but more basic. In the "classic" presentation of the issue, nineteenth-century liberal theorists separated out "economic man" as an analytic category for explaining social action, and buttressed by Marxian analysis, the "dismal science" was used to challenge the "master science." In these theories when problems of "causality" or historical development were addressed, politics was typically relegated to a position of diminishing importance, a mere reflection of underlying economic or technological forces.

Those old hypotheses should have passed into the files of useful heuristic devices, but their self-justifying perspective still survives. A well-known economist, for example, speaks of the "confection of self-regulating growth models" prevailing in his science. "In such constructs," he observes, "political factors and forces are wholly absent; if they play any role at all, it is that of spoilers" (Hirschman 1971, pp. 15-16).

Among developmental scholars and practitioners, economic growth has become the *idée fixe*. New social institutions are sometimes depicted as important auxiliary factors, and the diffusion of more "modern" cultural norms is pictured as a significant vehicle, but politics plays little role. A scholar illustrates the point in extrapolating national cohesion from economic "production and exchange."

> The hope is that, as economic interdependence within the nation increases, so too will grow the sense of common endeavor, that an attitude will come to prevail in which one's co-nationals are not distinguished from oneself on grounds of race, language, class or region, but that each citizen will come to feel that each other citizen is potentially a partner in the tasks of production and exchange (Anderson 1967, pp. 48-49).

There is no quarrel with hope (or any other virtue for that matter), but this approach to building national identity and communal solidarity does invite criticism.

If economics is the chosen science in these contemporary developmental fabrications, its handmaiden is public administration. The mania for administrative solutions combines the "politics is inefficient" charge with the naive claims of Weberian theorists who posit that administration can be separated from political considerations and influences. This ideological school conjures the vision of a benevolent, scientifically trained elite manipulating a baffling array of economic and social inputs, outputs, investments, diseconomies, exchange rates, payments, and savings. All are clearly programmed on a near-miraculous flow chart in a sterile and supposedly objective environment uninfected by the troublesome intrusion of political bacteria.

Participation

Condemnation of popular participation flows from the case against politics. It ranges from skepticism about human nature to the contemporary critique of the nature of undisciplined social mobilization and political decay. The most widely held prejudice posits that most people are not intelligent enough to take on the responsibilities of citizenship. The familiar argument pictures the masses as entangled in their own passions, whims, and selfishness. Governing is too important to be left to their incompetent and distorted judgment. At times the nonwhite inhabitants of the southern hemisphere are depicted as even less apt than their northern brethren. Writing in defense of Indira Ghandi's power-grab, an Indian philosopher is reported "expatiating on the 'congenital unfitness of Indians for democracy' " (Selbourne 1976, p. 31).

This line of reasoning usually holds that increases in participation serve the unwelcome purpose of including those with undesirable attributes: the incompetent, uninformed, authoritarian, alienated. Participation becomes self-defeating; further doses require coerced regimentation (with consequent loss of liberty) and supposedly lead to disruption of the prevailing participatory arrangements. In order to avoid this situation, self-styled benevolent elites isolate the masses, lest they fall prey to their own instincts or to the machinations of deceitful demagogues. The Peruvian generals, who talk much of participation, add a variation on this theme in calling for "free and active" participation, but "without the influence of imported ideologies" (Plan Inca 1974, p. 46). Even in "enlightened" competitive systems, "elitist democratic theory," as it is sometimes labeled, advances the corollary idea "that the role of the people is to produce a government." Participation is restricted to "that institutional arrangement for arriving at political decisions in which individuals acquire the power to decide by means of a competitive struggle for the people's vote" (Schumpeter 1950, p. 269). All significant decisions are left to elites.

As is well known, elitist theory has flourished in some parts of social science (Kariel 1970; Thompson 1970). Using as its standard example the Weimar

Republic's collapse and the subsequent horrors of Nazi rule, the new scientific "realism" has proposed that increases in participation tend to unleash destructive forces rather than promote rational and just policies. Studies of voting behavior have attempted to confirm the public's ignorance and apathy and to show that voters are often motivated by irrational considerations. Apathy is then praised as a normal sign of public contentment, a "cushion" protecting a stable society from violent change. Citizens and social scientists are invited to lower expectations about participation that stem from the "traditional" democratic theory of Rousseau, Jefferson, Mill, and others—a theory thought to be too naive and optimistic to account for the latest evidence.

Bringing the argument closer to problems of development, participation is condemned for introducing and encouraging divisiveness, if not outright disloyalty. The higher good for the critics is national unity. Political participation centering on corporate group, class, region, religion, or tribe is interpreted as threatening the national community. Analyzing the rise of African military regimes, a student of the subject notes that "the goal seems to be the achievement of homogeneity by political fiat, as if the rulers genuinely believed that the absence of conflict somehow produces national integration" (Zolberg 1968, p. 87).

All of these real and imagined bugaboos of participation have been gathered up and embellished in the last dozen years or so in the contemporary language of development: social mobilization-cum-praetorianism-cum-political decay. Socioeconomic modernization is said to mobilize the undisciplined masses. They then place unmanageable demands on weak governments which fall to other weak governments. The process continues ad nauseam and culminates in political decay, if not total collapse. Mobilization generates participation, which outstrips institutionalization, thus leaving the nation in chaos. In short, participation represents a "crisis," not an opportunity.

Given such scenarios, it is no wonder that participation has fallen on hard times and that the call for political order based upon coercive power has emerged as the most salient goal of the development process. The message is as simple as its proponents are glib: A strong and stable government is both logically and chronologically the first principle of successful development. Underdeveloped systems are so rent by divisions, indiscipline, and shortsighted demands for instant gratification that effective government based on shared values and popular support is impossible. Hence, order cannot evolve through the political process of debate, discussion, and participation. However regrettable (and however temporary), order must be grounded in domination by tightly organized authoritarian government.

The Renewal of Politics and Participation

Like the heresies of old, the case against politics and participation commits numerous sins of omission and commission. It fails to understand the fundamental nature of the political order and the omnipresent fact of political intercourse. It misconceives the relationship between politics and economics and is ingenuous anent the science of administration. Even more unfortunate, the criticisms convolute human priorities and refuse to grasp the functional contributions of popular participation.

Understanding the primacy of politics and the value of participation in development requires a more general clarification of concepts. The practices of politics and participation may display a range of variation in actual situations, but the variations are always of degree and not of kind. Some basic definitions help illuminate the concepts' main characteristics and establish their particular significance in the development context.

Politics and Participation Defined

While differing in subtlety and intellectual focus, all of the viewpoints recited above may well be united in a common misconception about the nature of politics, political community, and political authority. As a point of departure, politics should be conceived as a special kind of human activity that uses discussion and authority for arriving at decisions over conflicting purposes (Chapman and Scaff 1976, pp. 547-54). Political relationships appear when individuals associated in community act jointly on public affairs, notwithstanding significant disagreements, and without one will being violently imposed on the rest. What Dewey called "methods of discussion, consultation and persuasion" (1927, p. 207) are distinctively political and must be encouraged in any political environment.

Politics must not be confused with a monopoly on the means of force or violence. Polities use force, but it is not the distinctive means of political decision making and policy execution. Indeed, when force appears it signals the erosion of the intrinsic modes of political activity. It means that political community has disintegrated, that public debate and persuasion have proved wanting, and that political authority is in jeopardy.

Authority in a political system may assume many guises. As Arendt points out, it is "the most elusive of these phenomena and therefore . . . most frequently abused" (1969, p. 45). The term should suggest the important sense of moral obligation and the "rightness" of political arrangements that underlie any legitimate political system. Authority identifies and highlights the reciprocal relationships of accountability that connect citizens and governmental officeholders. Community and concomitant authority, in sum, are the crux of politics and, of course, must be the crux of political development. It is foolhardy to assume that political community and authentic authority will arise naturally out of economic development. On the contrary, politics is a distinctive human project which elicits its distinctive processes and its special genius.

Participation is the most tangible and efficacious mode of action for cultivating political relationships in a community. Like politics, it is fraught with many vexing conceptual conundrums, not all of which can be resolved in this brief exposition (see Scaff 1975). It is still important to set out several crucial propositions. In the first instance, participation implies conscious and voluntary activity that contributes or attempts to contribute to making public decisions in a context of conflicting purposes. It always has some public consequences, even though actors' motives and interests may be private. It promotes the active side of citizenship, involving the free exercise of rights rather than passive reception of benefits from the state. Verba and Nie are correct in insisting that participation should be distinguished from mere "support" orchestrated by a regime to celebrate its rule (1972, p. 2; also Verba 1967, pp. 55-56; Verba, Nie, and Kim 1971, pp. 9-10). Beyond their definition, however, it should be emphasized that participation has interactional as well as instrumental orientations. That is, it may be characterized by attempts to influence governmental decision making, but it may also be directed toward sustaining the process of communication itself. These are mutually reinforcing aspects of participation's effect on politics.

Secondly, a clear distinction must be maintained between political activity and the several variants of socioeconomic participation. Participation in corporate and group life is no doubt meaningful, but its political significance must be demonstrated. Actions performed and attitudes acquired in the role of worker, student, family, or church member may well have an effect on the political role of citizen, but it should not be assumed that any kind of activity or involvement automatically qualifies as participation in political life. To carry the argument one step further, it is quite conceivable for a full and open system of participation to prevail in corporate groups, but for the "political" system to remain closed or restricted. This situation obtained in the medieval communes and to some extent it is also illustrated by the post-1968 Peruvian experiment.

Thirdly, it is particularly important for an analysis of participation in developing areas to posit a distinction between local and national activity. In the developmental context localized participation should be viewed as a subordinate part of the larger imperative. National government is almost always the all-important initiator and implementer of policies and programs, for it enjoys a monopoly on legal-administrative skills and economic resources. Participation which fails to influence national government should be suspect. Writers in the Jeffersonian tradition have rightly advocated action at the local level as a stepping-stone to more ambitious achievements, but the developing nations count different ideological orientations and differing practices. Hence, political activities in these countries must eventually focus on the national level if they are to be credible and meaningful instances of participation.

The Primacy of Politics

The fully developed defense of participation must proceed from the Aristotelian idea of the "primacy of politics." Aristotle did not say that politics was better than other dimensions of the human condition, nor did he claim mastery for it because of a monopoly on the means of coercion. Rather, he described the scope of politics as an organizing, coordinating, and directive principle. The political order set out a framework of rules and institutions in which the entire community operated.

Building upon the Aristotelian foundation, the primacy of politics should also be understood to include cultivating the instrumentalities of politics, the methods of discussion, persuasion, and participation. Creating legitimate authority and gaining a monopoly on the means of force are important tasks in new states. But the former should be accomplished by agreement with the political arrangements in a society, not by fiat. Legitimacy is nothing more than a cruel joke without discussion and participation as minimal necessary conditions. This does not deny the salience of monopolizing "the use or threat of use of legitimate physical coercion," as one text records it (Almond and Powell 1966, p. 18), but any state that becomes preoccupied with this task simply reverses the priorities of development, placing compulsory stability ahead of politics.

Amending Aristotle's view in this way suggests that politics has certain "presuppositions" without which political practice is difficult to sustain. Three are particularly important: (a) social relationships, expressing the presence of a human association; (b) relationships of community, expressing shared associational norms and identity; (c) a degree of diversity and stress within the association, too tenacious to be handled by innocent conviviality. The actual existence of such presuppositions is problematic, especially in the developing nations. Often the task of development is interpreted to involve creating norms and identities around which a sense of community can grow. But this is still a task requiring political direction and political methods. Mistakes are made when elites want to interpret the presence of internal stress as justification for antipolitical policies of repression which they believe will lead to that unity of norms and purposes missing earlier.

The constituting act and the ongoing impetus to development is not the expansion of the economy or the secularization of society, but rather the organization of the polity. As Adam Smith wrote, to proceed from the "lowest barbarism" to the "highest degree of opulence" called for three political requisites—"peace, easy taxes, and a tolerable administration of justice" (quoted in Hirschman 1971, p. 2). The simple idea of a "market," characterized by self-interest and competition, was hedged in by political rules. Even in Smith's day the "invisible" self-regulating laws of exchange were a convenient fiction, not a description of a world without politics. Reflecting on this actual Smithian world of economic growth, W. W. Rostow gives the point added historical depth:

> Although the period of transition . . . saw major changes in both the economy itself and in the balance of social values, a decisive feature was often political. Politically, the building of an effective centralized national state—on the basis of coalitions touched with a new nationalism, in opposition to the traditional landed regional interests, the colonial power, or both, was a decisive aspect of the preconditions period; and it was, almost universally, a necessary condition for takeoff (1962, p. 7).

A distinguished contemporary political economist crystallizes and expands the argument in discussing the developmental process. Economic progress, he contends, depends on a number of conditions determined by public policy:

> At any one historical stage, the economy functions within a given political and institutional framework; on the basis of and owing to this framework, economic forces left to themselves can achieve some forward movement, but beyond a certain point further development becomes more difficult and eventually is held back by the unchanging political framework which, from a spur to progress turns into a "fetter" . . . (Hirschman 1971, p. 16).

Whatever the causes of change and the origins of relevant groups, struggles over policy will take place in the political arena, and results will be a matter of political choice.[1] Furthermore, a Platonic rescue is an extreme improbability. In Hirschman's words,

> . . . the need for corrective public policy measures could be obviated by the timely arrival on the scene of creative Schumpeterian entrepreneurs, who are able to perceive that change in circumstances or the new opportunities that go unrecognized by their more routine-ridden and prejudiced contemporaries. My point here is precisely that in some key situations, *the likelihood of such a providential appearance is infinitesimal* (1971, pp. 24-25; emphasis added).

If the chances for salvation emanating from the wizardry of "Schumpeterian entrepreneurs" provides little hope, the pseudoscience of the public administrators is equally wanting. The advocates of a suprapolitical public administration are blind to myriad unanticipated consequences because they refuse to understand the omnipresence of the political. If these utopians had read Weber carefully, they would have discovered that their science's founder clearly perceived that efficient decisions sometimes lack both rationality and justice. Moreover, he understood that bureaucracy has inherent political defects. Administrative norms of decision and action, guided by fixed rules and jurisdictions, are simply unable to handle problems of political accountability and initiative (Weber 1968, III, pp. 956-1005, 1381-1469).

In sum, the entire developmental process goes beyond economics and public administration. The drive toward development at its very core calls for effective utilization of scarce material and human resources which is essentially a task for political organization.

Participation Defended

The third part of the argument analyzes and defends participatory politics as the correct developmental strategy—both in normative and functional terms. It demonstrates the intrinsic and extrinsic merits of participation, defending it as a primary value in its own right and in terms of contributions to other politically relevant ends.

Participation and Justice. The denial of popular participation in the polity betrays a convolution of values. The purpose of the polity should be conceived as creation of an environment in which justice can be pursued. Evolution of order or creation of wealth may be elements of this larger charge, but they must be interpreted as subordinate parts of the whole. In rejecting justice in favor of order, the advocates of authoritarianism alter the first question of politics to read " 'What is the stable society?' Order is not considered a prerequisite for achieving the highest political good, but itself becomes the highest political good" (Kesselman 1973, p. 142).

When the primary purpose of the polity is bastardized, the entire conceptualization of the political process is set askew, and the normative connotations and policy implications of the developmental critique are corrupted. When order becomes the end-all and be-all of politics, then, ipso facto, governors bend every effort to establish their preconceived idea of order and squelch whatever activity seems to jeopardize it. All forms of political opposition and every petition for free participation are interpreted as threatening order-cum-developmental progress-cum-order, the now intellectually sanctioned *summum bonum*. Suppressing political parties, outlawing labor unions, exiling journalists, creating "death squads," torturing nuns, or consciously contributing to the maldistribution of wealth are all excused as "necessary" aspects of the search for developmental progress.

The entire panoply of developmental theory lends legitimacy to tyrannical institutionalized violence because it begins with a mistaken interpretation of the nature of politics and its relationship to justice. "My objection is not to describing how authorities attempt to maintain dominance," charges a critic, "but rather to the implicit espousal of their cause: the literature of political development might be assigned reading in Silone's school for dictators" (Kesselman 1973, p. 144).

This particular defense of participation can be clarified and made more accessible by using some of the ideas in John Rawls' *A Theory of Justice* (1971). This work shows in detail that participation is more consistent than any alternatives (e.g., repression, coercion) with the principles of justice. Rawls' revisionist liberal theory starts from the initial situation of choice, the "original position," in which individuals choose (without foreknowledge of their social position) principles that govern their associations with others and the distribution of advantages. Two principles are selected: (1) "each person is to have an equal right to the most extensive basic liberty compatible with a similar liberty for others;" (2) "social and economic inequalities are to be arranged so that they are both (a) to the greatest benefit of the least advantaged and (b) attached to offices and positions open to all under conditions of fair equality of opportunity" (1971, pp. 60, 83).

Principles at this level of generality do not speak for themselves, of course, and much interpretation is needed before ambiguities can be clarified. It is evident that the different principles may conflict with each other. One of the tasks of a theory of justice is to show how equality and efficiency can be reconciled, how individual liberty can be combined with social order. It should be stressed that the first principle of justice, sometimes called the "principle of (equal) participation" (1971, p. 221), is to have *priority* over other competing principles. This means, in effect, that citizens must have an equal right to take part in politics because such a right is a sine qua non of our ideas about justice, which are in turn a statement of the political association's *raison d'être.*

These ideas are important as a restatement of the central purpose of politics and as a proposed standard for evaluating different forms of rule. Applied in the development context, the analysis suggests that one ought in principle to prefer a society characterized by political rule that maximizes participatory opportunities or, minimally, a government committed to promoting such opportunities. Thus, the dignifying condition of participatory self-government becomes the gauge by which developmental progress is measured.

The exercise of free speech, the right to criticize government, and popular participation generally are manifestly moral imperatives. Other goods in competition with them may sometimes lead to their modification, and these situations demand recognition and study. However, these enduring moral imperatives of human association should not be shunted aside in promiscuous pursuit of authoritarian order. Developmentalists should be concerned with the priority of participation and affiliated values like justice and liberty, not merely with the preservation of stability and order alone.

Relating the principle of equal participation to development, Peter Berger identifies the core of the critique:

> Development is not what the economic and other experts proclaim it to be, no matter how elegant their language. Development is not something to be decided by experts, simply because there are no experts on the desirable goals of human life. Development is the desirable course to be taken by human beings in a particular situation. As far as possible, therefore, they ought to participate in the fundamental choices to be made, choices that hinge not on technical expertise but on moral judgments (1976, p. 59).

Development, in other words, ought to be returned to those it affects most, and its content ought to emerge from the participatory process. Developmentalists are fond of thinking in quite different terms, proposing for instance that development's task is to "manage the tensions" and "contain the participatory and distributive demands" that may erupt in a society (Coleman 1971, p. 78). This is the language of manipulation and control, not the language of participation, and is a pale reflection of the principles defended here.

The Functions of Participation

These affirmations may be obvious (indeed, sacred) to many, but it is necessary to recognize that the values of participation can no longer claim the validity of revealed truth. Hence, a full defense must explicate the extrinsic practical contributions of a participatory political system in the developmental process.

Political Communication. In the first instance, political participation forms the nub of an efficient communications system providing information about the values, prejudices, ambitions, and aspirations of the national community. Since intelligent and effective governing is based in part on accurate information, developmental strategy is well advised to nurture participatory input to increase its competence. Listening to what people say, in this sense, is more than acknowledging their innate dignity; it is a necessary means of improving policy and understanding the boundaries of the prudent and the possible.

At the most basic gradation of prudence, attempting to undertake the impossible is fraught with deleterious consequences and may well lead to massive collapse—the final manifestation of political decay and inane developmental policy. Bernard Crick makes the point in discussing the causes of revolution:

> For the most usual cause of revolutions, when all is said and done, is not that some band of zealots . . . has pushed the old government away . . . but just that the old government, probably for a great variety of reasons, simply ceased to govern. And the most usual cause of failing to govern is simply not knowing what the governed want or will settle for, not giving them adequate representation (1964, pp. 114-15).

The more usual circumstances do not, of course, involve actual revolutions, but are instead characterized by counterproductive policies and plain ignorance. Failures are often caused simply by inadequate or incorrect information, itself a result of elites' unwillingness to listen to anyone but themselves. The trash heaps of developmental policies are filled to overflowing with just such examples of well-laid plans gone agley. In a discussion of Brazil's increasing economic difficulties, for example, *Latin America* reports that "many investment decisions can now be seen to have been unwise, and some were undoubtedly taken on the basis of who paid the most to the official involved. . . . There is, too, a misplaced faith among the Brazilian elite in the efficacy of technocratic solutions" (1975, p. 285). In the same vein, the Brazilian authoritarians place little credence on the productivity of open discussion and debate which might correct developmental policy decisions and diminish corruption. "It has become obvious," according to the same source, "that the problem cannot be separated from censorship of the press, the arbitrary appointment of state governors and other officials, the lack of parliamentary checks on the actions of ministers, and the general exercise of unlimited power by a dictatorial government" (1975, p. 285). Across the Amazon basin, the well-known Peruvian novelist Mario Vargas Llosa testifies to the same situation in arguing that "the revolution is in danger of becoming fossilized" because "the Government has isolated itself from public debate" (Kandell 1975, p. 7).

Legitimacy. In analyzing developmental policy, the Brazilian economist Celso Furtado points toward a second cluster of functional benefits from participation:

> All genuine developmental policies derive their power from an amalgamation of value judgments upon which the ideals of the community are concentrated. And, if a community does not have political organs capable of interpreting the legitimate aspirations of the community, it is not equipped to undertake the tasks of development (Furtado 1970, p. 24).

Although citizens in underdeveloped lands may often be denied legitimate government, the concept is still a viable one. After all, university students, journalists, intellectuals, and other elites advocate legitimate government; authoritarian regimes that outlaw participation are constantly condemned as illegitimate. Suppression of participation erodes the possibility of evolving authentic long-term governmental legitimacy because it evokes dissatisfaction in the polity tending to polarization and fissiparous disintegration.

In the final analysis, indeed, political instability is increased rather than moderated by the politics of authoritarian order. The Peruvian case exemplifies the point. One analysis argues that "Such repression as there is doesn't eliminate opposition, but simply channels it into secretive or violent outlets" (Adams 1976, p. 47). Writing before the 1975 coup, another sympathetic source agreed that "the absence of a bond between government and masses, insofar as the Peruvian Revolution was undertaken for but not with them, tends to create areas of conflict that are becoming the Achilles heel of the whole transformation process" (*Comercio Exterior* 1975, pp. 97-98).

The posturing in search of popular participation in post-1968 Peru was explicitly confected "to mobilize enough strength to undertake and endure the heavy task of national development and to resist external pressure and conspiratorial machinations" (Jaguaribe 1973, p. 513). The warning against external pressure also highlights a sin of omission by those frightened by the menace of undisciplined participation and political decay, for causes of instability are frequently found in the larger context of international politics. According to the summation of one commentator,

> Political development in the Third World cannot be dissociated from its colonial origins and the contemporary international context. Western military, economic and spiritual conquest has been a major cause of instability. Moreover, the fragility of rulers is due as much to external intervention and the cold war contest. . . . The picture is less than complete if one treats developing countries as isolated and autonomous, without reference to foreign military assistance, covert external political intervention and overt military invasion, the power of multinational corporations over the political and economic processes of third world countries, dependency relationships more generally, and the manipulation of the international monetary system and trade relationships to favor the interests of the wealthy and powerful nations (Kesselman 1973, pp. 149-50).

In responding to these pressures participation can evolve increasing resiliency and strength in the overall system. The incorporation of new participants may encourage "greater consensus or congruence among those who have power and those who seek it as to procedures, institutions, and demands" and it may bring about "a new capacity for coping with a new range of problems," including both internal and external challenges to legitimate authority (Weiner 1971, p. 194).

Of course, one must distinguish between manipulating citizens in order to induce regime support and creating legitimacy for a national political system through participatory arrangements. Some developmentalists stumble into absurdities like ". . . governmental institutions derive their legitimacy and authority not from the extent to which they represent the interests of the people or of any other group, but to the extent to which they have distinct interests of their own apart from all other groups" (Huntington 1968, p. 27). Possessing "distinct interests" and manipulating citizens in accordance with them should be called what it is—manipulation—and not be sugarcoated with the language of legitimacy.

Those who oppose participation and offer stability as the primary political value misconstrue this relationship. Participation does not depend on stability, but rather assists in its foundation through the evolution of legitimate, systemic authority. The long-term expectation is that *regularized* participatory channels tend to moderate system demands and defuse potentially revolutionary frustrations and ambitions.

Political Education and Efficacy. Political education forms another nexus in the positive attributes of participation. Proponents of participatory democracy have long emphasized a sort of on the job training designed to evolve attitudes contributing to a just and well-ordered political system. As part of a larger socialization process, participation teaches the citizenry procedural skills and, more importantly, brings about increased awareness of politics and enhances the capacity for dealing with political problems.

Political education in this sense is not equivalent to indoctrination or covert socialization. Instead, the concept is useful for designating increases in individual knowledge and awareness of participatory opportunities. Although its portrait of "modernized man" is sometimes too good to be true, a recent work is on the right track when it proposes that certain "personal qualities" are the result of participation: "openness to new experience," "readiness for social change," "disposition to form or hold opinions," and learning to control one's environment are listed as important possibilities (Inkeles and Smith 1974, pp. 19-25).

Furthermore, such qualities are often the result of participation in a variety of socioeconomic institutions, not just in the political arena proper. For example, the same authors conclude that "the factory not only changes men's styles of political participation, but also increases their knowledge of subjects ordinarily assumed to be the distinctive focus of classroom instruction" (1974, p. 259). Cultivating participation in the industrial setting may well have profound political effects, as much evidence demonstrates (Pateman 1970; Jenkins 1973; Greenberg 1975).

The individual's sense of identity and worth as a citizen—in a word, his sense of "efficacy"— is closely allied with political education; it would be difficult to imagine one developing without the other. As indicated above, this function of participation is not confined to narrowly conceived political acts, such as voting. Participation in both the polity and the economic enterprise tends to enhance personal self-images resulting in increased individual efficacy. The message is significant: not only does participation lead to improved political relationships, but it is also important in contributing to a more vibrant society and a more productive economy.[2]

The value of these phenomena for developing nations is, of course, crystal clear. If increased economic output be a crucial part of their developmental strategy, then it ought to follow that they should institutionalize participation across a broad range of political and socioeconomic institutions in the national system.

Conclusion

However obvious it may be, it is also poignantly true that the basic questions governing human affairs are seldom put to rest. Sometimes in differing contexts and often in different idiomatic guises, they return to haunt almost every generation, evoking learned and polemic rhetoric in another dreary reenactment of debates and disputations seemingly lost in the obscure annals of history.

Post-World War II developmentalism has catalyzed another reincarnation of that historic precedent in its challenge of two essential truths of Western theory and practice: to wit, that politics is the master science, and that participatory freedom is both better and more productive than authoritarian order. As the frustrations and failures of the developmental experience have accumulated, moreover, it appears that the anti-political authoritarians have emerged as a major force in both the halls of academe and the corridors of power. It has been the purpose of this effort to respond to their position by restating the theoretical and practical arguments favoring participation within the context of contemporary developmental progress.

The conclusions have been sufficiently clear as the analysis has unfolded and want only a brief summation. In the first instance, this essay has demonstrated that economic policy is subordinate to and dependent upon the contextual and organizational parameters defined by the political order. There is no economic growth, that is, without political innovation; the primacy of politics is as applicable in post-war developmental theory and practice as it has always been.

The second focus of this essay has analyzed the failings of developmental strategies characterized solely by authoritarianism and the desire for stability. It has claimed, by way of corrective argument, that equal participation in the polity is a higher value than tyrannical control. The developmentalists ought to begin with a concern for justice rather than a dogmatic commitment to order. Beyond the essential rightness of participation, moreover, experience indicates that participatory developmental strategies encourage significant functional contributions to the developmental process in a society. One should expect improvement in political communication, legitimacy of the political system, and political education and personal efficacy when participatory policies are pursued.

Notes

1. The primacy of politics does not mean, however, that a political framework invariably "determines" economic growth or the character of economic factors. Deterministic language is misleading in this respect; the old materialist and idealist arguments are both partly correct. Causality in history should be viewed as a two-way street, a process of reciprocal or "dialectical" interaction. In Hirschman's words, when "fetters" appear, ". . . at that point, political-institutional change is not only necessary to permit further advances, but is also highly likely to occur, because economic development will have generated some powerful social group with a vital stake in the needed changes" (1971, pp. 16-17).

2. Informed by this view, even typically conservative industrial managers have embraced schemes of worker participation in hopes of improving industrial efficiency and productivity. Within the American context a political scientist reports that the likes of General Foods, Texas Instruments, Corning Glass, the Bell System, Polaroid, Monsanto, and Bankers Trust of New York have instituted workers participation programs and "all . . . report significant improvements in economic indicators and labor relations" (Greenberg 1975, p. 194).

Of course, the "management" school of thought advocates participation mainly for reasons of economic expediency. The profit motive is still much in evidence, and the scope of worker participation is generally quite limited. (For example, profit sharing schemes for workers are rare.) Consequently, one must view these developments in industry with considerable caution. For informed critiques see Blumberg (1969), Pateman (1970), Dahl (1970), and Jenkins (1973). A fascinating account of an experiment with "industrial democracy" in the Scott Bader Commonwealth in England can be found in Blum (1968).

II
The Citizen and Participation

The authors argue that compulsory suffrage in Venezuela has weakened the well-documented linkages between social status, political efficacy, and voter participation. They identify three modes of campaign activism, and their analysis shows that campaign efficacy does not increase with socioeconomic status but varies more closely with attitudes about the regime. Involvement is predominantly but not an exclusively partisan mode of campaign activism, and socioeconomic factors have their greatest impact on levels of exposure.

4.
Dimensions of Campaign Participation: Venezuela, 1973

ENRIQUE A. BALOYRA and JOHN D. MARTZ

One justification for the study of campaigning and voting is that, in truly competitive situations, they influence the distribution of public goods. Recent disciplinary efforts have attempted to put these "classical" aspects of political participation in sharper perspective, emphasizing other participatory activities of more direct influence on the distribution of public goods. This emphasis was long overdue but there remain some aspects of classical participation which deserve further analysis and cross-cultural validation.

Utilizing the case of Venezuela, we show that in a context of compulsory voting, partisan and attitudinal factors may become more important determinants of participation than the social circumstances of individuals. Following the seminal work of Verba and Nie (1972) we try to generalize their analytical approach to the arena of campaign activities, showing that there are three different dimensions of individual reaction to campaigns. Throughout the discussion we try to demonstrate how the Venezuelan context alters the web of relationships that seem to characterize this type of participatory behavior.

Our emphasis on campaign behavior is intended to call attention to its multidimensional nature. In a previous report (Baloyra and Martz 1976b), we considered campaigning and voting simultaneously and found that, as a result of popular compliance with compulsory suffrage, little can be said about the variation of voting participation in Venezuela.[1] On the other hand, our findings about null voting and withdrawal from electoral participation, aspects which have received only superficial and impressionistic treatment in the literature, deserved more ample and separate reporting.[2]

We believe that the Venezuelan campaign and general election of 1973 meet minimum standards of relevance which justify their study. The 1968 race proved the closest in Venezuelan history. The Social Christian candidate, Rafael Caldera, was proclaimed the victor by a margin of 31,000 in an electorate of 3.7 million. His 29 percent of the vote was 0.8 percent ahead of the government candidate Gonzalo Barrios of the *Acción Democrática* (AD) party. The 1968 campaign, marked by intense competition, was the first in which the outcome had been in doubt and in which an incumbent administration was voted out of office.

The situation appeared similar in 1973. There were few "natural" or automatic candidates on the scene. Given the anticipated closeness of the race, the two major parties engaged in strenuous organizational efforts. Carefully designed strategies were reevaluated constantly. For two years, voters were inundated with an outpouring of propaganda. By 1973, the sheer cost of campaigning had reached such proportions as to lie beyond all but the Social Christian (COPEI) and Social Democratic (AD) parties; we estimate the total cost of the campaign to have exceeded one hundred million dollars. Political polling was utilized extensively, giving the major campaigners feedback on the closeness of the race, as well as ample opportunity for controversy and partisan accusations of falsification. Our analysis of the behavior of campaign actors suggests that no other political campaign in Latin America comes close to the richly endowed, media-oriented Venezuelan campaign of 1973 (Martz and Baloyra 1976).

The Venezuelan case poses an interesting array of theoretical questions because, after all, what kind of testable hypotheses obtains under conditions of compulsory suffrage? How can one test the socioeconomic or any other model of participation in a situation where virtually everyone votes? What kinds of paradigms have operational and existential validity in such a context? What is the meaning of nonparticipation under these circumstances? Would nonparticipant Venezuelans resemble, in their attitudes and social circumstances, their counterparts in industrialized countries? Could the verification of the equalizing effect of compulsory suffrage be used to argue that compulsory suffrage is itself a public good, a socially equitable version of one-man one-vote? We cannot explore all of these here but merely suggest their theoretical relevance while emphasizing the democratic context of classical participation in Venezuela.

The Data Base. We pretested our instrument during the summer of 1973 and collected a total of 1,521 interviews during the fall of that same year. The interviews were drawn from a progressively stratified random sample of eligible Venezuelan voters. We stratified for age, sex, size of residential community, and social status, and 47 percent of the interviews were verified. Primary sampling units varied with the size of the community. In urban and metropolitan areas, the *barrio* and the *urbanización* served as the primary sampling unit, while the community itself was utilized in the rural areas. The former were drawn with a random numbers table matching a master list prepared by DATOS, C.A. of Venezuela, a firm specializing in market and public opinion research which was in charge of the field work. Rural communities were selected from a list of communities of the same size, although some changes were made to maximize geographic variation.[3] Baloyra personally trained and discussed the instrument with the supervisory personnel and the field teams that conducted the interviewing. The instrument had a total of 113 different items requiring 145 responses; average duration of an interview was about 50 minutes.

Determinants of Participation: The Variables

The structure of the Venezuelan party system, the overlapping between party loyalties and societal cleavages, the monopoly exerted by parties over most modes of political participation, and our dissatisfaction with the current theoretical treatment of the political orientations of the mass public, led us to proceed with considerable caution in selecting possible correlates of campaign participation in Venezuela. Individual traits including socioeconomic and cultural differences, modes of partisan involvement, patterns of evaluation of the performance of the administration in power, of the role of professional politicians, of the institution of elections, and of the regime, plus attitudes and orientations of a political nature such as political capacity, political agility, ideological tendency, and participatory mood, were all indispensable components of the list. Each group of factors included responds to one or more of the extant sociological, psychological, and political explanations of participation. However, following Verba and Nie, one may dichotomize these into "social circumstances," and "attitudinal factors," as illustrated in figure 1 where both are depicted as having a direct influence on participation.

FIGURE 1. A Preliminary Model of Participation

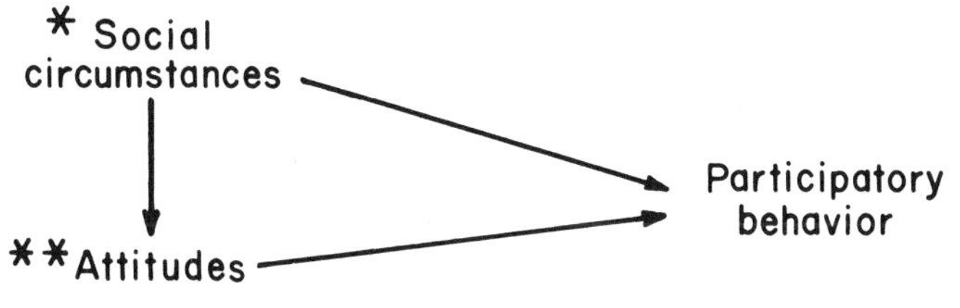

*Include social class image and social stratification of individuals, generational cohort, gender role, within-family status, region and size of community of residence, religiosity, reference group identification, and party membership.

**Include evaluations of different aspects of the political regime such as policies of the regime, elections, party politicians, and the administration in power; predispositions such as ideological tendency, political capacity, political agility, and participating mood; and partisanship.

Social Circumstances of Individuals. Discussion of those individual characteristics likely to have an impact on participation should depart from the explicit recognition that when one is dealing with such characteristics attention is being diverted to the cleavage structure of the society. Following Dahrendorf (1959) and other contemporary political sociologists, the analysis could emphasize the conflict potential of groups of individuals sharing one or more characteristics. Lipset and Rokkan's (1967) discussion of cleavage structures would also be useful, in that it offers a series of assumptions concerning the relative importance of these factors, their interconnectedness, and their impact on political conflict. The literature of consociationalism could also be cited, for it has identified the impact of language, religion, and regionalism on the politics of the smaller European democracies.[4]

We measured *social class images* in open-ended fashion, and dichotomized them into lower and middle class.[5] Our measure of *social stratification* was derived from a linear combination of standardized scores of income, education, and occupation, yielding six different strata: agricultural poor, manual poor, manual middle class, lower white-collar, upper white-collar, and professional.[6] Demographic traits with actual or potential significance include sex and age, and from a cultural standpoint their implications for *gender role* and *generational* differences; since these were two of the four variables utilized for sample stratification, we are rather close with our estimates to the actual population parameters. Regionalism and urbanization were measured respectively by *region of residence* and *size of community* of residence. Both have been identified as sources of cultural cleavage in the literature. Finally, three other individual traits worthy of inclusion because of their theoretical relevance are "religiosity," "primary group identification," and "status of the individual within the family."

Two observations appear relevant at this point. First, political roles may be imposed on individuals with different combinations of traits. Dependent women and young people are usually assigned different participatory roles than middle-aged males who are heads of household. Upper white-collar persons normally have more frequent opportunities to participate in politics outside the electoral arena than manual laborers. But common social circumstances may or may not lead individuals to share the same attitudinal outlook. Second, given the historically high rates of voting participation in Venezuela,[7] we are suspicious of the universality of the paradigm that equates higher social and economic status with "civic" attitudes and higher levels of participation. Compulsory suffrage has effectively wiped out these differences insofar as voting participation is concerned in Venezuela. On the other hand, the structure and organization of Venezuelan political parties resemble the European more closely than they do the North American. Thus they may have loosened even further the connections implied by the socioeconomic model.

Attitudinal Factors. In discussing attitudinal factors which may influence campaigning and voting, we are forced to deviate from the standard interpretation of "feelings of efficacy," and similar "civic attitudes" which are supposed to increase participation rates. This departure from conventional practice is not simply a matter of analytical convenience. We feel rather uncomfortable with the unstated assumption that somehow the individual must recognize that the government "usually does what is right." Even more disturbing is the analytical treatment of the respondent's failure to recognize this "fact" as a symptom of disorientation or lack of empathy with "civic" norms. This betrays a profound misunderstanding of the interaction between the political experience of the individual, and the attitudinal evaluations and predispositions that result from such experience. After all, participation may be ineffective.

Thus we treat some of our attitudinal measures as *evaluative* instead of normative orientations learned through socialization. This puts the emphasis on the individual's *actual* experience in dealing with government officials, party politicians, and other agents of the regime, for it is individual evaluation of the different aspects of the regime which gives theoretical coherence to the attitudes included in our models of campaign activism.

We measured *ideological tendency* as a six-point ordinal scale derived from respondents' choices among three types of economic systems (communism, socialism, and capitalism), and individual self-placements on the Left-Right continuum.[8] We are aware of treatment of ideology as a cleavage factor with cultural implications but, in the Venezuelan case, are not convinced of the permanence of the tendencies included in our scale.

Overall evaluation of the democratic regime was measured with a Guttman scale constructed from four items measuring opinion about the "impact of the policies of the governments of the last fifteen years on the nation" (beneficial or detrimental), "adequacy with which those governments have utilized the fiscal resources of the nation" (adequate or wasteful), who "the main beneficiaries of those policies have been" (the people or powerful groups), and the "honesty of the officials of those governments" (honest or crooked). In a sense, the scale measures the public's evaluation of the impact of the policies of the regime and the impact which, judging from the distribution of respondents among the scale types, seems to be rated negatively: very critical 30 percent, critical 27 percent, ambivalent 20 percent, and supportive 23 percent. The coefficient of reproducibility was .90 and the coefficient of scalability was .70.

What Dennis (1970) has called "support for the institution of elections" was operationalized with four opinion items dealing with "importance of the vote in politics," the "necessity of elections in a democracy," the fact that "elections make government officials worry about the problems of the people," and whether "candidates elected care about the problems of the people who elected them." The items were scaled following the Guttman technique, producing the following distribution: critical 7 percent, moderately supportive 19 percent, supportive 28 percent, and very supportive 46 percent. The coefficient of reproducibility was .94 and the coefficient of scalability was .73.

Comparison of the frequencies of the two scales shows that while Venezuelans perceive serious shortcomings in the policy outcomes of the democratic regime, they are highly supportive of this essential feature of the regime. Obviously, discontent with policy outcomes has not translated into a high level of criticism of elections. This is important because it could be argued that, given the compulsory nature of suffrage, voting participation in Venezuela is *mobilized,* not *voluntaristic.* Therefore, dissatisfaction with the regime *cannot* find expression through withdrawal. This does not seem to be the case, however, since the two attitudes do not correlate very highly (simple r = .29).

More interesting, perhaps, is the fact that if one treats this distribution as evidence of the fact that support for elections is a "consensus" value in Venezuela, one must conclude that this "civic" attitude is sufficiently widespread that it is not "more characteristic" of persons of higher socioeconomic status, which indeed proves to be the case (simple r between support for elections and stratification is .09).

Evaluation of the role of professional politician is another aspect which concerned us. Party politicians are, after all, prime movers and beneficiaries of a situation of competitive politics; public dissatisfaction with them could lead to a decrease in some types of participatory activities. It is entirely possible that for large segments of the public, especially in a country like Venezuela, party politicians are the most visible agents of the regime. We asked our respondents whether they believed that "politicians care about national problems," "help the community," "care about people's problems," and whether they "talk much and do nothing." The Guttman scale built from these items yielded the following distribution: very critical 35 percent, critical 19 percent, ambivalent 20 percent, supportive 18 percent, and very supportive 8 percent. Reproducibility was .89, scalability .70.

We found Venezuelans to be more irritated with the performance of politicians than with any other aspect of the regime; 35 percent of our respondents were included in the category of highest level of criticism for politicians. This is higher than the 30 percent who are very critical of the policy outcomes of the regime, and much higher than the 7 percent who are very critical of elections. Thus, one would expect criticism of politicians to be a more relevant factor than criticism of elections and of the regime's policies in reducing participation.

Regime performance must be distinguished from the performance of the government in power, and we tried to accomplish this with a series of questions testing opinion about the Christian Democratic administration of President Rafael Caldera, its impact on the economic situation of the respondent's family, its impact on the respondent's reference group, plus opinion about the manner in which the administration had handled major national issues. We standardized the responses, recovering a four-point scale of *evaluation of the Caldera administration.*[9] We found this attitudinal dimension to be mildly related to the socioeconomic circumstances of the respondents (simple r's between the scale and class image and stratification were −.24 and −.28, respectively).

Political efficacy presented some conceptual problems stemming from the treatment in the literature of this aspect of the general political orientations of the public. Ever since Campbell and his associates (1954) first introduced the concept, political efficacy has been measured in the same fashion. At issue here is the implicit assumption that participation increases the sense of personal political efficacy. Stated in this fashion the concept is not very useful—it cannot be applied to instances of unsuccessful participation which may lead to a decreased sense of personal efficacy. In other words, we believe that the linkage between efficacy and participation depends on past participatory experiences of the individual and his/her salient reference groups, as has been suggested by Cornelius (1975, pp. 108-34).

Furthermore, we found that the scale of political efficacy seemed to lack cross-cultural validity in Venezuela. We included the customary items measuring efficacy in our instrument, and were unable to scale them in Guttman fashion.[10] This suggested that we were not dealing with the same qualitative phenomena, and that the Venezuelan context altered the validity of the items. Secondly, we found that two of the items measuring efficacy had high inter-item correlations with two of the items measuring the perceived influence of the respondent's reference group. We standardized the responses to these four and, taking advantage of the fact that their wording including reference to the influence of "people like you," treated them as measuring different aspects of the same dimension, "the influence of yourself and of people like you." We treated this as a scale of *political capacity.*[11]

Political agility refers to the individual's level of information, but we could not measure this aspect in terms of the individual's ability to name or recognize elected officials. The nature of the Venezuelan electoral system makes this exceedingly difficult, since most elective positions are filled from party lists. Instead, we simply counted the number of "don't know" responses for each respondent as an indicator of that individual's ability to understand political questions, and dichotomized the range by identifying as "informed" those who were below and as "uninformed" those who were above the sample average. Capacity and *agility*, or efficacy and level of information, as they are usually called, were treated as factors with a direct impact on participation; the lower their levels, the lower the level of participation.

Last but not least, we wanted to develop a measure that would combine capacity and opinion about the regime, usually treated as efficacy and trust. The literature suggests that certain combinations of trust and efficacy characterize, or are conducive to, certain levels of participation. Gamson (1968) argued that high efficacy and a low degree of trust yield an optimal combination for mobilization. In our case, capacity and opinion about the regime were dichotomized and combined to differentiate four types of *participatory mood*: (1) *supporters* who have high capacity and evaluate the regime positively, (2) *deferents* who are positive evaluators of low political capacity, (3) *discontents* who are negative evaluators with low capacity, and (4) *critics* who are negative evaluators with high political capacity.[12]

Findings

Dimensions of Campaign Behavior

Verba and Nie demonstrated that political participation is multidimensional; as far as campaign activism goes, we could not agree more. Twelve items measuring different aspects of campaign activity were selected for a test of this working hypothesis. We wanted to discriminate three different aspects of individual reaction to campaigns through this procedure, and the resultant configuration satisfied this purpose. We scaled the items following the Guttman criterion and recovered the three-dimensional configuration presented in table 1. The coefficients of the scales suggest that the modes are unidimensional and cumulative, and that they measure *exposure* to, *involvement* in, and *perceived efficacy* of the campaign. Only one item, asking whether "someone tried to influence (the respondent) to vote for a particular party or candidate," could not be incorporated into any of the three scales.

Exposure to the campaign deals with the more passive or spectatorlike reaction to campaign stimuli, including such activities as "reading," "watching," and "listening." Significantly, one-fourth of the public failed to register any "activity"—if one can call it that—of this kind. *Involvement* in the campaign refers to a more demanding aspect of activity: working as a campaign volunteer, admission of being very interested in the campaign, effort to communicate and influence others, and attendance at rallies and other campaign events. One-half of our respondents failed to undertake any of these activities. Thus, one could assume that this second aspect of individual reaction to the campaign is more demanding than the first. Finally, *perceived efficacy* of the campaign measures the attitudinal aspect of activism.

We are aware that participatory attitudes are not "activities," but want to treat this aspect explicitly for two reasons. First, although the literature emphasizes the distinction between participatory activities and participatory attitudes, the latter have received little analytic treatment. Second, we want to measure the relationship between the two aspects and thus introduce a more immediate connector between social circumstances and political attitudes, on the one hand, and participatory modes on the other. It occurs to us that participatory attitudes specific to one or more aspects or modes of participation are more relevant connectors between social circumstances and participation than those predicated on notions of efficacy, even though the latter are also included in the analysis. However, it is likely that no single attitude or *participatory mood* may summarize individual predisposition to participate. In other words, it is necessary to examine the attitudinal correlates of different participatory modes, for these may vary with the individual's previous experience.

Inspection of the frequencies of the different categories of the scales gives the impression that although the majority of the public was not highly exposed to or involved in the campaign, it perceived the campaign to have been moderately efficacious. The immediate question that arises is, "Are these the same or

TABLE 1. MODES OF CAMPAIGN ACTIVISM

Table 1a. Exposure to the Campaign

Y_1	Y_3	Y_2	scale score	freq.	per-cent	intensity of exposure
1	1	1	3	209	13.8	high
0	1	1	2	559	36.8	medium
0	0	1	1	343	22.5	low
0	0	0	0	409	26.9	none

coefficient of reproducibility = .93
coefficient of scalability = .78

Table 1b. Involvement in the Campaign

Y_5	Y_8	Y_7	Y_4	scale score	freq.	per-cent	intensity of involvement
1	1	1	1	4	71	4.7	very high
0	1	1	1	3	110	7.3	high
0	0	1	1	2	164	10.9	moderate
0	0	0	1	1	339	22.6	low
0	0	0	0	0	819	54.5	none

coefficient of reproducibility = .92
coefficient of scalability = .60

Table 1c. Perceived Efficacy of the Campaign

Y_{10}	Y_{11}	Y_9	Y_{12}	scale score	freq.	per-cent	perceived efficacy
1	1	1	1	4	494	34.4	high
0	1	1	1	3	454	31.6	moderate
0	0	1	1	2	262	18.2	low
0	0	0	1	1	195	13.6	very low

coefficient of reproducibility = .90
coefficient of scalability = .64

Note: "Reporting that someone had tried to influence their vote" (1 = yes; 0 = no) did not scale on any of the three modes. This was possibly due to the fact that this item referred to an activity by someone other than the respondent.

different individuals?" That is to say, do the same individuals register similar levels of scope and intensity on all three dimensions? The correlation coefficients measuring the relationships between the three suggest not. *Exposure* did not appear to lead to comparable levels of personal *involvement* (simple r between them is .36), nor to evaluate *campaign efficacy* in terms of level of exposure (simple r = .28 between exposure and perceived efficacy). On the other hand, involvement and perceived efficacy were related more closely (simple r = .51). It may be assumed that the relatively low magnitude of the coefficients is indicative of considerable individual differentiation. Furthermore, one can also infer that increasing volumes of campaign appeals, communications, and messages did not result in significant increases in the efficacy attributed to the campaign by the public. The strongest link was for persons highly involved to perceive greater efficacy than those less involved.

A necessary test of the validity of the three-dimensional configuration recovered through the Guttman procedure is available with a factor analysis of the twelve items measuring individual reaction to the campaign. Two reasons recommend this type of verification. One is that factor analysis *simultaneously* partitions the variance into a linear combination of components. Another is that replications of the Verba and Nie approach to participation have utilized factor analysis consistently. The results of this verification appear in table 2, where the unrotated and (varimax) rotated three-factor solutions are presented. The unrotated solution suggests that all but two items—being influenced by others and opinion about the importance of the election outcome—load on the first component, the "exposure" factor. This would lend some credence to the unstated assumption utilized in most references to campaigning as unidimensional. However, the rotated solution shows otherwise.

The configuration recovered through the orthogonal rotation unveils basically the same clusters identified by the scalogram Guttman analysis. Notable differences between the two solutions require some clarification. First of all, we could not include "being influenced by others" in the Guttman solution. Ideally, this item should have clustered within the exposure dimension, but now appears as part of the involvement factor. The wording of the item was sufficiently clear to rule out the possibility of massive response error. Furthermore, the magnitude of the correlation between "persuading others" and "being influenced by others" does not support such an interpretation ($r = .25$). A further complication stems from the distribution of the loadings of "campaign interest" and "attendance at rallies" which seem to fall primarily on the involvement factor, but also on the evaluative and exposure factors respectively.

In short the factor analysis results are congruent with the scalogram analysis although some discrepancies remain between the two solutions concerning involvement. We believe this to be the result of the larger number of items included in the factor analysis, and also of differences between the computational procedures of the two techniques.[13] Essentially, the factor-analysis solution validates the Guttman solution as to the number of recoverable dimensions and their qualitative nature, and we will utilize the latter to explore variation of individual reaction to the campaign.[14]

Determinants of Campaign Activity

One area of electoral participation in which Venezuelans are not constrained by legal requirements, and in which they can minimize partisan obligations, is that of campaign activity. Compulsory suffrage does not extend to campaign

TABLE 2
FACTOR-ANALYIC SOLUTION OF
INDIVIDUAL REACTION TO THE CAMPAIGN

	Unrotated Solution			h²	(Varimax) Rotated Solution		
	I	II	III		I	II	III
EXPOSURE:							
Watching (Y₃)	.54	.56	−.27	.68	.81	.08	.09
Listening (Y₂)	.57	.52	−.27	.67	.80	.10	.13
Reading (Y₁)	.53	.45	−.08	.49	.66	.23	.05
INVOLVEMENT:							
Influenced (Y₅)	.69	−.12	.33	.60	.17	.71	.24
Volunteered (Y₇)	.68	−.10	.33	.58	.18	.70	.24
Interested (Y₈)	.74	−.19	.13	.61	.21	.60	.44
Influenced (Y₆)	.30	.05	.51	.35	.03	.57	−.16
Attended (Y₄)	.52	.16	.15	.31	.35	.42	.09
EVALUATION:							
Choosing (Y₉)	−.49	.42	.35	.55	−.06	−.10	−.73
Outcome (Y₁₁)	.56	−.34	.15	.46	.09	.29	.60
Importance (Y₁₂)	.24	−.26	−.51	.39	.10	−.20	.58
Impact (Y₁₀)	−.54	−.37	−.10	.43	.05	.31	.43
Eigenvalues	3.65	1.37	1.09				
% of variance	31	11	9				
N=	1,415						

activity—although it is a crucial factor in plotting campaign strategy— and the most severe party discipline means little to the unaffiliated members of the public. Campaigning is also one area of participation in which the "social circumstances" and the attitudes of individuals could be more detectable determinants of participation. We regressed these two types of determinants on the three dimensions of individual reaction to the campaign. In order to control for the effect of partisanship we ran separate multiple regressions for three different types of constituents: party identifiers, independents, and apoliticals.[15] Such differentiation is required by the omnipresence of parties in the Venezuelan context, as well as by the theoretical convenience of comparing the reactions of partisan and nonpartisan individuals to campaign stimuli. Should the socioeconomic model be applicable to the Venezuelan case, it would more likely be to independent and/or apolitical individuals since they are less constrained by partisan factors.

Determinants of Campaign Exposure. We utilized stepwise multiple regression to generate the path-analytic models of campaign exposure presented in figure 2, which summarize the more relevant findings in graphic form. We will not discuss all the linkages of all the models, but only those having some theoretical relevance to the variation of the dependent variable, level of campaign exposure. Our terminology and graphic representation are congruent with the usage found in the literature.[16] The explanatory power of the models of campaign exposure is relatively satisfactory, although weak in the case of the *apoliticals* (figure 2C). It is important to point out that partisan factors *are not* conspicuous in any of the three models. On the other hand, criticism of politicians was the only attitude found to influence exposure. This leaves us with a basic pattern in which socioeconomic status is the more relevant factor regardless of the degree of partisanship of the individual.

Among *party identifiers* (figure 2A) persons of higher socioeconomic status, those favorably disposed toward politicians, and, in general, males seemed to have been more exposed to the campaign. Notice that these are three different groups of party identifiers, not a single group of identifiers sharing the three characteristics. The lack of covariation between these determinants, and the minimal differences between the magnitudes of the original correlation coefficients r_{13} and r_{14} and paths P_{13} and P_{14}, suggest that this is the case. Thus we have a four-variable model with three exogenous and independent sources of variation.

The model of campaign exposure of *independents* (figure 2B) includes a well-established relationship characteristic of the mass public in Venezuela and elsewhere—the relationship between socioeconomic status and opinion about the regime, in this case criticism of politicians. Independents of higher socioeconomic status *and* more favorable disposition toward politicians were more exposed. In the model of campaign exposure of *apoliticals* (figure 2C) exposure to the campaign depended solely on social circumstances, such as individual location on the strata and gender role. The fact that opinion about the regime is uniformly critical among apoliticals would explain why attitudinal factors are not included.

Further reflection on the theoretical implications of the models of exposure leads to two inferences. First, if campaign exposure is a public good, this is not shared equally by the public. More specifically, inequality of exposure parallels social inequality, and not even the tremendous magnitude of the Venezuelan campaign of 1973 could equalize access to campaign information. Undoubtedly those of higher socioeconomic status sought more campaign information; however, there were no intervening attitudes in this relationship. In other words, their higher levels of exposure may not have been determined by their "more civic" attitudes but simply by easier access to media. On the other hand, regardless of party connections, those who were more critical of politicians had less exposure and, therefore, sought less information than the rest. Was this because they thought that nothing new would emerge from increased exposure that might change their orientation to the regime? Thus if one cannot unmistakably label the more intense exposure of the upper strata "civic," neither can the lower levels of exposure of the more cynical be termed "disoriented."

FIGURE 2. *Path-analytic Models of Campaign Exposure.**

A. PARTY IDENTIFIERS (n=389)

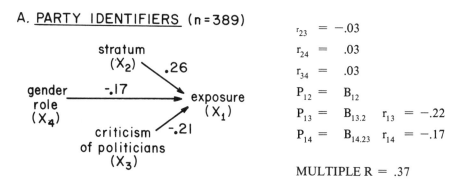

$r_{23} = -.03$

$r_{24} = .03$

$r_{34} = .03$

$P_{12} = B_{12}$

$P_{13} = B_{13.2}$ $r_{13} = -.22$

$P_{14} = B_{14.23}$ $r_{14} = -.17$

MULTIPLE R = .37

B. INDEPENDENTS (n=123)

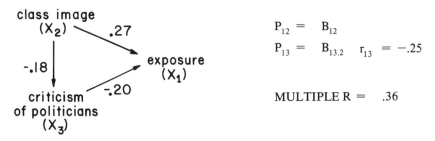

$P_{12} = B_{12}$

$P_{13} = B_{13.2}$ $r_{13} = -.25$

MULTIPLE R = .36

C. APOLITICALS (n=211)

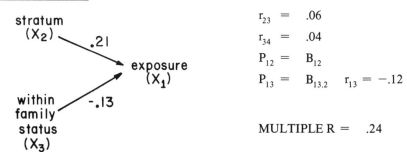

$r_{23} = .06$

$r_{34} = .04$

$P_{12} = B_{12}$

$P_{13} = B_{13.2}$ $r_{13} = -.12$

MULTIPLE R = .24

*Note for figures 2 through 5:
  Path coefficients are expressed in standardized form. All paths are significant at .01, and are identified by the symbol P.; beta weights with B. Straight arrows are paths, curves without arrows identify non-causal covariation, curves with arrows are unanalyzed correlations, and absence of any lines signifying no linkage whatsoever. To simplify the diagrams we do not identify paths nor covariations smaller than .10.

Determinants of Campaign Involvement. In contrast with campaign exposure, campaign involvement was relatively free from socioeconomic influences, and related more closely to partisan and attitudinal factors. The path-analytic models of individual involvement in the campaign appear in figure 3. Among *party identifiers* (figure 3A), higher levels of involvement were more characteristic of party members. Criticism of politicians had direct and indirect impact on involvement. Apparently, even though this attitude influences the decision to become a party member, membership status reduces the number of potential campaigners who would be inactive due to their criticism of politicians. Thus, membership increased the level of involvement of party identifiers regardless of attitudinal predispositions or participatory mood.

Among *independents* (figure 3B), involvement was influenced by two factors independent of one another, gender role and participatory mood. Thus, when partisan constraints are removed, the level of female participation decreases and the importance of the individual's participatory mood becomes more relevant than evaluation of any specific aspect of the regime. The model of individual involvement of *apoliticals* (figure 3C) includes a familiar relationship between opinion about the administration and community size. Generally, students of Venezuelan politics agree that support for the regime is stronger in the smaller communities where the two dominant parties, AD and COPEI, have managed to maintain the clientelistic bonds of their political machines (Myers 1975). These bonds are weakened by individual mobility of a geographic or social nature which put the individual in the context of a more complex set of relationships. The overall causal pattern described in figure 3C identifies opinion as the most significant influence, whether one utilizes this model or an alternative one which would have stratification as the predictor of highest causal order but without a significant direct path to involvement.

One additional comment concerning the three models of campaign involvement should be made. Even though Verba and Nie showed that "campaigners" in the United States are predominantly upper status residents of big cities and suburbs—to mention two of the characteristics that are directly comparable with our data—this does not seem true for Venezuela. There, the more active campaigners in 1973 were party members, males, residents of smaller communities, and individuals with more positive attitudes toward the regime. Notice that we do not say individuals with "civic" attitudes because, although our general model of campaign participation is predicated on the nexus between social circumstances and individual attitudes (see figure 1), we treat the nexus as an evaluative rather than learning process. In other words, our models of individual participation through direct involvement in the campaign suggest that when party influences are present they tend to equalize participation regardless of status, and that when the influence of partisanship is not relevant—as is the case with independents and apoliticals—unequal participation is due to gender role and attitudinal differences, not to socioeconomic circumstances.

FIGURE 3. Path-analytic Models of Campaign Involvement.*

A. <u>PARTY IDENTIFIERS</u> (n = 389)

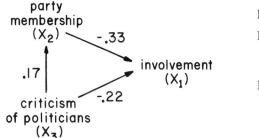

$$P_{12} = B_{12}$$
$$P_{13} = B_{13.2} \quad r_{13} = -.28$$

MULTIPLE R = .43

B. <u>INDEPENDENTS</u> (n = 123)

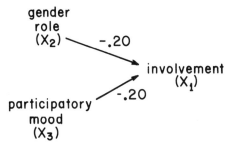

$$P_{12} = B_{12} \quad r_{23} = -.07$$
$$P_{13} = B_{13.2} \quad r_{13} = -.18$$

MULTIPLE R = .27

C. <u>APOLITICALS</u> (n = 211)

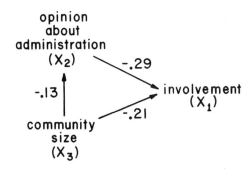

$$P_{12} = B_{12}$$
$$P_{13} = B_{13.2} \quad r_{13} = -.17$$

MULTIPLE R = .34

*See figure 2 for explanatory note.

Determinants of Opinion about Campaign Efficacy. Given the long struggle to legitimize suffrage in Venezuela, its incorporation as an essential feature of the regime through compulsory voting, and the high levels of popular support for the institution of elections, one could treat the latter as a "civic" attitude in the most rigorous sense. We have not found pronounced differences between the strata in their levels of support for elections. Thus, one could well contend that this is a widely shared attitude, if not a consensus value in Venezuela. Furthermore, our data show that two-thirds of our respondents rated the 1973 campaign "moderately" or "highly" efficacious, probably a direct consequence of the high level of support for elections. Since this seems to be the case, what differences could be found comparing the evaluation of campaign efficacy of individuals with different kinds of partisan involvement? Our results are presented in figure 4.

Regardless of party connections or social circumstances, our respondents' evaluations of campaign efficacy were mediated by their attitude toward elections. Such is clearly the case for *party identifiers* (figure 4A) and for *apoliticals* (figure 4C). Party membership seems to reinforce support for elections among the former. Thus, party identifiers who are not members and are more critical of elections seemed to have participated less. However, we found opinion about elections to be an indirect influence on membership; moreover, we had to treat the relationship as unanalyzed covariation because there are sound theoretical reasons to suggest reciprocal causation between the two.

Individual location on the strata tends to produce similar results among *apoliticals:* upper strata apoliticals are more critical and thus were less likely to perceive the campaign as efficacious. The causal pattern of the *independents* (figure 4B) is less problematic, for it includes a more obvious nexus between criticism of elections and criticism of politicians. The direction of causality between the two, at least for this group, is likely to run from the latter to the former. That is, among independents, support for elections diminishes as a result of a negative evaluation of politicians, and both tend to reduce the perceived efficacy of electoral campaigns. After all, opinion about politicians is one of the factors that influences the individual's overall orientation to politics—that is, the political self-image of the individual. Consequently, it is no surprise to find this attitude influencing their opinion of the campaign most decisively.

Perhaps the most obvious and relevant comment concerning campaign efficacy is that its close links with opinion about elections suggest that campaigns may by perceived by the Venezuelan public as "efficacy tools" (Seligson 1977c) of elections, regardless of partisan preferences or social circumstances. In other words, this is not merely another instance of one attitude serving as the best predictor of another, but one in which an opinion about one aspect of participation—voting—influences the perceived efficacy of another aspect of participation, namely, campaigning.

FIGURE 4. *Path-analytic Models of Opinion about Campaign Efficiency**

A. <u>PARTY IDENTIFIERS</u> (n = 389)

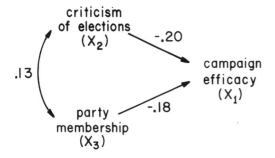

$P_{12} = B_{12}$

$P_{13} = B_{13.2}$

$r_{13} = -.20$

MULTIPLE R = .28

B. <u>INDEPENDENTS</u> (n = 123)

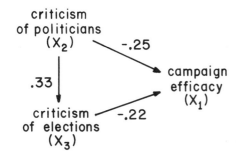

$P_{12} = B_{12}$

$P_{13} = B_{13.2}$

$r_{13} = -.31$

MULTIPLE R = .39

C. <u>APOLITICALS</u> (n = 211)

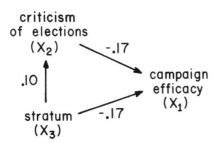

$P_{12} = B_{12}$

$P_{13} = B_{13.2}$

$r_{13} = -.19$

MULTIPLE R = .26

*See figure 2 for explanatory note.

A Model of Campaign Activism

It would be possible to review the features of the nine models presented in our discussion and try to utilize the more important inferences as guides for theory construction concerning campaign activism. However, the nine models concern three different aspects of this activism—seeking information through exposure, becoming involved through overt behavior, and coming to a conclusion about the efficacy of the campaign—for three different degrees of partisanship. There is value in a general model which would include the latter, as well as interrelationships among the three aspects of campaign activism. Such a model, generated through path-analytic methodology, is presented in figure 5.

The model depicted in figure 5 is unusual in two senses. First, it has a large number of variables. Second, we have deviated from established practice by deleting all paths and covariations smaller than .10. This allows us to handle the large number of relationships included in the model. We have identified the proportion of unexplained variance for the three dimensions of activisim, although for *party membership* (X_4) and *political self-image* (X_5) we have not done so even though we derived their more explicit causal paths.

Examining the paths converging on campaign *involvement,* in figure 5, it seems apparent that campaigning is primarily although not exclusively a partisan activity. It is a male-dominated activity as well, even though we do not find differences between the social circumstances and attitudes of males and females. Furthermore, it is also obvious that campaign involvement increased with *exposure* and with the opinion that the campaign was efficacious. The paths leading to *exposure*, on the other hand, were dominated by social circumstances, represented in the model by gender role and stratification. Partisan factors did not have much direct influence on *exposure* ($P_{24} = -.09$, not represented in the figure). Due to the lack of covariation between gender role and party membership and between the former and stratification, the causality of exposure is greatly simplified. Exposure is undoubtedly the aspect of campaign activism most affected by social inequalities. Yet this was not the case with respect to involvement, thanks to the influence of the partisan factor.

The attitudinal aspect of campaign activism, represented by campaign efficacy, was not at all subject to the influence of social circumstances. Instead, the causal paths leading to efficacy originated in the partisan factor or in individual attitudes. More importantly, social circumstances also had little impact on the latter. There is little relationship between gender role and the two attitudes which could be construed as civic: opinion about elections and campaign efficacy. Stratification is not related to efficacy ($P_{36} = -.08$, not significant) and is mildly related to opinion about elections. This is important because contemporary social science has come to regard as "normal" the relationship between high socioeconomic status, civic attitudes and high sense of personal efficacy, and participation. Our data show that the direct links between higher socioeconomic status and higher involvement are weak, and

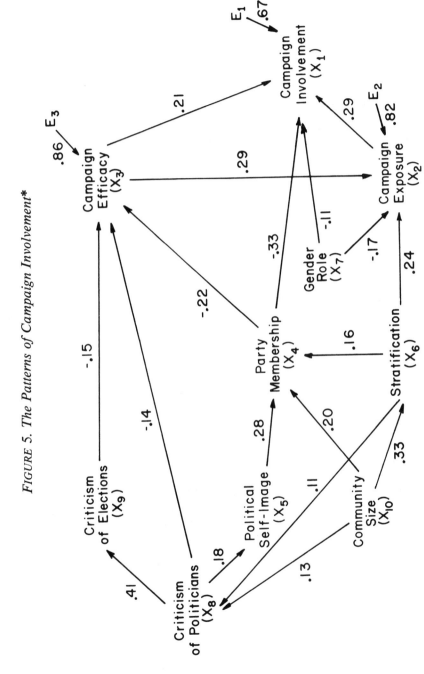

FIGURE 5. *The Patterns of Campaign Involvement**

*See figure 2 for explanatory note.

that those between the former and civic attitudes relevant to campaign participation are also weak. Furthermore, the model does not confirm direct linkage
between high support for elections and high levels of involvement—the former
do not seem to be enough for the latter; what exists between the two is an
indirect relationship through what could be called the "efficacy tool" of
opinion about elections, namely, opinion about campaign efficacy.

Three different patterns of participation seem to emerge from the model
presented in figure 5. Two have their ultimate antecedent in the individual's
attitude toward politicians, which seems an important conditioner of attitude
about elections and exerts some influence on political self-image, the most
important determinant of party membership. The three causal paths, and the
nature of the relationships which they involve, could be treated as *autonomous, mobilized,* and *manipulated involvement.*

Autonomous involvement is a pattern of campaign activism dominated by
individual attitudes; opinion about politicians, about elections, and the perceived efficacy of the campaign stand in a simple causal sequence in which only
the latter has direct impact on involvement. Autonomous involvement seems
independent of social circumstances and, to a large extent, of partisan
connections. It is "autonomous" to the extent that it is not "organized," is not
connected with institutional or societal factors.

Mobilized involvement is partisan and is represented by the causal paths
occupying the center of figure 5. Even though social circumstances such as
stratification and size of community of residence have an impact on party
membership, they lack any direct causal links to this type of involvement; the
same is true of attitudinal factors. Thus, mobilized involvement reduces
socioeconomic differences among these kinds of participants, and seems relatively free of attitudinal influences.[17]

Manipulated involvement is represented by the causal flow depicted at the
bottom and lower right-hand corner of Figure 5. Even though manipulation is
undoubtedly present in the other types of campaign involvement, we stress the
manipulative character of this third type on the following grounds. First, it is
mediated by exposure. Second, with the exception of campaign efficacy, it is
not affected by attitudinal factors. Third, it seems to include a group of participants more susceptible to "presentational campaign techniques,"[18] given their
lack of partisan connections or unique attitudinal predispositions toward the
regime. Consequently, it presupposes a type of involvement which could be
induced largely on the basis of exposure.

Conclusion

Our findings seem to contradict an impressive body of evidence reported in the
literature showing a relationship between high socioeconomic status, high

sense of political efficacy, and higher levels of political participation. Our examination of this relationship, also described as "the standard socioeconomic model of political participation," focused on campaign activism in Venezuela. Popular compliance with compulsory suffrage prevents meaningful analysis and discussion of the question in reference to voting participation.

Among a set of predictors included in the literature, we found it convenient to alter the conceptual standing of "efficacy" and "trust" in order to increase their validity in the Venezuelan context, and combined both measures into a third which we called participatory mood. We differentiated three related, but separate, aspects of campaign activism: involvement, exposure, and efficacy. We regressed the predictors on each of these, controlling for partisanship. In general, we found that socioeconomic factors were more relevant in predicting levels of campaign exposure, that the predictors of levels of involvement varied tremendously among different types of partisans, and that efficacy was but mildly influenced by socioeconomic factors. A general model of patterns of campaign participation confirmed the existence of three different modes of campaign involvement, and that campaign efficacy and campaign involvement did not increase with status, that involvement was predominantly but not exclusively a partisan mode of participation, and that socioeconomic factors were more relevant in predicting levels of exposure, although campaign efficacy was the most relevant predictor of the latter.

We are not certain that our findings vindicate Alan Wertheimer's claim that, given the social inequalities which coexist with our present system of voluntary participation, a legal form of compulsion would be less coercive (1975, p. 278). Of all the "public goods" offered by the Venezuelan democratic regime, the electoral system seems to enjoy the highest degree of popular support; this in spite of the high levels of criticism for other aspects of the regime. Support for elections seems at "consensus" level in Venezuela, but we do not find a host of "civic" attitudes associated with it, nor can one observe significant differences between the socioeconomic strata in their support of this value. Our findings suggest that the standard socioeconomic model of participation is not totally inadequate in explaining campaign activism in Venezuela, but they fail to substantiate some of the better-known links predicated by that model. On the other hand, even though the analysis identifies partisanship as an institutional factor of great importance, campaign activism seems to go beyond mobilization and politicization by parties. Our model suggests that other avenues of involvement are open to the public, in response to the agitation by parties but beyond their manipulation. Being overly ambitious, we could contend that the Venezuelan case offers considerable support for Wertheimer's contention. Being realistic we will consider this analysis a first, and relatively successful, attempt at formalizing the dynamics of the Venezuelan campaign of 1973 which we have discussed in considerable detail elsewhere (Martz and Baloyra 1976).

In closing, we must make one final observation about our findings. The literature has contended that most members of the mass public do not know what they want from politics, that their low levels of efficacy deflate their rates of participation, and that the full mobilization of these kinds of individuals would have unforeseeable and unpredictable consequences. The Venezuelan experience of the last seventeen years suggest otherwise: full mobilization through compulsory voting and highly articulated parties has apparently wiped out the primacy of class-related factors from the correlates of mass participation. Perhaps the mass public is not as disoriented as we have been led to believe; perhaps if masses were given the opportunity to participate on equal terms, and were fully mobilized, we would see the disappearance of some of the relationships that are now taken for granted and that help to rationalize the perpetuation of the conditions which created those relationships in the first place.

The Venezuelan experience suggests that partisanship may constitute a more relevant baseline for the analysis of political participation than the social circumstances of individuals. However, our greatest concern is not with obvious differences in context but with the political and intellectual implications of the profile of the average person produced by contemporary social science. For such a profile questions the internal attitudinal consistency, sustained interest in issues, ideological coherence, and commitment to democratic values of the average person. It is, in short, a vision which puts in doubt the value and ultimate relevance of popular participation in democratic politics, and cannot accommodate the insights of ordinary citizens. Thus, the agenda for the comparative study of political participation in Latin America should aim to criticize and reinterpret this dominant view, and not to reconcile the "idiosyncracies" of the area with the leading assumptions of a paradigm that is in dire need of further clarification.

Notes

1. We were confronted with a situation in which an almost nonexistent amount of variance in the dependent variable—voting— did not allow for any meaningful explanation.

2. These were two aspects which lent themselves to causal analysis and more elegant manipulation of the data.

3. Description of the sampling plan and a discussion of validity and reliability of the instrument are available in Baloyra and Martz (1976b, pp. 13-23).

4. For a critical review see Obler and Steiner (1977).

5. Our question measuring social class images was "Today much is written about social classes; to which social class do you belong?" Responses were: high (1.1 percent), middle (57.3 percent), working (4.0 percent), low (6.2 percent), and poor or humble (24.6 percent); 2.5 percent of the respondents refused to answer the question, while 4.4 percent did not understand the question.

6. Frequencies for these categories were as follows

	absolute frequency	relative frequency	adjusted frequency
(1) agricultural poor	218	14.3%	16.0%
(2) manual poor	280	18.4	20.5
(3) manual middle class	338	22.2	24.8
(4) lower white collar	202	13.3	14.8

(5) upper white collar	128	8.4	9.4
(6) professional	198	13.0	14.5
out of range	157	10.3	missing

7. In order to document this statement, see a discussion of the subject in Martz and Baloyra (1976, pp. 46-48).

8. Frequencies for the different tendencies are:

	absolute frequency	relative frequency	adjusted frequency
(1) Radical Left	215	14.1%	15.4%
(2) Left	105	6.9	7.5
(3) Center Left	181	11.9	13.0
(4) Center	151	9.9	10.8
(5) Center Right	155	10.2	11.1
(6) Right	588	38.7	42.2
out of range	126	8.3	missing

The procedure utilized is described in considerable detail in Baloyra and Martz (1976b, chapter 5).

9. The distribution of respondents along the different categories of evaluation of the performance of the Caldera administration was:

	absolute frequency	relative frequency	adjusted frequency
(1) very satisfied	261	17.2%	18.1%
(2) satisfied	440	28.9	30.5
(3) dissatisfied	559	36.8	38.7
(4) very dissatisfied	183	12.0	12.7
out of range	78	5.1	missing

10. See Robinson, Rusk, and Head (1969, p. 459) for the actual wording of these items.

11. The four items utilized were "How much influence do (people like you) have in Venezuelan political life ... ?:" none = 195, little = 528, enough = 312, great = 414, don't know = 72; "Do you believe that, at the present time, the influence of (people like you) is ... increasing (570), remaining about the same (503), or decreasing (373)?" (don't know = 75); "Do you believe that people like you have power to influence what the government does?" (yes = 414, no = 1,002, refused to answer = 5, don't know = 99); and "Finally, do you believe that voting is the only way you can influence what the government does?" (yes = 984, no = 453, refused to answer = 8, don't know = 76).

	absolute frequency	relative frequency
(1) very incapable	176	11.6%
(2) incapable	708	46.5
(3) capable	444	29.2
(4) very capable	193	12.7

12. The frequencies of these four categories were:

	absolute frequency	relative frequency	regime evaluation	political capacity
(1) supporters	267	17.6%	positive	high
(2) deferents	396	26.0	positive	low
(3) discontents	488	32.1	negative	low
(4) critics	370	24.3	negative	high

13. The Guttman procedure requires that all items be dichotomized, while the factor-analytic technique is not predicated on such manipulation.

14. We dropped the "being influenced by others" item and repeated the factor analysis but the results remained unsatisfactory.

15. We operationalized this variable with responses to the question, "In Venezuela there is much talk about the independents, about the independent vote. Nowadays, in Venezuelan politics, do you consider yourself an independent, a sympathizer of a party, or a person who is not interested in politics . . .?"

	absolute frequency	relative frequency	adjusted frequency
(1) sympathizers	739	48.6%	48.7%
(2) independents	291	19.1	19.2
(3) unconcerned (apolitical)	487	32.0	32.1
refused	2	.1	missing
do not know	2	.1	missing

We believe that this question summarizes, in the Venezuelan context, what is usually identified as "psychological involvement in politics" (Verba and Nie 1972, p. 83), and is measured by a host of items. Our usage is more simplistic but based on a question which has great contextual validity— "Are you an independent?"—in Venezuela. Furthermore, we believe that if there is one basic orientation utilized by individuals to establish their position in the society, such as class identification, it is worth exploring a similar concept which would summarize the individual's basic orientation to politics. Obviously, ours may not be *the* best possible way to measure this hypothetical construct, but we have found it an extremely useful predictor of partisan attitudes and behavior (Baloyra and Martz 1976b, chapter 7).

16. For a discussion of path analysis see Duncan (1975).

17. Any doubts concerning the interpretation of the signs of the paths included in this pattern should be put to rest by the clarification that these stem from coding (*self image*: 1, identifiers; 2, independents; 3, apoliticals; *membership*: 1, members; 2, nonmembers), and not from any theoretical misconception. Thus, criticism of politicians accompanies nonpartisan self-images, lack of party membership, and decreased involvement.

18. "Presentational campaign techniques" are those which rely very heavily on the use of media. See Martz and Baloyra (1976, pp. xxxviii-xl) for a discussion.

Biles examines the structure, extent, and sources of conventional democratic political participation in urban Uruguay before the 1973 military coup. His analysis supports recent cross-national findings that participation is multidimensional. Four modes of participation are defined. He demonstrates that particularism and its institutionalized form, patronage, have had a profound effect in shaping Uruguayan participation and in modifying the impact of causal factors common elsewhere.

5.
Political Participation in Urban Uruguay: Mixing Public and Private Ends

ROBERT E. BILES

During the three decades preceding the 1973 military coup, Uruguay was considered one of the three leading democracies in Latin America (Wilkie 1974, p. 482). A wide range of opportunities for conventional democratic participation was available, and citizen participation was high. The purpose of this paper is to determine the types or modes of that participation, the amount of participation, and the factors producing it. The study supports the findings of Verba, Nie, and their associates (1971, 1973) that political participation is multidimensional, that is, that there are alternative modes by which citizens may seek to influence the distribution of public goods. However, the study also shows that the strong role of patronage and particularistic concerns in Uruguay produced a different set of modes than those found elsewhere and also suggests that the dominant role of these private ends eventually proved dysfunctional for the survival of democratic participation.

The Setting: Uruguay, 1970. The primary data for this study were collected in 1970, a year before a national election and less than three years before the military coup which ended a thirty-year period of competitive, democratic politics. Elections were regular and meaningful. Political communication through the media was widespread and until the closing years of the period quite free. The party system offered substantial opportunities for campaign participation with two long-established major parties, several small parties, and elections featuring large numbers of factions and candidates. Long-established traditions of interest-group activity and political patronage provided multiple opportunities for noncampaign-related participation aimed at influencing government or expressing individual and group demands. On the other hand, by the mid-1960s Uruguay was also marked by considerable turmoil, to which the government responded with suppression of certain groups and activities and some press censorship—thus changing the environment and the margins of permissible conventional participation (Weinstein 1975; McDonald 1972b, 1975). The setting of the study, then, is one of conventional democratic politics during a period of considerable stress and eventual decline.

A striking feature of Uruguay is the relative homogeneity of its small population (2.9 million). Uruguayans share a common tradition, with no distinct regions or significant minorities. Middle-class values are widespread, and Montevideo serves as a focal point for the diffusion of news and cultural values (but see Weinstein 1975). The population is also highly urban. According to the 1963 census, 45 percent of the population lives in urban Montevideo, 36 percent in the small cities and towns of the interior, and 19 percent in rural zones (Dirección General de Estadística y Censo 1969). Survey data indicate that political behavior in Montevideo and the urban parts of the interior are similar, but there are few empirical data available on the political behavior of the rural population.

The Data Base. The study utilizes data from my 1970 survey of the adult population of Montevideo. Additional data on Montevideo and the urban interior are drawn from surveys conducted by an Uruguayan polling agency, Gallup Uruguay. My survey used multistage cluster sampling, while Gallup Uruguay used stratified three-stage area probability samples. Out of a target sample of 1,000, my survey produced 852 interviews. Interviewing was done by experienced Uruguayan interviewers under my supervision.[1]

The Analysis

The Modes of Participation

Political participation is defined here as activity influencing or designed to influence the distribution of public goods. Public goods include those goods distributed both by the formal political institutions and by communities which are provided by public expenditure and the use of which, once supplied, is difficult to restrict (Booth and Seligson, chapter 1).

While in the past political participation was often thought of as unidimensional, research by Verba, Nie, and others (1971, 1972, 1973) clearly indicates that participation is, in fact, multidimensional. What this means is that "there are meaningful alternative modes of citizen participation, modes whereby citizens press claims on the government in quite different ways" (Verba et al. 1973, p. 238).

To determine the structure of participation in Uruguay, ten participation variables were selected from my Montevideo survey. Seven of the variables were similar to those forming the modes of participation found by Verba and

Nie. To measure voting, respondents were asked whether they had voted in each of the last four elections. Two indicators were then taken for this analysis—turnout in the last (1966) election and turnout in the other recent elections. To determine campaign activity, respondents were asked if they had worked actively for some political candidate or contributed money for an election campaign. Group activity, even by ostensibly nonpolitical organizations, has been another means of influencing the distribution of public goods. In my survey, respondents were asked if they belonged to any of six different types of organizations—consumers or producers cooperatives, professional or merchants associations, labor unions, religious organizations, social clubs, and sports clubs. This was not a completely satisfactory indicator of political activity because it did not ask for active membership nor did it ask about involvement in community problems. Nevertheless, the number of organizational memberships has served as a useful surrogate for more direct measures in other studies (e.g., Almond and Verba 1965). An additional membership—in a *political club*—was considered as a separate variable (i.e., it is not included in the variable "number of memberships"). In Uruguay, political clubs were important as focal points for patronage and recruitment of campaign workers but also served as social centers.

Although often neglected in trádicional participation studies, another means to influence is contacts with officials initiated by the individual to resolve a personal or family problem. To measure this *particularized contacting,* respondents were asked whether they had received or could receive favors through the political clubs—a major channel for resolving individual problems with the bureaucracy.[2] These questions, of course, do not tap the full range of channels for obtaining influence, and they are tied to a particular institution.

Because of their more restrictive definition of political participation, Verba and Nie do not consider political communication. However, as a source of prestige and influence, it falls within the broader definition used here (action affecting the distribution of public goods). Three means of *political communication* were considered here: (1) talking about political matters with other people, (2) informing oneself about political affairs by reading newspapers, and (3) by listening to radio or television.

To determine the modes of participation in Uruguay, the ten measures of political participation were factor analyzed (Biles 1976a). The results supported the notion of the multidimensionality of participation (table 1). The variables formed four distinct clusters, indicating four different avenues of citizen participation. However, a major difference in the particular modes found sheds important light on the nature of the Uruguayan political system. In research covering seven nations and three continents, Verba, Nie, and their associates have consistently found the same four modes with only minor variations attributable to differences in political systems (Verba, et al. 1973). However, two of the modes found in other nations formed a single mode in Uruguay. These are campaign activity and particularized contacting. In other

TABLE 1
FACTOR ANALYSIS (VARIMAX ROTATED MATRIX) OF TEN
PARTICIPATION VARIABLES, MONTEVIDEO[a]

	Campaigning and particular- ized contacting	Voting	Political communi- cation	Communal activity	h²
Could receive favors through political club	.830	.035	.088	.020	.70
Have received favors through political club	.796	.004	.068	−.089	.65
Did campaign work or con- tributed money	.625	.009	.226	−.280	.53
Voted in 1966 election	.019	.920	.095	−.049	.86
Voted in other recent elections	.077	.915	.105	−.052	.86
Follows political affairs in newspapers	.069	.127	.842	−.077	
Follows political affairs on radio or TV	.059	.069	.803	.026	.65
Talks about political matters with others	.246	.083	.672	−.202	.56
Number of other organizational memberships	.051	.088	.111	−.898	.83
Member of political club	.478	.074	.091	−.562	.56

[a]The smallest component used had an eigenvalue of 0.91.
N=840.

nations, particularized contacting—resolving individual problems through personal contact with officials—is a distinct activity and is least related to the other modes. However, in Uruguay the two questions concerning seeking favors through the political clubs formed a single mode with the question concerning campaign work and contributions. All three must be considered manifestations of the same underlying dimension in Uruguay.

Two of the modes found in Uruguay were essentially identical to those found elsewhere: voting and communal activity (participation in groups). The two voting variables formed a distinct mode, as did belonging to a political club and the number of memberships in other types of clubs. As expected, they represented distinct vehicles of participation. A fourth mode of participation in Uruguay, political communication, was formed by questions concerning talking about politics and following it in newspapers and on radio or television. While this type of activity was not considered by Verba and Nie, Booth found a similar mode in Costa Rica (1976). Broadening the definition of partici- pation, then, does not alter the fact of multidimensionality but simply adds further modes.[3]

Participation: How Much?

One of the most important findings of recent studies of participation is that participation is more widespread than had been previously assumed

(Verba and Nie 1972; Verba, et al. 1973; Seligson and Booth 1976, p. 101). This was no less the case for Uruguay. Only 3 percent of my Montevideo respondents reported that they "never" or "almost never" followed politics in the media. Before sanctions were imposed for nonvoting, only 12 percent reported having voted in none of the last four elections for which they were eligible. The vast majority of urban Uruguayans, then, participated at least occasionally in politics. As table 2 makes clear, a majority participated on a regular basis. Moreover, there was a tendency to participate in more than one mode. Sixty-six percent reported doing at least two of the following: voting in all elections, belonging to a political club, doing campaign work, or talking politics at least occasionally.

TABLE 2

PROPORTION REPORTING PARTICIPATION BY ACTIVITY, MONTEVIDEO

Act	% Active
Voted in 1966 election	82
Follows political affairs on radio or TV every day[a]	66
Voted in all other recent elections[b]	63
Belongs to at least one organization other than political club[c]	54
Follows political affairs in newspapers every day[d]	39
Talks about political matters with others every day[e]	17
Did campaign work or contributed money	13
Could receive favors through political club	12
Have received favors through political club	9
Member political club	6
Number of cases	(852)

[a]Once a week or from time to time, 30%; almost never, 4%.
[b]Some, 25%; none, 12%.
[c]None, 46%; two, 18%; three or more, 11%.
[d]Once a week or from time to time, 47%; almost never, 13%.
[e]Once a week or from time to time, 55%; almost never, 28%.

For a fuller understanding of the extent of participation, the modes were examined individually. During the 1960s, Uruguayan voter turnout was moderately high. Calculating the age structure of the population from 1963 census data and eliminating foreigners ineligible to vote, I estimate that 73 percent of the eligible national electorate cast valid ballots in 1966 and 75 percent did so in 1962, a turnout lower than European levels but comparable to U.S. and Canadian turnout in the period.[4] There has been considerable debate in the literature as to the effect of place of residence on participation (Milbrath and Goel 1977, pp. 106-10). In Uruguay, the nonmetropolitan interior has had a slightly higher turnout rate than has Montevideo, the one metropolitan area in the country. Turnout in Montevideo was 72 percent in 1962 and 70 percent in 1966, compared to 76 percent in the interior for both elections.

Although an exact comparison of all parts of the nation cannot be made from available data, it is clear that political communication was widespread in urban Uruguay but lower in rural areas. In Montevideo, 72 percent discussed politics at least occasionally, and 97 percent followed it in the media at least occasionally. The amount of exposure, however, varied considerably. Over one-third (37 percent) followed politics every day in both newspapers and radio or television, while another third (32 percent) "almost never" followed in one media form and followed "once a week" or less in the other. Montevideo and the urban interior had identical proportions who listened to news on the radio and listened to the 1971 candidates by radio. However, smaller proportions of the urban interior read newspapers regularly and fewer followed the 1971 campaign by television and by newspapers.

Political communication in rural zones was lower. While in urban Uruguay 89 percent listened to radio news, a study (CLEH 1963) of the rural dispersed population showed that 80 percent listened to the radio but only 26% preferred news. One-third (32 percent) of the rural dispersed population read newspapers at least once a week, while 42 percent of Montevideo residents followed politics in newspapers with the same frequency. No exact statement, then, can be made about the level of political communication in all of Uruguay, but it does appear to have been higher than the levels found in Italy and Mexico and not substantially lower than those of Britain (Almond and Verba 1965, p. 56; Gallup Uruguay 1962a, 1962b, 1966a, 1968c, 1971; CLEH 1963, pp. 427-30).

Organizational membership was also a common means of participation in Uruguay. In my 1970 survey of Montevideo, 54 percent reported belonging to at least one organization, while four years earlier a Gallup Uruguay survey found that 45 percent each of Montevideo and the urban interior belonged to at least one organization (1966c). It was more difficult to compare the level of membership between urban and rural respondents because of the lack of information on total memberships per rural individual. However, for each type of organization, urban residents had a higher proportion of members than did rural residents (CLEH 1963, pp. 421-26). It appears, then, that in Uruguay urbanites participated slightly more in organizations than did rural residents but that the size of the city (metropolitan area vs. small cities and rural dispersed vs. rural villages) made little difference. Combining the 30 percent of the rural population which belonged to at least one cultural organization with the 45 percent of urbanites found by Gallup Uruguay to belong to any organization, at least 42 percent of Uruguayan adults belonged to at least one organization—a proportion which approached that of Britain and Germany and exceeded that of Italy and urban Mexico (Almond and Verba 1965, p. 246).

Loading on the same mode with the number of group memberships is a more specifically political variable—belonging to a political club. In 1970, a nonelection year, 6 percent of my sample of Montevideo adults said that they belonged to a political club, compared with 11 percent at the time of the 1966 elections (Gallup Uruguay 1966c). In 1962, also an election year, 3 percent of the rural dispersed population and 8 percent of rural villagers said they belonged to "political groups" (CLEH 1963, pp. 421-26). Political club members, then, are few but are found in both urban and rural areas.

In Uruguay, election campaign activity and particularized contacting formed a single mode; however, for the sake of comparison, their indicators are discussed separately. In response to the question "Have you worked actively for some political candidate or contributed money for an election campaign?" 13 percent of my Montevideo respondents said yes. At the time of the 1971 election, 11 percent of Montevideo respondents said that during the campaign they had worked in a campaign, 20 percent had gone to the political club of their party, 21 percent had tried to convince others, and 33 percent had attended political meetings. The proportions for the urban interior were similar (5, 21, 31, and 40 percent [Gallup Uruguay 1971]). Problems of comparability of the questions and the absence of data for the one-fifth of the population which was rural makes exact comparison impossible. But it appears that the proportion attending political meetings and working actively in a campaign compared favorably with proportions in the U.S., while fewer Uruguayans attempted to persuade others to vote a certain way (Flanigan and Zingale 1975, p. 155; Robinson et al. 1969, pp. 602-5).

Empirical evidence on favor seeking as an indicator of particularized contacting is difficult to obtain, for many individuals are reluctant to admit having sought or received favors. Nine percent of my respondents said they had received favors, a proportion similar to that found for urban Uruguay (11 percent). However, 62 percent of my sample failed to respond to either question concerning favors! Of those who did respond to either question, 40 percent replied that they either had received or could receive a favor from a club. In the department of Canelones, which adjoins Montevideo, a similar proportion, 44 percent, said that they knew some politician from whom they could ask "some small favor if it were necessary." Of those Canelones respondents who said that they or a member of their family was a public employee, 38 percent said that the employment was obtained through one of the parties (Gallup Uruguay 1968b, 1966a). The data from candid respondents, then, imply that favor seeking is extensive in Uruguayan politics.

The Sources of Participation

Why people participate politically and why they choose a particular mode of participation may be examined on four levels: systemic influences, exchange theory, social forces, and psychological motivation. The first, the systemic argument, is that the level and type of participation are shaped by historical patterns and the channels available. In Uruguay prior to 1973, for example, elections were the normal means of changing leaders, and parties provided channels for resolving individual problems. The second explanation, exchange theory, emphasizes rationality in balancing benefits and costs (e.g., Chaffee 1976). Individuals participate because they desire a certain outcome. The scope of that outcome will affect the mode of participation chosen. Particularized contacting produces benefits for the individual, while voting tends to produce more generalized consequences. Two important costs affecting the participation decision are the degree of initiative required and the degree of conflict encountered (Verba et al. 1973, p. 236). The third explanation, the social forces argument, is that individual characteristics such as social status, sex, and age expose one to social conditions which shape one's participation. Higher status persons, for example, generally tend to participate more because they have more opportunity, resources, and participatory pressures. A fourth explanation of participation is psychological motivation. Individuals may vote, for example, because they feel it is a citizen's duty, or work in a campaign because they identify with a party.

All four explanations had some validity in Uruguay. But their manifestation was shaped by a systemic factor—the predominance of particularism and its institutionalized form, patronage. Patronage had long played a key role in Uruguayan politics. In this century, conflicts between the Colorados and Blancos were resolved by pacts dividing patronage rather than territories, as was done in the nineteenth century. Employment in both government and private business was largely based on particularistic ties (Solari 1967, p. 167). In addition to providing jobs, the political parties provided aid in making the highly inefficient bureaucracy function—for the recommended. This historical experience had two important consequences. First, it produced a system dominated by particularistic channels of influence—through parties, groups, and personal contacts. Second, it contributed to a predominance of particularistic over universalistic values (Taylor 1960a, pp. 57-63; Weinstein 1975, pp. 50-84).

What this means for exchange theory is that the benefits and costs of participation tend to be calculated primarily in personal terms, which in turn influences the social forces argument. The distinctive behavior of different social classes, for example, is muted if individuals perceive their interests as bound up in parties, groups, and personal connections which cut across class lines. The psychological motivation argument is also affected. Some of the psychological orientations such as the sense of citizen duty, trust in government, and the sense of the relevance of government have universalist elements which may reduce their motivational force in Uruguay when they conflict with more particularistic orientations such as party identification.

As measures of some of the forces shaping participation, sixteen variables mentioned in the literature were chosen from the author's survey. They were then subjected to factor analysis to group together those that co-varied. Five factors emerged: socioeconomic status (family income, occupation of head of household, class self-identification, and education), political involvement (political information level, interest in politics, political efficacy, sense of citizen duty, strength of party identification, and sex), personal relevance of government (how often government is right, perceived change of family's economic situation, and how much government affects one), general relevance

TABLE 3
RELATIVE IMPORTANCE OF SELECTED VARIABLES IN EXPLAINING
MODES OF PARTICIPATION IN MONTEVIDEO

PARTIAL BETA COEFFICIENTS* IN REGRESSION
PROBLEMS ON VARIABLES:

	Could Receive Favors	Campaign Work or Contribution	Voted in Recent Elections	Follows Politics in Newspapers	Number of Organization Memberships
Problem 1:					
Family Income (SES)	−.10	−.07	−.03	.03	.14
Political Information Level (Involvement)	.16	.27	.28	.29	.24
How Often Government Is Right (Personal Relevance)	.02	.04	.08	.01	−.04
Relevance of Elections to Economic Recovery (General Relevance)	.03	.05	.07	.05	−.05
Political Disagreement With Friends (Cross-Pressure)	−.01	.03	−.06	.09	.02
Multiple Coefficient	.17	.28	.30	.34	.30
Problem 2:					
Strength of Party Indentification	.22	.24	.25	.06	.11
Interest in Politics	.10	.16	.17	.37	.07
Political Efficacy	.03	.08	.10	.03	.21
Multiple Coefficient	.27	.36	.38	.40	.28

*Underlined coefficients are significant:
Partial coefficients $\geq$ .07 are significant at the .05 level.
Partial coefficients $\geq$ .10 are significant at the .01 level.
All multiple coefficients are significant at the .01 level.

of government (relevance of elections to economic recovery), and cross-pressures (political disagreement with friends and age).

In order to explore the correlates of the modes of participation in Uruguay, the highest loading variable from each independent factor was subjected to multiple regression analysis with representative variables from the modes of participation (table 3, problem 1). In addition, three variables theoretically related to specific modes were also analyzed (problem 2). Although particularized contacting loaded on the same dimension as campaign work, the two variables were treated separately in this analysis to further test the linkage between them. Examination of table 3 shows that while receiving favors generally had a lower relationship with the independent variables, it had much the same pattern of relationships as did campaign work, thus suggesting that the two were motivated by much the same forces. The other three modes showed differing causal structures, thus indicating their distinctiveness.

In Problem 1, three of the independent factors—personal relevance of government, general relevance of government, and cross-pressures—showed only insubstantial relationships with the participation modes. They did not appear to play a major independent predictive role for any of the modes. Socioeconomic status, as measured by family income, showed a weak but significant relationship with two of the measures of participation. It thus appeared to play some role. However, the sense of political involvement showed the strongest relationship with each of the modes. It would seem that the perceived importance of political outcomes in Uruguay (relevance) was insufficient to promote participation when the affective bonds of involvement were held constant.

To clarify the nature of the impact of political involvement, three of its facets with theoretical linkages to the modes were examined in problem 2 of table 3 (Verba et al. 1971, pp. 44-53). The first involvement variable was political interest, which should associate with concern for broad as opposed to particularistic issues. Thus, it correlated moderately with each of the measures except particularized contacting and this particular measure of communal activity (belonging to groups, not necessarily for political reasons). Probably because political communication has less tangible payoffs, political interest was its strongest correlate. Based on experience elsewhere, political efficacy was expected to correlate with the range of participation but to be most important for those activities requiring more initiative, such as campaigning and communal activity. However, it correlated strongly only with organizational membership and was not related to the campaigning-particularized contacting mode (the most particularistic mode).

As expected in a democratic system with electoral linkages, the strength of the respondent's party identification correlated with voting and campaign work. On the other hand, in most polities, one would not expect partisanship to have much to do with particularized contacting. However, in Uruguay the patronage system institutionalized parties as a major channel for resolving individual problems. Hence, partisanship and particularized contacting were correlated. This particularistic linkage helps to explain why the expected relationship between political efficacy and campaign work did not emerge when the strength of party identification was held constant. It was not one's universalistic feelings that counted most in producing campaign work but rather one's particularistic connections.

This brief comparison of the correlates of the modes confirms their distinctiveness, supports the finding of joint occurrence of the contacting and campaigning mode, indicates the centrality of political involvement in motivating participation, and demonstrates the modifying influence of particularism on the impact of other independent variables.[5]

Conclusions

The major finding of this paper was the central role of particularism and patronage in shaping political participation in pre-1973 Uruguay. All four common explanations of participation—systemic, exchange theory, social forces, and psychological motivations—proved applicable to Uruguay. Non-particularistic motivations played a role. However, the strength of particularism as a value and the existence of highly institutionalized channels of patronage and clientelism served as systemic factors modifying the impact of exchange, social, and psychological forces. With respect to exchange theory, particularistic considerations were dominant when payoffs were specific (personal) and tangible—that is, for campaigning and contacting and to a lesser degree for voting. When payoffs were diffuse or symbolic, universalism often prevailed, as with political communication and to a lesser degree with communal activity. The impact of social forces acting on the characteristics of the individual was also muted when particularistic connections cut across class, sex, and age lines. This happened particularly with voting and campaigning-contacting. On the other hand, those modes less influenced by particularism—communal activity and political communication—were affected by social characteristics. The essentially affective psychological dimension of involvement was dominant over the more rational or evaluative dimension of relevance of government for all modes of participation. Holding involvement constant also largely eliminated the small bivariate impact of cross-pressures on voting. Within the involvement dimension the more particularistic variable, strength of party identification, dominated the campaigning-contacting mode and voting, while the less particularistic variables, interest and efficacy, affected political communication and communal activity, respectively. Uruguayan political participation was, in short, the product of mixing public and private ends.

This study replicates the work of Verba and Nie and supports their findings in other nations, that political participation is multidimensional. Participation in Uruguay fell into four modes with distinct causal structures. The study further refines the concept of multidimensionality by confirming that systemic differences may produce variations in the modes, in this instance the joining of the campaigning and particularized-contacting modes. It also broadens the definition of participation to include political communication and shows that this mode may be usefully accommodated to those usually examined.

In most polities, campaign activity and particularized contacting are distinct modes. However, in Uruguay the use of well-developed patronage channels as a primary means of obtaining campaign workers together with the affective bonds of partisanship blurred the boundaries between the activities and produced a common mode. Campaigning and contacting loaded on the same factor and had similar causal structures. The union of the normally "apolitical" particularized contacting activities with campaigning strongly demonstrates the interest-based nature of Uruguayan politics and the central role which political parties played in it.

The political communications mode introduced in this study vied with voting as the most common political activity in Uruguay. Less affected by system characteristics specific to Uruguay, it showed patterns similar to those found elsewhere.

The study adds further evidence that political participation in Latin America is not substantially lower than in other regions. Uruguayan voter turnout and campaign activity were comparable to U.S. levels, while organizational membership and political communication were comparable to or slightly below British levels. Moreover, in spite of some variation, participation was common among all major urban Uruguayan demographic groups. Rural residents, however, showed less participation in at least communal activity and political communication.

In addition to building a clientele, the Uruguayan patronage system at first contributed to social stability by absorbing unemployment and providing social welfare (Solari 1967, p. 147). However, the system suffered from two major faults. First, it was dependent upon economic growth for its finance. By the mid-1950s, Uruguay began an economic decline and had increasing difficulty supporting the system. Second, the system was self-defeating. It produced such an inefficient bureaucracy that by the 1960s the system worked poorly even for those receiving the benefit of party recommendation. Perhaps more importantly, the substitution of private for public concerns made it impossible for the political system to serve national needs. Neither parties nor congress could aggregate national interests. Serving short-term clientelist interests substituted for long range rational decision making. Hence, the system was incapable of dealing with the economic and social crisis of the 1960s and 1970s. Discredited as incompetent and venal, politicians were replaced by the military, and their instruments, the parties, were reduced in role. Patronage and interest-based politics, then, contributed to the collapse of Uruguayan democracy. Interestingly, however, while the form of rule has changed, the particularistic substance remains. The number of interests represented has been severely limited, but the private ends they serve remain (Weinstein 1975, pp. 132-36; McDonald 1972b, 1975).

Notes

1. Using 1963 census data, interviews were proportioned among 19 sampling areas according to population. Then, using random selection procedures at each stage, blocks, housing units, and individuals were chosen. A total of 129 blocks were selected with eight proposed interviews per block. Interviewing covered two months (Biles 1972, pp. 451-86).

2. "One of the functions for which political clubs generally serve consists of helping people speed administrative procedures so as not to lose time, or to obtain pensions, telephones, jobs, etc. Have you or some member of your family been able to make use of one of these functions of the political clubs?" "If you should eventually find yourself in difficulties, is there some political club to which you could go for help?"

3. Factor analysis of only those variables comparable to those used by Verba and Nie (that is, excluding the political communication variables) does not appreciably alter the findings (Biles 1976a, pp. 15-16).

4. Because of serious uncertainty about population changes, similar calculations were not made for 1971. However, because of the passage of legislation to enforce the constitutional requirement to vote, the total number of valid ballots cast increased 35 percent over 1966. Voters as a percentage of registrants increased from 74 percent in 1966 to 89 percent in 1971, a proportion that would rank Uruguay second in Latin America (Dirrección General de Estadistica y Censo 1969; Solari et al. 1966; Fabregat 1964, 1968, 1972; Taylor and Hudson 1972; Russett et al. 1964; Biles 1972, pp. 169-81).

5. A more extended discussion of the correlates (and individual variables) of participation may be found in the original version of this paper (Biles 1976c).

Many scholars have doubted the political rationality of most Latin Americans. Some theorists argue that all mass publics are probably irrational, while others believe that the nature of Latin American society insures irrationality. Booth tests these suppositions by comparing the behavior of a national sample of Costa Ricans to a hypothetical model of rationality based on goal-oriented behavior. His data reveal that Costa Ricans behave rationally in the areas of national, local, and community government, contrary to the expectations of the theorists. His findings show that wealthier citizens and urbanites participate more in national institutions, while the poor and rural citizens concentrate their activity in the local and community governments.

6.
Are Latin Americans Politically Rational? Citizen Participation and Democracy in Costa Rica

JOHN A. BOOTH

Little of the research on political participation and citizen rationality has touched upon Third World societies, and still less on Latin America. The vast majority of such analysis has come from studies of electoral behavior in the United States and Western Europe. The conventional belief, however, is that Third World mass publics are very unlikely to follow rational patterns of political action (Nelson 1969; Portes 1972). Since the capacity of citizens for rational participation is important for all political systems, the lacunae regarding nonelectoral forms of citizen action and participation in Third World societies in general is indeed unfortunate. This essay attempts to shed some light upon the question of Latin American mass publics' capacities for reasoned political behavior through an analysis of recent data from the Central American nation of Costa Rica. The findings reveal that Costa Ricans by and large do act rationally in public affairs, as do mass publics in other societies, suggesting important implications for certain widely held images of Latin American politics and for a current theoretical debate regarding the most appropriate definition of democracy.

Comments by Richard N. Adams, Thomas A. Baylis, Richard J. Moore, Karl M. Schmitt, and Mitchell A. Seligson have greatly improved earlier versions of this paper.

Research on Citizen Action and Rationality in Latin America

An important scholarly image holds Latin Americans to be politically irrational due to the political culture of the region (Booth 1977a; Booth and Seligson, chapter 1). Latin America's political culture consists of a complex web of sociopolitical values, attitudes, and behavior patterns strongly influenced by emotionalism, dogmatism, and a "cultivation of the intellect" that bars pragmatic problem solving:

> The certainty of the "true" solution and the quick description of the malady leads to a certain myopia which is visible in party politics, labor-business disputes, public versus private sector conflicts, and adds to a general malaise in intercountry disputes. (Ranis 1971, p. 155)

Among the cultural traits usually viewed as barriers to the sort of pragmatic, realistic pursuit of political goals commonly regarded as rational are the following: parochialism, disdain for pragmatism (Almond and Verba 1965; Lipset 1967; Williams 1973); *machismo* (Ramos 1962), paternalism, patron-client relationships (Powell 1970; Strickon and Greenfield 1972; Willems 1975), personalist ties (Scott 1959, 1965; Willems 1975), emphasizing the "expressive rather than the instrumental; (Lipset 1967, p. 7) traditionalism, deference to elites (Lipset 1967, pp. 7-8; Scott 1967), and authoritarianism (Tallet 1969).

Some important exceptions to the Third World participation research gap have recently appeared on two fronts, however. First, seminal studies on the structure of citizen action in India and Nigeria (Verba et al. 1971; Kim et al. 1974), have demonstrated that participation there resembles that in First World nations to a surprising degree, both in its levels and dimensions. Studies on Latin American nations have tended to confirm these findings for Costa Rica (Booth 1976; Seligson and Booth, forthcoming-c), Uruguay (Biles, chapter 5) Venezuela (Baloyra and Martz, chapter 4 and 1976a), Peru (Dietz and Moore 1977). Second, separate studies by Portes (1972), Cornelius (1974), and Dietz (1974) have dealt with the question of participant rationality. Although these studies suggest that participation may conform to rational patterns, they focus only upon the urban poor of a few major cities and upon a rather narrow range of political activities. This essay expands the analysis of citizen rationality in Latin America by examining several types of participation among a representative national sample of Costa Ricans.

Costa Rica provides a particularly appropriate setting for such a study because its political system had functioned as a liberal constitutional democracy for some twenty years at the time of the study in 1973. It thus provides a unique opportunity to compare citizen participation in an open, constitutionally governed Latin American polity with the landmark participant rationality studies, most of which have been set in the U.S. (see below). The constitutional environment controls for the possibility that an authoritarian or repressive political environment might confound key relationships or distort behavior patterns. By contrast, for example, should Guatemalans or

Argentines exhibit irrational political behavior patterns, one would not know whether they truly stemmed from the nature of Latin political culture or derived from the effects of dictatorial rule. Since no such repression characterizes Costa Rica, the findings can provide a necessary benchmark for further research in the region's nondemocratic polities.

The Debate Over Citizen Rationality

The differences just discussed, between the conventional wisdom on political rationality in Latin America and some suggestive recent research, reflect important aspects of a larger debate among political theorists. Students of politics have long disputed whether masses can participate rationally in public affairs, and consequently how much they should participate. This issue receives considerable attention from social scientists today. One side in the debate regards masses as inherently irrational and would therefore restrict mass participation. The other side sees masses as rational within the limitations of the political system.

While no clear school of thinkers stands out as completely representative of democratic theory (Pateman 1970; Danielson 1974), one may easily identify the key elements of democracy. Aristotle (1962, pp. 74-81) defined democracy as that constitution in which those who are poor and free form a sovereign majority and thereby exercise decision-making power in ruling and adjudicating disputes. This description touches upon the major elements of democracy, a process for the government of a social entity in which its own members play an active decision-making role (Cohen 1973, pp. 3-6). This basic definition receives support from the writings of Thucydides (1962, p. 425), Rousseau (1962), and Jefferson (1935, p. 83). The classical definition of democracy, then, is rule by the people.

On the other hand, however, many political thinkers have doubted the capacity of mass publics to govern themselves. Both Aristotle (1962, pp. 160-161) and Hamilton (1961, pp. 56-57) have attributed the failure or perversion of democracy to the people's inability to resist demagoguery and basic human passions. Several contemporary democratic theorists have agreed, questioning the capacity of masses rationally to engage in politics. Moved by the failure of the Weimar Constitution at the hands of a totalitarian mass movement, these social scientists[1] have proposed to "correct" classical democratic theory to fit the empirical social conditions they have observed in contemporary societies (Pateman 1970, pp. 3-4). Members of this group, henceforth to be referred to as the "empirical theorists of democracy," have reported on the basis of their survey research that informed, active electoral participation (voting and campaigning) commonly occurs primarily among persons of higher income, educational, and occupational status levels (Lipset 1963, pp. 64-178; Campbell et al. 1960; Milbrath 1965, pp. 110-41). The empiricists report the poor to be inactive in general, but ill informed when they do take part. Lower- and middle-class citizens allegedly lack ideological consistency, are rather authoritarian, and are unlikely to apply democratic values in real life (Campbell et al. 1960; Converse 1968; Prothro and Grigg 1960; Berelson et al. 1954; Lipset 1963; Almond and Verba 1965). More than anything else, an individual's place within the socioeconomic status hierarchy determines his capacity for reasoned political activity; the mass public in Western societies, in comparison to socioeconomic elites, tends toward irrationality, antidemocratic values, and inherent political apathy, except for occasional voting.

These findings about mass publics led the empiricists to reconsider the value of popular political participation in democracy: they began to view it more as a danger than an asset in liberal constitutional polities. The empiricists thus became democratic "revisionists" since their fear of mass participation led them to turn to sociopolitical elites, supposedly far more democratic and rational than masses, for the maintenance of democracy (Prothro and Grigg 1960; Converse 1968). Political elites thus became the key to this redefined concept of democracy, while mass nonparticipation was reinterpreted as a desideratum. The empiricists thus reduced the role of mass political activity in democracy from an ideal of active engagement in all levels of collective decision making to simply taking part in leadership selection in elections (Berelson et al. 1954, pp. 306-18; Dahl 1956; Lipset 1963, pp. 27, 123; Milbrath 1965, pp. 142-54; Milbrath and Goel 1977, pp. 144-50).

The empirical democratic theory school has, however, come under attack in two major areas. First, critics accuse the empiricists of defining politics too narrowly, including only electoral phenomena. This narrow definition plus the tendency to focus on "democratic values," say the critics, have caused the empiricists to overlook considerable amounts of relevant political activity (Euben 1970, pp. 14-17; Pateman 1970, pp. 21, 52-45; Cobb and Elder 1972, pp. 5-10; Bachrach 1966, p. 99). Second, the critics attack the conceptual underpinnings of the empiricists' research on reasoned behavior as defining rationality too narrowly. The critics contend that such narrow ideas of rationality (usually conceived as either "consistency" between ideology and specific issue positions or between democratic principles and hypothetical applications of such principles) *predetermined* the finding that mass publics are irrational, not due to the attributes of the citizens themselves but rather to the structure of the tests (Cobb 1973; Mason 1973; Brown and Taylor 1973; Walker 1966; Lipsitz 1970). In fact, several recent studies have reassessed the empiricists' work and concluded that methodological and conceptual problems, as well as changes in the attitudes of the U.S. population over time, led early research falsely to conclude that mass publics generally act irrationally (Key 1966; RePass 1971; Bennett 1973; Nie and Andersen 1974; Frohlich et al. 1974). In short, new evidence has given ample reason to question the conclusions of the empirical democratic theorists regarding both the capacity of mass publics and their proposed redefinition of democracy.

Reason and Political Participation

These scholarly images of political participation in Latin America and the debate over the definition of democracy together suggest two fundamental issues for analysis. One thread running through both literatures suggests that mass publics do not behave in politically rational ways, and the other suggests that higher socioeconomic status usually accompanies higher levels of rationality. Does mass political behavior in Costa Rica follow rational patterns? Is social position the major determinant of political rationality? The following analysis seeks answers to these queries, attempting to avoid some of the empiricists' pitfalls by examining citizen rationality for a multitude of non-electoral forms of political behavior within three different arenas of participation—the national system, local government, and the neighborhood. The analysis begins with a narrow, tightly defined approach to reasoned political behavior (the goals-saliency model), and through empirical analysis utilizing this model identifies several criteria for improving tests of participant rationality by heightening sensitivity to the sociopolitical context of participation.

The goals-saliency rationality model. The disagreements in the findings of the empiricist theorists of democracy and their critics stem in part from the critics' development of the concept of *saliency.* The basic insight involved in the critique is that one cannot judge the rationality of a political act without considering whether the actor perceives some institution as a useful path toward his goals. As employed here[2] saliency means the perceived relevance of a particular political object or institution for the realization of personal goals (Czudnowski 1968). Saliency implies that one must judge the rationality of individual political activity in terms of its appropriateness for seeking the goals of the actor. The basic aspects of this means-ends model of reasoned behavior are: first, that an individual must have goals for the future; second, that he/she must see some political institution as relevant (salient) for pursuing those goals; and third, that he/she must then act in a manner consistent with both his/her own goals and the saliency of the particular institution (see also Touraine and Pécaut 1970; Almond and Verba 1965; Lane 1959). Rational behavior thus involves participating in an institution if one has politically relevant goals (ends) and also perceives that institution (means) as relevant for realizing his/her goals. Irrational behavior would therefore consist of either low participation when both goals and saliency are high, or high participation when neither high goals nor saliency are present.[3] The basic hypothesis of the analysis, then, is that Costa Ricans do participate rationally in political affairs. In the aggregate, therefore, participation should be highest among individuals who both have goals and perceive some institution as relevant for realizing these goals. Levels should be lowest among individuals with neither high goals nor saliency.

Arenas of participation. One important consideration for testing such a model of rationality is that the measures of salience and goal levels be contextually relevant for the type of participation analyzed. Political participation is defined here as behavior influencing or attempting to influence the distribution of public goods (Booth and Seligson, chapter 1). In this connection, participation in Costa Rica clearly takes place in different sociopolitical contexts, or arenas. Three arenas of participation have relevance here: national government institutions, local or municipal government, and politics internal to communities. A brief explanation is necessary, because although the distinction between the national arena and the others is obvious, that between local government and community politics is perhaps less so. The lowest level administrative unit in Costa Rica is the *municipio,* or *cantón,* roughly the equivalent of the county government in the U.S. The municipal government consists of a council of voting *regidores* and nonvoting *síndicos,* and a bureaucracy headed by the municipal executive who oversees municipal service delivery. Municipalities have broad responsibilities for collecting certain taxes and for basic public services from roads to water supply to electricity, thus affecting most citizens directly. A municipality usually contains several communities (towns and villages), each of which has internal politics connected with community improvement activities, health and nutrition programs, and local schools. Community politics may sometimes be unrelated to municipal (county wide) politics, but at other times does concern municipal institutions as sources of power or resources. The participation indices used below measure activity which attempts to influence the distribution of public goods in each arena.

Testing the model. Data for the following analysis come from a 1973 national probability sample of Costa Rican family heads.[4] The dependent variables, community, local government, and national participation, are scales constructed from multiple items for each arena of activity.[5] Community participation, for example, combines discussing local problems, membership in community improvement associations, and taking part in community improvement projects. Local government activity combines contacting local officials and discussing local politics. National participation includes partisan activity, contacting national public officials, discussing national politics, and membership in voluntary associations. In order to make the scales on the different types of participation comparable, they have been standardized, thus expressing each of the indicators in terms of its own overall variation.

The first dependent variable is participation in the local government arena. Some 12.6 percent of the respondents reported having sought assistance from the municipal executive, 10.6 percent from a municipal councilman, and 9.0 percent from the police; 21.4 percent reported they discussed local politics at least from time to time. The number of changes an individual desires in his community provides an index of his goal orientation for the community.[6] An index of the saliency of local political officials comes from a question designed

to elicit the respondent's perception of the relevancy of the municipal government and its representatives for the solution of important local problems.[7]

The specific hypothesis to be tested here is that if Costa Ricans behave
rationally in the local political arena, the average level of contacting local
officials should be at its highest among those with both a high level of
community goals and who believe the local government is relevant for solving
local problems. Furthermore, participation should be lower among those
fulfilling only one of these conditions, and lowest of all among those with low
goal levels and no perception of local government saliency.

Table 1 displays the mean standardized levels of the index of participation
in local government. For each successive level of goal orientation, the level of
local government participation increases. Participation is much higher
(0.261) among those desiring three or more changes in their communities than
among those desiring no change (−.189). The data also demonstrate that the
saliency of the municipality affects participation in local government: those
who see the *municipio* as relevant for resolving local problems take part
somewhat more (0.013) than those who do not perceive its relevance
(−.015). Citizens with both a high goal orientation and who perceive the
municipality as salient participate at a level (.315) many times higher than
that of citizens lacking both goals and the saliency perception (−.191). Data
from the local government arena therefore support the hypothesis that Costa
Ricans use means-to-ends calculation in determining their political activity.
Rational calculation appears to play an important role in contacting local
officials and discussing local politics.

Taken alone, these findings do not seem particularly worthy of note.
However, when we recall that a major trend in political theory and research
denies the likelihood of such simple rational political behavior, especially in a
Latin American political culture, these seemingly mundane observations take
on much greater importance. The findings challenge the conventional wisdom
that argues that ordinary citizens are inherently incapable of goal-oriented
political behavior. If similar patterns appear for both the national and the community arena participation, these findings should lead us to question the
common assumption that because of their cultural heritage, Latin American
masses are politically irrational.

Continuing to the second arena, Costa Ricans are quite active within the
contexts of their communities: 55.9 percent reported having taken part in
some community improvement project, 42.2 percent having discussed local
problems at least from time to time, and 16 percent belonging to a formal
community development group. The test for the index of community (neighborhood) participation resembles that for the local government arena: Taking
part in problem solving within the community usually requires interaction with
one's neighbors, whether as coparticipant in some project or simply discussing
local problems. Thus, a measure of the perceived relevance of neighbors for
the resolution of local problems provides the necessary saliency index.[8] As

TABLE 1
POLITICAL PARTICIPATION^a BY GOAL LEVEL AND SALIENCY

Saliency^{c,d,e}	Arena of Participation	Intensity of Goals^b			
		0	1-2	3+	Total
Not Salient	Local government	−191 (290)^f	078 (374)	206 (73)	−015 (737)
	Neighbors	−207 (365)^f	017 (437)	234 (78)	− 71 (881)
	National government	−253 (122)^f	−134 (371)	152 (248)	−050 (740)
Salient	Local government	−186 (265)	116 (311)	315 (68)	013 (644)
	Neighbors	−120 (196)	207 (247)	605 (66)	141 (479)
	National government	−306 (102)	−040 (335)	424 (218)	073 (655)
Total	Local government	−189 (555)	095 (685)	261 (141)	(1381)
	Neighbors	−108 (562)	086 (684)	493 (144)	(1390)
	National government	−275 (224)	−090 (706)	292 (466)	(1395)

^{a}Participation levels are Z-scores for local government, neighborhood, and national government participation indices.

^{b}Goal intensity is the total number of local changes desired for the local government and neighborhood arenas, and the total number of national problems perceived for the national arena.

^{c}Perceives local government as relevant for problem solving in the community.

^{d}Perceives neighbors as relevant for problem solving in the community.

^{e}Perceives national government as relevant for problem solving in the community.

^{f}Values in parentheses below each participation score are the number of cases in each cell.

before, the total number of changes the person desires for his community or neighborhood will serve to measure his goal orientation.

The evidence for the neighborhood arena in table 1 again confirms the hypothesis of rational participation. The average level of activity increases notably for successive levels of goal orientation (from. −.108 to .403). Further, persons perceiving their neighbors as potential sources for local problem solving reported much more activity (.141) than those who did not share this view (−.071). Finally, those who both have community goals and view their neighbors as salient for these goals participated most of all (.605); those who neither have goals nor see any problem-solving relevance in their neighbors were the least active group (−.207). Here, again, is substantial evidence that in the aggregate Costa Ricans act rationally in politics. A person with a desire to improve his community is likely to discuss local problems and to work for such change if he believes that his fellow citizens provide a potentially effective resource.

A similar test can be applied to participation in national political institutions. Once again, the basic hypothesis is that if citizens have both goals or desires for Costa Rica, and believe national institutions salient political objects, they will participate in politics more than persons who meet neither or only one of these conditions. The activities included in the index are political party membership (reported by 21.5 percent), contacting national officials (10.3 percent contacting a National Assembly deputy, 3.4 percent the president, etc.), discussing national politics at least "from time to time" (27 percent), and membership in voluntary associations (66.1 percent members of at least one group). Voting in national elections is not included because voting is mandatory in Costa Rica. In order to be rational, behavior must be freely chosen. The requirement to vote and the possibility of legal sanctions for noncompliance probably greatly reduce the appropriateness of this model of behavior for studying rationality of voting.

For this test, the total number of national problems perceived measures goal orientation.[9] Orientation toward the national government for solving important local community problems provides an index of saliency.[10] Once again, the participation level scores confirm the hypothesis of rationality (see table 1). The level of activity among those not seeing the national government as salient is lower ($-.050$) than among those who saw it as relevant ($.073$). Participation rises from a low among those with no national goals ($-.275$) to a high among those reporting three or more goals ($.292$). The highest national level participation comes among those with both high goals and the saliency perception ($.424$). Thus, for national arena political activism, Costa Ricans, in the aggregate, exhibit rational behavior.

To sum up, the answer to the first question of this analysis—"Does mass political behavior follow rational patterns?"—must be affirmative. The test of the narrowly defined model of means-to-end goal oriented behavior in each of three arenas of action has revealed rational aggregate behavior patterns. These findings cast serious doubt upon the accuracy of the literatures discussed earlier. The conventional view of Latin American political culture and the empirical democratic theorists would both have predicted irrational behavior patterns, but the tests done here reveal not irrationality, but rationality.

Social Position and Goals-Saliency Levels

The second question of interest concerns the belief of the empiricist theorists of democracy that social position is a major determinant of the capacity for reasoned political calculation—i.e., that rationality occurs much more commonly among elites than masses. This section explores this question by looking at how the Costa Rican's position within society affects his/her levels of goals and saliency.

The goals-saliency level model can be transformed into a linear variable in order to permit the use of regression analysis. This variable will be called "goals-saliency level," alluding to its principal characteristics. Persons with neither goals nor a perception of institutional saliency (for some relevant arena of political action) recieve a low score. Persons with either goals or the saliency perception (but not both) receive a score of intermediate range, and those with both of these attributes are scored the highest. This variable will permit testing the empiricists' claim that rational behavior is largely confined to persons of higher status levels. This claim suggests that persons close to the center of society (high in wealth, income, education, or geographically close to metropolitan centers) will be more likely than those on society's periphery to have high levels of goals and to perceive institutions as salient for problem solving. If the empiricists' hypothesis is correct, then, such status indices should all correlate positively with the goals-saliency level.

Table 2 presents correlations among the three goals-saliency indicators for the local government,[11] community,[12] and national government[13] arenas and several variables indicative of individual socioeconomic status and socio-political context. There we see that three indices of status (income, education, and occupational status) correlate not similarly but differentially with the various goals-saliency indicators. National goals-saliency correlates moderately with the objective status measures, neighbors goals-saliency somewhat less strongly, and local government goals-saliency very weakly. The ecological position variables also relate differentially to the three goals-saliency levels. Costa Ricans who live far from the national capital or in small towns are less likely to have high levels of national arena goals-saliency. But on the other hand, none of these contextual variables appears to affect goals-saliency formation for the local government or neighborhood arenas.

TABLE 2. ZERO-ORDER CORRELATES OF GOALS-SALIENCY LEVELS

	Goals-Saliency Level		
Variables	*National Government*	*Local Government*	*Neighbors*
Status			
Education	.23	.01(NS)*	.14
Income	.20	.02(NS)	.12
Occupational Status	.16	.07	.13
Ecological Conditions			
Distance from the capital	.12	.01(NS)	−.01(NS)
Distance from the *cabecera municipal*	−.11	.01(NS)	−.04(NS)
Town size	.11	−.02(NS)	.01(NS)
N	1395	1381	1390

*Not significant at the .05 level

These findings have two important implications. First, they lead us to reject the hypothesis derived from the empirical democratic theorists that high levels of goals-saliency should correlate uniformly and positively with status measures in all arenas of political activity. It is clear that in Costa Rica at least, the high goals-saliency condition which leads to participation is not predominantly confined to higher status groups. The capacity for rational political behavior (measured here as the concurrence of high goals and saliency) is, then, distributed throughout the Costa Rican population. Masses *do not* appear to be inherently incapable of reasoned political action.

The second implication of the findings has to do with the pattern observed in the correlations in Table 2. This pattern suggests an alternative explanation for goals-saliency levels among Costa Ricans to that of the empiricists. Status alone does not determine goals-saliency for all arenas as it should were the empiricists' belief in the inherent irrationality of masses correct.

Rather, an individual's position within the society seems far more important. Isolation from the center of Costa Rican society—by being poor, uneducated, or in a low status job, by living far from the capital, a municipal seat, or in a small town—tends to lower individual goals-saliency levels with respect to national institutions. Local government and community goals-saliency, however, remain uncorrelated with these ecological factors and have lower correlations with the status items as well. Local concerns, occurring regardless of where one lives, thus transcend geographical centricity, and are much less fixed by the status system.

These findings about the formation of goals-saliency suggest that a broader approach to reasoned political behavior might be useful. Apparently the structure of political institutions and one's location in the society influence what types of public goods a citizen may attempt to have. Though position in the status hierarchy does not appear to bar access to municipal government, status seems materially to influence orientation to the national government— the lower one's status, the lower his national goals-saliency level. Likewise, the extreme centralization of national political institutions in the capital and larger towns restricts access to national institutions for those in small towns and isolated areas. Such barriers, however, do not appear to affect orientation toward the community and the municipal government because they are much more accessible and can provide at least some services throughout the nation. In contrast, the complex and centralized institutions of national government provide services primarily to the more urbanized areas of Costa Rica's *meseta central* (central plateau), so that orientation toward national institutions requires substantial personal economic, educational, and status resources, as well as an advantageous geographical location. The low utility of national institutions and the high costs of gaining access to the distribution of public goods controlled by these institutions apparently act as barriers to important segments of mass interest. Low national goals-saliency among the poor, small town, and rural residents—especially those outside the meseta—logically stem from the nature of national institutions. While the empiricists have suggested an inherent deficiency of political reasoning among mass publics as the cause of low mass interest and participation in national politics, these findings lead one to reject that explanation. Rather than individual deficiencies, it is the very structure of Costa Rican social and political institutions which provides barriers to national politics for many citizens. These barriers are less severe or nonexistent for local and neighborhood politics.

Toward a Broader Approach to Rationality

We have seen (1) that mass participation follows generally rational (means-to-ends) patterns, and (2) that position with respect to sociopolitical institutions (rather than an innate but unequally distributed capacity for political ratiocination) influences citizens' political interests. But while the goals-saliency rationality model has proven useful so far, it remains a very narrowly defined construct which could well profit from amplification. The goals-saliency model isolates only two attributes of Costa Ricans to evaluate the rationality of their behavior—their goal orientation and their perception of institutional relevance. Both of these factors have proven useful, at least partly because of their sensitivity to the individual's perception of his sociopolitical context. But there is no reason to believe that goal intensity and saliency alone exhaust all the perceptions which the individual employs to decide whether and how to participate.

In searching for other factors which Costa Ricans may take into account in deciding to participate, many individual and contextual variables have been examined employing multiple regression analysis. While the details of this analysis consume too much space to present here (see Booth 1977b), some of the findings bear relating. First of all, two factors which contribute to participation independently of goals-saliency levels include socioeconomic status and political knowledge, both reflections of the individual's resources for political participation. Other important characteristics appear to reflect some of the costs associated with the context in which the citizen must participate—the size of one's community and the distance one resides from San José, the capital, and from the seat of his municipio. More elaborate models of citizen rationality should attempt to include such ecological and personal attributes.

A second finding was that the major effects upon participation varied according to the political arena in question. Socioeconomic resources, for example, were particularly critical for national level activism, but not at all important for community improvement work. The availability of basic public services, greatest in Costa Rica's metropolitan center and in larger towns, associated negatively with community improvement activism. These findings further buttress the notion that participation in national politics is somewhat more likely to be the domain of socioeconomic elites because they are both served by and have the resources to deal with the national government in San

José. That same national government is both geographically remote and a poor supplier of services in the hinterlands (Booth et al. 1973; Booth 1974). Once again, the need to make the rationality model sensitive to specific contextual conditions stands out.

A third finding of this analysis was that in the more intimate context of the community the explanatory power of the goals-saliency calculation increases. Rational calculation contributes much more to community improvement activity and discussing local problems than to participation in the more remote municipal and national frameworks. More than likely one may hold specific goals and evaluate the potential utility of an institution more easily in the context of his/her community or neighborhood than in the more remote contexts of the nation and the municipality.

And finally, the degree to which political action serves as a useful instrument for pursuing goals may also affect the influence of rational calculation on participation. For example, for a Costa Rican, the act of discussing local politics has very low utility for pursuing concrete goals, whereas in contrast community improvement activity and contacting local officials work much more specifically and directly toward political objectives. Goals-saliency calculation was observed to contribute more strongly with the more clearly utilitarian activities—those useful for pursuing a concrete goal. Thus, future rationality studies would do well to try to measure the perception of the citizen as to how useful specific acts may be for pursuing particular types of objectives.

Conclusions

These findings differ dramatically from the expected dichotomy between rational elites and irrational masses. On the whole, Costa Rican mass political behavior follows rational patterns. This finding strongly contradicts the negative image of mass behavior expected in Latin America from the writings of the empirical theorists of democracy and of many students of Latin American political culture. Costa Rican masses appear to be not irrational but rational in their behavior. Citizens throughout the system, both masses and elites, take part in politics in salient arenas, taking actions they believe useful for pursuing their particular goals. Further, the contextual correlates of participation suggest that this reasoning process is even more complex than the model tested could measure, sensitive to a broad range of individual and social factors.

How do these Costa Rican data compare to findings from other nations? Several studies were cited above which strongly suggest that voter rationality is widespread among citizens of the United States and Britain. While the goals-saliency model of rationality differs from that approach, those findings nonetheless suggest reasoned behavior among mass publics.

But what about Latin America? Portes' (1972) research on slum dwellers employs the issue consistency approach to demonstrate that organizational behavior, housing improvement activity, and party choice follow both non-radical and rational patterns in several countries. Cornelius (1974) and Dietz (1974) discuss tests of a version of goals-saliency rationality (somewhat more complex than the one employed here) among the urban poor of Mexico City and Lima. They report in detail the complicated chain of perceptions and calculations involved in demanding community improvement help from government agencies. The process reveals the considerable ingenuity with which the poor pursue political solutions to their most pressing problems. All in all, then, other studies support the Costa Rican data by suggesting that mass publics can and do conduct themselves rationally—both in the First World and in Latin America.

A first implication of these findings thus runs contrary to the normative arguments of the empiricists. The basic ability to participate rationally exists among Costa Ricans, among other Latin Americans, and probably among masses in general. While this proposition may still not sound surprising to some, its significance lies in the fact that a major trend of political thought would reject such a statement as implausible. The ultimate implication of such elitist theories has usually been that mass irrationality either justifies the partial or complete exclusion of all masses from political decision making, or explains why most Latin Americans are ruled by generals. But if the empiricist argument's foundation in social reality falls before more valid, reliable, and consistent evidence, as it apparently has, the elitists' normative recommendations for political organization must be seriously reconsidered. There would appear to be no convincing argument (based on capacity for rational political action) for excluding the majority of citizens from political decision making.

In light of these findings, therefore, political scientists should seriously reexamine the conflicting definitions of democracy. If citizens are not irrational, why should "democratic" theorists wish to restrict their participation? Nonparticipation in national institutions apparently results from barriers built into the sociopolitical system (complexity, centralization, service discrimination, high cost of activism, etc.). Such nonparticipation should not be regarded as a virtue for a polity, but a serious flaw—indeed, an obstacle to democracy and not the source of its salvation. Defenders of the classical definition of democracy, for years outnumbered and apparently ovewhelmed by misleading early findings, seem now to have gained the upper hand in the debate as the balance of empirical evidence has tipped in their favor.

The second major implication concerns Latin American political culture and its supposed effect on political behavior. Evidence from Costa Rica (with a liberal constitutional tradition) and from several other Latin American nations (some with authoritarian regimes) reveals rational patterns of political activity. Although these findings do not necessarily disprove contentions that Latin Americans may be emotional, dogmatic, personalistic, or paternalistic in their political culture, they do cast considerable doubt upon the common conclusion that the accompanying political behavior is therefore necessarily irrational. A more reasonable interpretation would recognize how the complexity of human motivation, culture, and the individual's social and physical environment must affect his/her decisions and actions (Seligson and Booth 1976, chapter 1). Latin Americans should not, therefore, be accused of political irrationality so long as the impressions to that effect stem not from hard evidence of behavior but from certain erroneous assumptions made by students of their culture.

Finally, these findings suggest that political scientists might do well to consider how existing governments might enhance democracy. Latin Americans have long accused North American political scientists of theoretical perspectives which work counter to democracy in the region (Flores Olea 1967, pp. 168-73). Political scientists should jettison the culture-bound and elitist assumption that mass publics, of the Third World as well as the First World, are inherently unfit for democracy. Ridding ourselves of such bias could well serve as a first step toward rectifying the unhappy tradition that has made us so often unwelcome abroad.

Notes

1. Major authors within the empirical democratic theory camp are Dahl (1956), Berelson et al. (1954), Lipset (1963), Prothro and Grigg (1960), Campbell (1962), Campbell et al. (1960), Milbrath (1965), Converse (1968), and Milbrath and Goel (1977).

2. Another approach to saliency is that of students of ideology and belief systems. They employ saliency to refer to the degree of importance an individual attributes to an issue. For example see Cobb (1973), Bennett (1973), Nie and Andersen (1974) and Lipsitz (1970).

3. The goals-saliency model of rationality does not account for the *accuracy* of citizen perceptions about the appropriateness of institutions for problem solving. Rationality consists of congruence among goals, actions, and *beliefs* about reality, not reality itself. Thus, rational behavior may not always be *correct* from the standpoint of goals. However, human behavior tends to be adaptive in the long run; people use their intelligence to survive in a complex world.

4. These data come from a survey conducted for the Costa Rican *Dirección Nacional de Desarrollo de la Comunidad* by Acción Internacional Técnica in 1973. The sample was a two-stage stratified random design using the probability proportional to size (PPS) technique (Kish 1967). The target population was all Costa Rican family heads. From a stratified random sample of 20 of Costa Rica's 391 districts with a population of over 300, dwelling units indicated on recently updated census maps were randomly sampled from within each community. Further description and discussion of the sampling may be found in Booth (1975a, pp. 425-29).

5. The community arena activism index consists of the mean of the standardized values (Z-scores) for responses to three questions about discussing local problems at least "from time to time," membership in community improvement associations, and the total number of community betterment projects participated in. Similarly, the local government arena index combines Z-scores for having contacted the municipal executive and a municipal councilman. The national government arena index combines Z-scores for membership in a political party, contacting the president, contacting a Legislative Assembly delegate, discussing national politics, and level of activity in voluntary associations.

6. This is the number of changes mentioned in response to the question "What things would you like to change about this place (community)?" Note that this index does not measure the intensity with which any single goal is desired, but rather the overall goal orientation of the citizen for his community.

7. The index is constructed by awarding one point to a response related to municipal government elicited by the following question: "Whom would you approach if you wished to resolve the most important problems of this community? The national government, the munici- pality, your neighbors in the community, or some other special person?"

8. Neighbor saliency is tapped through the following item: "Suppose that a community is divided because one group wants to build a new football field, but another group doesn't want it built. Who is most capable of resolving this dispute? A policeman, the municipal executive, a municipal councilman, neighbors, the local "boss" (*gamonal*), the parish priest, someone else, or no one?" Mentioning the neighbors as the potential problem solver is construed to indicate neighbor saliency.

9. This is the total number of separate items elicited by this question: "In your opinion, what are the most important problems for Costa Rica?"

10. National government saliency is measured by a response mentioning national political leaders or institutions to the question in note 7 above.

11. The goals-saliency index for interaction with local government was constructed in the following manner: Local goals were measured by the number of local changes desired, so that one or fewer changes were scored as 0 (low goals) and 2 or more were scored as 1 (high goals). Saliency was measured by perceiving the municipal government as relevant for problem solving (scored 1), or irrelevant (scored 0). See the above notes for these items. Cases with missing values on either variable were excluded (65 in all). The local government goals-saliency index is a linear combination of these two measures so that a score of zero means low goals-low saliency of local government, a score of 1 means either low goals-high saliency or vice versa, and a score of 2 indicates the high goals-high saliency of local government combination.

12. The goals-saliency index for community improvement participation was constructed in an analogous fashion. Saliency of neighbors and other citizens in the community is indicated by perceiving them to be relevant for problem solving in the community (scored 1), or irrelevant (scored 0). Goal intensity was measured as described above: low (scored 0) = one or fewer changes desired for the community, high (scored 1) = two or more changes desired for the community. Cases with missing values on either variable were discarded (56 in all). See previous notes for the items used. The final index is a linear combination of these items, producing a three value scale: 0 = low saliency-low goals, 1 = either low goals-high saliency or vice versa, and 2 = high goals-high saliency.

13. The goals-saliency index for national level political participation is constructed similarly. Saliency of national government is indicated by the respondent perceiving it as relevant for solving an important community problem (scored 1), or irrelevant (scored 0). Goal intensity was measured by the total number of national problems perceived (2 or more scored 1, 1 or none scored 0). See previous notes for these items. Cases with missing values on any variable were discarded (51 in all).

Participation in communist nations has traditionally been regarded as "inauthentic." LeoGrande's study of political participation in revolutionary Cuba attempts to ascertain how Cubans participate in politics and how that participation affects the formation of public policy. In recent years, "direct democracy" (implementing policies made by elites) has been replaced by greater emphasis on mass input into the process of policy formation. The practical result has been a considerable expansion and diversification of the participatory opportunities available to Cubans, particularly at the local level.

7.
Mass Political Participation in Socialist Cuba

WILLIAM M. LEOGRANDE

The study of political participation has traditionally focused almost exclusively on participation in developed Western nations. Participation in underdeveloped countries has been presumed to be restricted to political elites, except for periodic outbursts of mass violence (Seligson and Booth 1976). Participation in communist countries, on the other hand, has been acknowledged as being widespread, but it has been regarded as coerced, ineffective, and therefore inauthentic (Hough 1975; Little 1976; Baylis chapter 2). A number of recent studies (Seligson and Booth 1976; Hough 1976; Salisbury 1975) have challenged this conventional wisdom as ethnocentric, and have called for research to establish empirically the extent and effects of political participation in non-Western settings. This study is an examination of political participation in revolutionary Cuba which attempts to ascertain: (1) how the revolutionary leadership has conceived of the role mass participation should play in the revolutionary process; (2) what opportunities to participate in politics exist for the mass public in Cuba; (3) how many Cubans avail themselves of these opportunities; and (4) what effect mass participation has on the political process.

Cross-national studies by Verba, Nie, and their collaborators (Verba, Nie, and Kim 1971; Verba and Nie 1972; Verba et al. 1973) have demonstrated that political participation is a more complex phenomenon than the prevalent unidimensional conceptions of it had allowed. They identify various "modes" of political participation, and by showing that these modes cannot be scaled

The author would like to thank Hamilton College for research support.

hierarchically they establish that participation is multidimensional. Modes of participation are distinctive ways in which citizens relate to the government (Verba and Nie 1972, pp. 44-45), and they are distinguished by the degree of initiative required from the participant, the degree of conflict liable to be engendered with other participants, and the scope of the intended outcome (personal or community-wide).

Four modes of participation have been identified cross-nationally (Verba et al. 1973, p. 237): voting, campaign activity, personalized contacting of government officials, and communal activity (i.e., nonelectoral activity by which citizens try to influence policy). In Yugoslavia, another mode—self-management activity—has been identified (Verba et al. 1973), and in Costa Rica (Seligson and Booth forthcoming-c; see also Booth 1976) researchers found evidence of two additional modes: political communication and community improvement activism.

Our study of political participation in Cuba will utilize a modified version of the conceptual schema developed by Verba et al. (1973) in their study of Yugoslavia, since it is the only communist polity in which this sort of research has been conducted. In Yugoslavia, four modes of political participation were identified: voting, contacting, communal activity, and self-management activity. Participatory acts which in other nations formed the mode of campaign activity were found not to constitute a distinctive mode in Yugoslavia. Since the Cuban electoral process prohibits campaigning, there is no campaign activity mode there either.

In addition to these four modes, our study of Cuba will also consider the mode of supportive activity. Most studies of political participation concentrate solely on activity aimed at influencing the policy process. Participation is defined as behavior through which the populace articulates its interests and makes demands on the political system. Verba and Nie (1972, p. 2), for instance, define participation as "those activities that are more or less directly aimed at influencing the selection of governmental personnel and/or the actions they take." However, as Salisbury (1975), Baylis (chapter 2), and Booth and Seligson (chapter 1) point out, this is an unnecessarily narrow conception of participation. Behavior which is supportive rather than demanding can have implications which are as important for policy implementation as demand participation is for policy formation. Supportive participation (i.e., behavior in which people carry out policies) constitutes a political resource, and its absence can be a serious constraint on policy makers. If a given policy initiative is premised upon eliciting supportive participation, the success of the policy will depend upon the extent to which such participation is forthcoming. Consequently, supportive participation is deserving of investigation, and our study of Cuba will construe participation broadly to include supportive as well as demand participation.

This study defines political participation as behavior which influences or is designed to influence the distribution of public goods (on the concept of public goods, see Chaffee 1976; forthcoming), where public goods are taken to include not only goods distributed by formal political institutions, but also by the community (See Booth and Seligson, chapter 1).

Unconventional participation (e.g., strikes, demonstrations, etc.) is included in this definition, but will not be considered because adequate data are not available and because the evidence that does exist indicates that such activity has been of only minor consequence in Cuba since the early 1960s.

Unlike the Verba and Nie studies, which are based upon individuals' responses to survey instruments, the Cuban data are entirely aggregate. Data on the number of people engaged in various participatory acts are relatively plentiful, but individual-level data are nonexistent. This places several limitations on the study. Our conceptual schema of modes, though it has found empirical verification in other contexts, must be regarded in this instance simply as a means of organizing the available data rather than as a testable hypothesis about the structure of political participation in Cuba. Without survey data, it is impossible to verify that participatory acts in Cuba do, in fact, cluster together in the modes we have postulated. Our categorization of participatory acts as belonging to one mode or another will follow the categorizations found in Verba's study of Yugoslavia (Verba et al. 1973).

The aggregate character of the data also prevents any assessment of the degree to which some people participate in a wider variety of activities than do others. Nevertheless, the data suffice to establish the extent of participation in a wide variety of activities, and to do so using a conceptual framework that has been found to be applicable cross-nationally.

The Role of Participation in a Revolutionary Ideology

Promoting mass political participation has always been a key aspect of the revolutionary leaderhip's plans for building socialism and communism in Cuba. Participation is regarded as indispensable to achieving both the objective conditions (economic development) and the subjective conditions (new socialist man) for a revolutionary transformation of Cuban society. As Fagen (1969, p. 7) writes, "A primary aim of political socialization in Cuba is to produce a participating citizen, not just one who can recite the revolutionary catechism perfectly. The test of the new Cuban man is how he behaves." Nevertheless, the particulars of precisely *how* Cuban citizens ought to participate in the revolutionary process and the actual opportunities available for participation have changed considerably over time.

The earliest concern of the revolutionary government was to organize and mobilize the population to support the new regime and to protect it from both internal and external threats. While the revolutionary government enjoyed widespread popular support after the collapse of the old regime (Free 1960; Zeitlin 1970), few people had actively participated in the struggle against Batista (Bonachea and San Martín 1974). Moreover, there was no organizational vehicle to convert attitudinal support into behavioral support. Initially, then, the principal form of mass participation was the mass rally.

Dozens of such rallies, with tens of thousands in attendance, were held in the first few years of the revolution, and they were an important factor in the struggle between left and right wings of the anti-Batista coalition. The inability of the Right to mobilize mass support as could the Left contributed significantly to the Right's feelings of political isolation and impotence (Thomas 1971, pp. 1232-33, 1246-47).

The first formally organized vehicle for mass participation in revolutionary Cuba was the Militia, created in late 1959. At its peak in the mid-sixties, the Militia included half a million armed civilians, drawn largely from the working class (Blutstein, et al. 1971, p. 454). It constituted an important supplement to the military might of the Revolutionary Armed Forces (as demonstrated at the Bay of Pigs), and also acted as a politico-military counterweight to the armed forces. Since the mid-sixties, however, the status of the Militia has been reduced to that of a civil defense force and military reserve; it is no longer a significant vehicle of mass participation in politics.

The conception of how Cuban citizens ought to participate in politics and the range of participatory opportunities available have been inextricably linked to the revolutionary leadership's conception of socialist democracy. Throughout the 1960s, the concept of "direct democracy" predominated. This conception rested upon several distinct premises: (1) that the essence of democracy is the pursuit of policies which serve the interests of the people; (2) that democracy requires the active support of the people through their direct participation in the implementation of public policy; and (3) that a direct, informal, and noninstitutional relationship between the people and their leaders is sufficient to ensure governmental responsiveness to popular needs and demands.

In practice, direct democracy meant that virtually all organized political participation was supportive activity. Fagen (1969, p. 9) refers to this activity as mobilization participation and describes it aptly as "a matter of enlisting supportive hands in the service of national goals. . . . Mobilization as used here means 'getting the troops out' to do whatever the leadership feels needs to be done." With the exception of the brief interlude of Local Power (1966-68), which has been described elsewhere (LeoGrande 1976), there were no formal channels through which Cuban citizens could participate in policy formation or elite selection during the 1960s.

There was one informal way, however. Fidel Castro's numerous inspection tours throughout the countryside constituted the principal opportunity for the Cuban people to communicate with their leaders and thereby to exert some influence over policy. Frequent, usually unannounced, and always informal, these visits were an integral part of direct democracy. "No one could accuse him," wrote Hugh Thomas (1971, p. 1345), "as Fanon in *The Wretched of the Earth* did of so many leaders of new states, of retiring to the palace and never visiting the country. On the contrary, Castro never seemed to be in the capital, always travelling by helicopter, or jeep, or Oldsmobile, always looking at some new project, always speaking, encouraging, threatening, denouncing, never indifferent."

In his travels, Castro gave the ordinary Cuban direct access to the center of governmental power—himself. He would often spend hours with small groups of people discussing local problems, ordering action to solve the problems, or explaining why the problems were unsolvable. Not infrequently, he would take the side of the citizenry against abuses or inefficiency by local officials. Castro personally came to be regarded as a more reliable bulwark against governmental irregularity than any set of structural safeguards. González (1974, p. 184) writes:

> As the personal link between the rulers and the ruled . . . Castro also supplied an element of regime responsiveness to popular pressures. Constantly making personal inspection tours throughout the length and breadth of the island, he functioned, in effect, as an ombudsman for the populace. Only he possessed the singular ability to redress local grievances in a political system that had yet to develop truly responsive (as opposed to command) institutions. By the same token, he served as the regime's intuitive barometer of popular sentiment, sounding out public opinion and eliciting criticisms from among the rank and file regarding the performance of local party and government officials in the management of state enterprises.

Since direct democracy placed such emphasis on direct personal mass-elite relationships, institutional mechanisms for mass participation in policy making or to ensure elite accountability were virtually nonexistent.

The Cuban conception of democracy underwent substantial revision in the reorganization of the political system which began in 1970. The failure of the economic policies of the late 1960s, culminating in the failure to produce ten million tons of sugar in 1970, was a severe blow to the prestige of the revolution. These failures prompted a reassessment not only of economic policy, but also of the political system which had allowed such mistakes to be made. The problems in the economy were blamed, in part, on the weakness of Cuban political institutions and on the lack of popular participation in the formation of public policy (Castro 1970a). To remedy these failings, a total reorganization of the political system was initiated, a reorganization aimed at "institutionalization" (i.e., strengthening the institutional structure of the political process) and "democratization" (i.e., increasing mass participation in policy decision making). This new phase of the Cuban revolution marked a shift away from the precepts of direct democracy, and the recognition that more than supportive participation was required for building socialism:

> The people must be given the opportunity to decide the persons to whom they delegate their power and, moreover, the channels should be established through which every member of society may, to the greatest extent possible, participate directly in the governing of that society, in the administration of that society (*Granma Weekly Review* 1974a, p. 10).

In practice, this has meant an expansion of political participation and participatory opportunities beyond the narrow bounds of supportive activity which, during the 1960s, constituted by far the greatest part of political participation in Cuba.

One aspect of political participation in Cuba which has remained relatively constant over time is the boundary delineating the limits of legitimate participation. Since 1961 when Castro declared himself a Marxist-Leninist, the Cuban political system has been officially characterized as a proletarian dictatorship. As such, it is thoroughly antipluralistic; many political activities regarded as essential to pluralist democracy are beyond the bounds of legitimacy in Cuba's socialist democracy. Specifically, mass participation aimed at altering the form of rule (i.e., the basic ideological and institutional framework of the political process), replacing the existing political elite with a counter-elite, or blocking the implementation of policy are all regarded as strictly illegitimate. The formation of political organizations that might pursue such goals—e.g., opposition political parties, autonomous voluntary associations, or even organized factions within existing political structures—is likewise prohibited.

Political Participation in Cuba in the Early 1970s

Legitimate forms of political participation in Cuba are concerned primarily with influencing the allocation of public goods within the context of the existing political system. Such participatory activity is channeled through and structured by a variety of political institutions, three of which are especially important: the mass organizations, the Communist Party, and the elected government assemblies.

The mass organizations. Like all socialist countries, Cuba has a variety of mass organizations which organize people on the basis of common characteristics such as age, occupation, and gender. Four of these stand out as being, by far, the most important: the Committees for the Defense of the Revolution (Comités de Defensa de la Revolución—CDR); the Confederation of Cuban Workers (Confederación de Trabajadores de Cuba—CTC); the Federation of Cuban Women (Federación de Mujeres Cubanas—FMC); and the National Association of Small Farmers (Asociación Nacional de Agricultores Pequeños—ANAP). Together, these four organizations constitute the most important mechanism through which Cuban citizens participate in politics. The activities comprising three of the five modes of participation under consideration (supportive activity, communal activity, and self-management activity) occur largely under the rubric of these mass organizations.

During the 1960s, the mass organizations constituted virtually the *only* channel through which Cubans could participate, and the activity of these organizations was then concentrated primarily on mobilizing people for supportive activities. This emphasis characterized all the mass organizations from their inception: the CDR was created to mobilize supporters to defend the regime against internal opponents; the CTC was reoriented in 1961 to mobilize workers to raise productivity and thereby to accelerate economic development; the FMC was created to mobilize women to participate in all the various activities of the revolution; and the ANAP was organized to mobilize support among small private farmers. Indeed, the Cubans themselves portrayed the mass organizations as instruments of mass mobilization. "In order to organize and mobilize the masses," said party official Jorge Risquet in 1963, ". . . the Party depends upon the mass organizations, which are like its arms and legs" (Risquet 1963). Not until the political reorganization of the 1970s was the role of the mass organizations expanded to allow for any significant input to the policy-making process.

Today, the mass organizations are still the main vehicle for political participation. Mass organization membership is so extensive that virtually everyone belongs to at least one mass organization, and a majority of Cubans belong to at least two. Since their reorganization in 1961, the trade unions have had a membership of over 2 million, or more than 80 percent of the state sector work force (Castro 1976, p. 188). Similarly, the Farmers' Association has included nearly all small private farm owners since its inception in 1961; present membership stands at 232,000, or about 85 percent of private farmers and the members of their families (Castro 1976, p. 193; Mesa-Lago 1976, p. 283). The memberships of the CDR and FMC have grown more slowly. After burgeoning rapidly in the first two years of their existence (1960-1962), they settled into a fairly steady rate of expansion of about 15 percent per year. This continued into the early 1970s when membership in both organizations peaked at what appears to be a saturation point of 80 percent of the eligible populations. At present, the CDR has nearly 5 million members, and the FMC has over 2 million (Castro 1976, pp. 197, 201). Unlike the other mass organizations, the CDR is open not just to one social sector, but to anyone who supports the revolution. The CDR's goal is to incorporate the entire adult population into its ranks.

There is considerable social pressure to join a mass organization, thereby demonstrating that one is "integrated" into the revolution—i.e., that one is a supporter and a participant. Consequently, membership figures probably overstate the number of citizens who are actually participants in any mass organization activities. Intense organizational efforts to mobilize the entire membership of a mass organization (e.g., to elect delegates to a national Congress, or to discuss drafts of important legislation) typically result in a participation rate of about 85 percent (e.g., *Granma Weekly Review* 1968b, p. 8; 1974b, p. 3; Castro 1976, p. 192). At the other extreme are those members who participate a great deal. Such members are referred to as "activists" and comprise 19 percent of the CDR's membership, and 16 percent of the FMC's (*Granma Weekly Review* 1970, p. 3; 1975, p. 6).

The specific tasks undertaken by the mass organizations have been as diverse as they have been numerous, changing considerably over time as the national goals and policies of the regime have evolved. As memberships have expanded, the mass organizations have taken on a larger number and a wider variety of tasks.

Participatory opportunities available through the mass organizations fall primarily into the modes of supportive and communal activity. Both modes are extremely variegated and the constraint of space prohibits a full listing of all the participatory acts that comprise them. The three most important types of supportive activity, though, are voluntary labor campaigns (usually in agriculture at harvest time), work on community improvement projects (such as adult education, public health classes, vaccination campaigns, blood donation drives, school improvements, etc.), and socialist emulation (contests between individuals or groups to see who can fulfill or overfulfill their work plans most quickly). Since different individuals devote their time to different projects, it is extremely difficult to estimate how many people participate in these supportive activities taken together, although it appears to be a majority of the membership.

Communal activity is defined as nonelectoral behavior aimed at influencing policy, especially within the community. Much of the communal activity engaged in by Cubans involves internal decisions about how the mass organizations will conduct their various work programs. At the base level, branches of the mass organizations have considerable autonomy to organize their own programs of work and to elect their officers (Fagen 1972). Candidates for leadership positions in the mass organizations at the local level are nominated by the membership itself, with the requirement that there must always be at least two candidates for every position. The Communist party is prohibited from either nominating or endorsing any candidate. After a discussion of the merits of the candidates, the membership votes (in the trade unions, at least, this vote is by secret ballot). One indicator of the effectiveness of this process is the very high turnover in mass organization leaders at the local level. For example, in the trade union elections of both 1966 and 1970, three-quarters of the candidates elected had not previously held leadership posts (*Granma Weekly Review* 1966, p. 3; Mesa-Lago 1974, p. 77). Participation in this electoral process varies somewhat from one mass organization to another. About 84 percent of the trade unions' membership participated in the 1966 elections, while only about 60 percent participated in the elections of 1970 (*Granma Weekly Review* 1966, p. 3; Mesa-Lago 1974, p. 77).

Mass organization members also have some opportunity to influence the work of their organizations at the national level. National plans of work are adopted at a mass organization's national congress. "Draft theses," i.e., a proposed work plan, circulates throughout the organization before the congress convenes so that the membership can discuss it and suggest changes. In addition, most national congress delegates are drawn from the base of the organization; local units elect delegates to congresses in the way that they elect local leaders.

The degree of influence these procedures actually give the membership over national work plans is debatable; no doubt the Communist party and the national leadership of the mass organizations retain the ability to control this process. That, however, does not make participation by the general membership "inauthentic." The whole process is not merely a charade; rather, it is a way for the national leadership to assess the reactions of the membership to a program which depends for its success upon mass participation in its execution.

Mass organization members also have opportunities to influence policies outside the organizations themselves. The main mechanism for doing this is the mass discussion of drafts of laws. The process here is similar to the mass distribution of draft theses before a national congress, except that all the mass organizations are involved. Drafts of important legislation are discussed by mass organization members at the local level, suggested changes are solicited, and these changes are then communicated to the Council of Ministers for use in drawing up the final text of the law. In at least some cases, the suggestions that emerge from the discussion process have led to substantial revisions in the draft law. The mass discussions of draft legislation are typically attended by about 60-80 percent of the mass organizations' membership (Castro 1976, p. 192; *Granma Weekly Review,* 1968a, p. 1).

Individual mass organizations also serve a "watchdog" function in various settings. The trade unions are responsible for overseeing the behavior of plant managers, the CDR is responsible for maintaining a "patient advocate" service to assure proper treatment of people receiving medical services, and the FMC and CTC have created the "Women's Work Front" which is essentially a women's caucus within the trade unions. The Women's Work Front is responsible for seeing that the trade unions give proper attention to the concerns of working women.

Self-management activity in Cuba takes place almost entirely in the work place through the trade unions. While there were several experiments in worker self-management during the 1960s, they were largely ineffective. The trade unions, like the rest of the mass organizations, devoted most of their energy to mobilizing supportive activity. In the late 1960s, the trade unions were replaced by the Advance Workers Movement—a cadre organization of the most productive workers in a plant. The function of the Advance Workers Movement was to spur production. At its peak, the Movement included only 450,000 workers, about 17 percent of the labor force (Mesa-Lago 1974, p. 237). Thus the vast majority of workers had no mass organization of their own to represent their interests or through which they could participate in politics.

One conclusion of the post-1970 reassessment of the political system was that the replacement of the unions by the Advance Workers Movement had been a mistake (Castro 1970b). Beginning in 1970 and culminating in 1973 with the Thirteenth Congress of the CTC, the trade unions were rebuilt. The self-management activities now available stem largely from resolutions passed at the Thirteenth Workers' Congress (CTC 1973). Workers' participation in decision making within the workplace is exercised through three channels: production assemblies, management councils, and work councils.

Through the production assemblies, which are meetings of a plant's entire work force, workers have the right to participate in decisions concerning production quotas, individual work norms, overtime, working hours, socialist emulation plans, voluntary labor mobilizations, etc.

Proposals passed at production meetings are not binding on the plant manager, but rejections of such proposals must be justified at the next production assembly. The assemblies are held at least every two months, though many work centers hold them more frequently. Zimbalist (1975, p. 20) reports that worker attendance at production meetings is between 80 and 100 percent and that worker participation is "extensive and vocal." In interviews with Cuban workers, Pérez-Stable (1976, p. 40) found that 85.9 percent of her respondents said the workers must be consulted in enterprise management, 57.8 percent felt that workers' input through the production assemblies was influential, and 52.6 percent believed that the management had to respond to workers' proposals.

Management Councils offer an additional avenue for worker participation in plant administration. The councils are composed of the plant administrator, his/her top assistants, elected trade union representatives, a representative of the Women's Work Front, and representatives of the Communist party. The Management Councils do not have the power to overrule the plant manager, but all administrative matters must be brought before it for discussion. "From my interviews with administators, Party representatives, union representatives, and workers," writes Zimbalist (1975, p. 19), "it seems that the workers' input at these meetings is quite significant."

The Work Councils, on the other hand, are comprised entirely of workers elected by their coworkers. These councils handle all labor grievances, and their decisions are not subject to review by the plant management.

The Communist Party of Cuba. During the 1960s, the only avenue for political participation besides the mass organizations was the Communist Party of Cuba (Partido Comunista de Cuba—PCC). As a Leninist party, the PCC is a cadre party; membership is highly selective and limited to a very small portion of the population. Indeed, the Cuban party has been smaller than any other ruling Communist party. In 1969, it had only 55,000 members, about .7 percent of the population (Green 1970, p. 76). In contrast, the next smallest ruling party (Albania), included 3.0 percent of the population. At present, after a decade of rapid expansion, the PCC has reached over 200,000 members, about 2.2 percent of the population (Castro 1976, p. 234). Thus, the number of people participating in politics through the party has been and continues to be relatively small.

However, the PCC's unique method of selecting party members does provide the mass populace with at least some opportunity to participate in party affairs. Since 1962, PCC members have been chosen by the "mass method." Periodically, the workers in each plant meet to decide who among them deserves to be a party member. Nominations are made, discussed, and voted upon. Those who are approved are then recommended to the party for membership. If the party decides to accept these nominees, it must still return to the workers' assembly for ratification of the individuals' membership (*Cuba Socialista* 1962, pp. 129-32).

The Organs of People's Power: 1976 and Beyond

During the 1960s, all government officials in Cuba were appointed from above. There were no elections and there were no representative assemblies analogous to soviets in the USSR. This was consistent with the general absence of mechanisms for assuring elite accountability to the populace and it was consistent with the precepts of direct democracy. It meant, however, that the government institution provided no opportunities for mass political participation.

The shift away from direct democracy in the 1970s brought with it a thorough reorganization of the government and the initiation of "People's Power." Composed of elected delegates, these legislative assemblies constitute the primary organs of government at all levels of administration (municipal, provincial, and national), and all administrative agencies are, in theory, subordinate to them. After a two-year pilot project in Matanzas province, Organs of People's Power were instituted nationwide in 1976.

The stated purpose for creating People's Power was to provide the citizenry with more opportunities to participate in policy formation and elite selection, especially at the local level (R. Castro 1974). The delegates to the municipal assemblies are directly elected by the general populace. These delegates, in turn, elect the members of the provincial and national assemblies. The legal powers of these assemblies are formidable (Constitution of the Organs of People's Power 1975). The Organs of People's Power has the authority to set governmental policy, to oversee administration of that policy, and to appoint or dismiss administrative officials. The Communist party explicitly retains the "leading role" in the political process, however, and it is still too early to assess the degree of actual control over decision making that the People's Power Assemblies will be able to exercise.

The electoral process for municipal delegates is complex, but is worth discussing at length. Municipalities are divided into electoral districts called "circumscriptions." Each circumscription sends one delegate to the municipal assembly. Circumscriptions are divided into neighborhoods, each of which runs one candidate for the delegate seat of the circumscription in which the neighborhood is located. A mass meeting of all eligible voters is held in each neighborhood for the purpose of nominating that neighborhood's candidate. The meetings are chaired by a local resident who was himself elected to chair the nominating meeting at a prior meeting of the neighborhood's residents. Nominations are made from the floor; any number of people may be nominated, so long as there are at least two nominees. The Communist party is explicitly prohibited from making nominations or endorsing nominees, although individual party members may make nominations. The nominees are then discussed and voted upon by a show of hands. The nominee receiving a simple majority becomes the neighborhood's candidate for the delegate election. During the nominating process for the 1976 elections, 76.6 percent of the eligible voters attended these nominating meetings (*Granma Weekly Review* 1976a, p. 2).

Since each circumscription encompasses several neighborhoods, each delegate seat is contested by several candidates. Once candidates have been nominated by the neighborhoods, an election commission compiles their biographies and distributes them to all eligible voters in the circumscription. No other form of campaigning is permitted.

The first nationwide election of delegates to the municipal assemblies was conducted in 1976 with some 30,000 candidates contesting 10,725 seats. Voting was by direct secret ballot in closed voting booths. Although voting is voluntary (it was compulsory before 1959), voter turnout was 95.2 percent, the highest in Cuban history. Given the multiplicity of candidates, in many circumscriptions no one received a majority of ballots cast. Runoff elections had to be held to fill about a quarter of the delegate posts; turnout in the runoff election was 94.9 percent (*Granma Weekly Review* 1976b, p. 1; 1976c, p. 6).

The delegates' mission is to act as a "true vehicle of communication between the electorate and the muncipal assemblies" (Constitution of the Organs of Peoples' Power 1975, p. 22). Consequently, the Cubans have introduced a formal set of procedures to assure ongoing contact between delegates and the populace. Delegates are mandated to meet regularly with their constituents, both to report on governmental operations and to listen to people's complaints and suggestions. The principal forum for such contacts are the "Assemblies for Rendering Accounts." These are mass meetings of the delegate's entire constituency which are held every three months. Delegates are required to report on the actions of the municipal assembly, report on their own performance in the assembly, and to solicit the people's grievances and proposals. All proposals are submitted to a vote, and if they are passed, the delegate is required to introduce them to the next meeting of the municipal assembly. Finally, the delegate must report back at the next Rendering of Accounts what the disposition of the proposal was. Delegates are also required to meet every three months with all the CDR committees in their circumscription to receive input from those organizations. Finally, delegates are required to set aside several hours every week as "Consulting Hours," during which time members of the community can meet with them on an individual basis.

Since People's Power has only been recently created, it is still too early to evaluate the effectiveness of its mechanisms for increasing elite accountability and popular input to local policy making. Results of the two-year pilot project in Matanzas, however, offer preliminary indications that these procedures are functioning fairly well. The meetings for "Rendering Accounts" were held regularly and attended by between 50 and 70 percent of the electorate. People also took advantage of the consulting hours by visiting their local representative, though estimates as to the extent of such contacting are unavailable (Bengelsdorpf 1976; Casals 1975).

The creation of People's Power has significantly expanded the participatory opportunities of the Cuban population, and large numbers of people seem to be taking advantage of those opportunities. People's Power provides the first opportunity since 1959 for the Cuban people to vote for government officials; it provides several important new opportunities for communal activity (the nomination of candidates, the Rendering of Accounts assemblies, and the delegate meetings with CDR); and it provides a formal procedure to facilitate individual contacting of delegates (Consulting Hours).

Conclusion: Participation and the Allocation of Public Goods

The available data (summarized in table 1) clearly indicate that participatory opportunities in Cuba have expanded greatly since 1970, and that the vast majority of Cubans participate in politics in a variety of ways. The effects of this participation on the allocation of public goods is more difficult to assess, but several preliminary conclusions seem warranted.

Supportive activity has been and continues to be an important political resource for the successful realization of the regime's policy goals. Numerous accomplishments in such fields as housing, education, and public health would have been unattainable without active participation by thousands of citizens.

Electoral, communal, and self-management activity differ from supportive activity in that they are aimed directly at influencing policy—i.e., influencing the distribution of public goods by the state. Such participation in Cuba is not merely symbolic or manipulated, though the scope of its effectiveness is clearly limited by the ideological and institutional context in which it occurs. Fundamental challenges to the regime, its leadership, or its basic policy orientations are proscribed, as are political structures through which people might organize to pose such challenges. Virtually all opporunities for legitimate participation are provided by regime-sanctioned institutions. This does not mean that participation is therefore devoid of influence, but it does mean that popular influence is restricted to policy decisions about the allocation of particular public goods rather than the structure of the allocation process itself.

Since the institutions which structure participation in Cuba are organized on the Leninist principle of democratic centralism, there is also a significant difference between the effectiveness of popular influence at the local and national levels. Mass participation affords citizens considerable opportunity to affect local policy, local implementation of national policy, and even the composition of local elites. Above the local level, however, the role of the Communist party becomes increasingly important, and policy at the national level is undoubtedly the least responsive to popular influence.

TABLE 1: MASS POLITICAL PARTICIPATION IN CUBA: A SUMMARY

Activity	*Percentage of eligible population participating*
I. Voting	
1. For People's Power Delegates	95%[a]
II. Contacting Local Officials	
1. Formal contacting (Consulting Hours)	na[b]
2. Informal contacting	na
III. Communal Activity	
1. Mass Organization membership	90 (est.)[c]
2. Electing mass organization officials	60-85[d]
3. Discussing mass organization work plans	80 (est.)[e]
4. Discussing draft legislation	60-80[f]
5. Nominating People's Power candidates	77[g]
6. Meeting with People's Power Delegates (Assemblies for Rendering Accounts)	50-70[h]
7. Nominating Communist party members	na
IV. Supportive Activity	
1. Voluntary labor	60-75 (est.)[e]
2. Community improvement programs	na
3. Socialist emulation programs	90 (est.)[e]
V. Self-Management Activity	
1. Production Assemblies	80-100[i]
2. Management councils	na
3. Work councils	na

Sources: [a]*Granma Weekly Review* (1976b, p. 1; 1976c, p. 6).
[b]Not available.
[c] Refers to the estimated number of Cubans belonging to at least one mass organization. Memberships of individual mass organizations average about 80 percent of the eligible population. Data for each mass organization are reported in the text.
[d]*Granma Weekly Review* (1966, p. 3); Mesa-Lago (1974, p. 77).
[e] Author's estimate based on partial data collected from Cuban press sources.
[f] *Granma Weekly Review* (1968a, p. 1); Castro (1976, p. 192).
[g]*Granma Weekly Review* (1976a, p. 2).
[h] Bengelsdorpf (1976, pp. 3-18).
[i] Zimbalist (1975, p. 20).

Even national policy is not wholly impervious to popular demands, however. The expansion of participatory opportunities since 1970 reflects the national leadership's desire to provide policy makers with information concerning popular opinions and demands—information which is essential to the formulation of realistic policy at the national level.

The evolution of political participation in revolutionary Cuba has been toward increasing levels of participation, and toward greater participation by the populace in influencing the formulation of public policy. For Cubans in accord with the socialist character of the revolution, the expansion of political participation has provided extensive and meaningful opportunities to influence the allocation of public goods.

Neuse's study of women voters in Chile from 1952 to 1973 reveals interesting patterns of change. After the election of Salvador Allende in 1970, women voters, contrary to traditional expectations, formed well over half of the national electorate and supported Marxist politics in increasing numbers. Attributable partly to changes in how women perceived their place in society, the evidence suggests also that more women voted for Marxist candidates because of the increasing relevance of politics for them. After 1970, the male-dominated political structures made increasing efforts to speak to the issues that would attract the female vote.

8.
Voting in Chile:
The Feminine Response

STEVEN M. NEUSE

This study is a longitudinal evaluation of the evolution of Chilean female voting patterns between 1952 and 1973. The issue of female voting is particularly crucial regarding Chile, where it has become commonplace to suggest that "women have come to play an almost decisive role in Chilean elections" (Gil 1966, p. 214), and where mobilizing efforts by political forces of both the Left and Right up to 1973 produced an image of an increasingly politically aware and active female population. (Chaney 1974; Mattelart 1976; Petras 1973) While voting is only one of many modes of participation (Seligson and Booth 1976) it is possible that changes in voting patterns may be reflective of underlying structural and psychosocial forces contributing to changes in the political system.

The following analysis examines the patterns of female electoral behavior between 1952 and 1973, assesses the sources of electoral variation among women, and deals with the alleged changes in the direction and style of female voting. For analytical purposes the study is divided into pre- and post-Allende presidencies. I have done so for two reasons. In the first place, voting data suggest that the Allende election was a crucial signpost in the development of the female electorate in Chile. Before the Allende era, women had never comprised more than half of the total electorate nor had they ever supported the traditional Marxist parties in any national elections with more than 30 percent of their votes. By 1973, however, women comprised a large majority of the electorate and indicated through their vote a willingness to support that coalition in far greater numbers than ever before. Second, the analysis of this period was separated because the author regrettably was unable to obtain comprehensive results of the post-1970 elections from colleagues or official sources. Thus, he was unable to undertake as thorough a statistical analysis as on the previous elections.

In addition to official and complete returns from presidential and congressional elections between 1958 and 1970 (Dirección del Registro Electoral 1958, 1964, 1965, 1969, 1970), the study draws from census data (Dirección de Estadística y Censos 1964; Mattelart 1965) for basic socioeconomic indicators at the *comuna* (local political unit) level.

The literature on the relevance of sex differences to politics provides one with a number of leads to follow in analyzing female voting in Chile. Studies have found that, on the whole, women in widely varying national contexts tend to vote at lesser rates and for more conservative candidates and parties than men (see Duverger 1955 and Tingsten 1963 for the classic studies in this area). The evidence presented below suggests, however, that Chilean female voting patterns are far too complex to be characterized simply in terms of role-motivated limitations on voting or conservative-traditional (or at the other extreme, class-oriented) voting rationales.

Hopefully, this study can probe more deeply some of these time-tested (or perhaps in many cases, timeworn) assumptions regarding the *apparent* low level of female electoral participation and the conservative bias of that participation, and to determine more precisely the nature and import of socioeconomic factors which shape this mode of political participation.

Female Turnout

Findings and Assumptions. Between 1952 and 1970 dramatic changes took place in the Chilean electorate, changes which compel one to modify the image of the woman as less inclined to vote than her male counterpart. In the four presidential elections in that time period, the female percentage of the total vote rose from 30 to 49 percent. Moreover, in the highly urbanized local districts of the Santiago area in the 1964 and 1970 presidential elections, the female vote exceeded the male vote by a 52:48 percentage margin (even after controlling for a larger female population). In the urban areas of the northern and southern regions of Chile the female vote rose respectively from 32 percent and 35 percent of the total vote in 1958 to 48 percent and 50 percent in 1970. Only in the highly rural and mining areas did women fail to garner more than 40 percent of the vote by 1970. Thus, in this 18-year period, the gap—at first larger in all areas—between men and women voters had closed in most urban areas of the nation, and women formed almost 50 percent of the electorate nationally.

Two questions are raised by these findings: why did women in Chile participate less than men, and what factors account for the evident change in this pattern? The traditional answer to the former query is found in mostly pre-feminist era writings. Female political activities, it is suggested, have lagged behind those of men because of sexual role socialization patterns which enjoin most women from political activities. Religious values, familial concerns, and male disapproval of female participation inculcate a low sense of political efficacy, and the result is reflected in lower voting rates (Campbell, et al. 1954, p. 191; Currell 1974, p. 41; DiPalma 1970, p. 135; Milbrath 1965, pp. 75-76).

Numerous studies on Chilean women too point to the existence of a strong feeling among women (and men) that "politics is not an activity for the women" (Klimpel 1962, p. 128). Chaney found among politically active women a tendency to see their positions not in terms of role expansion but "as an extension of their traditional family role in the political arena" (1973, p. 104). The Mattelarts uncovered strong feelings among all female groups, except the upper urban sector, that women ought to leave political activities to men. Even a majority of their urban lower sector female subsample reacted negatively toward female political activities. Moreover, while most upper sector women did not reject political activities, few had a well-developed notion of the political role (Mattelart and Mattelart 1968, pp. 143, 158). Even in the tumultuous Allende period one researcher uncovered among male students and working-class men strong approval for the traditional female familial based role (Gissi 1976, p. 33).

While one cannot deny that to a certain extent traditional role constraints have had somewhat of a dampening effect on female political awareness and participation, it would be unwise to accept this as sufficient explanation. For example, Langton and Rappoport found, using Chilean data, that when controlling for religious belief (e.g., political Catholics, traditional Catholics, and those with no religion) not only were there no significant differences between the groups on measures of political involvement, but there were no differences between men and women in each category (1976, pp. 283-84). Too, it is difficult to account for the dramatic increase in voting in a short 18-year period by sole reference to the rejection of traditional roles and values. Even in the 1960s and 1970s women were encouraged by strong social (male) pressures to maintain certain role patterns (even Allende and his *Unidad Popular* coalition after 1970 continued to stereotype women—see below, discussion of Allende period).

More persuasive is the hypothesis that Chilean women have not been oriented toward electoral politics because politics has not been meaningful, and concomitantly that the rise in female voting has been, in part, a function of making the political arena more relevant to female interests and concerns. In her study of the Chilean female, Klimpel found that, at least up to the early 1960s, politically active women were isolated on the whole in their own sections within the political parties and were not really a vital part of party activities (1962, p. 122ff.). Jaquette claims too that politics has been less relevant to female needs. Quoting the Mattelarts' study she notes that at all class levels few women, in contrast to men, identified political issues as key problem areas for them (Jaquette 1976, p. 232). One can suggest then, that these findings regarding "leaving politics to men" show the combined result of women's rational assessments and limited role perceptions.

It may be possible then to account for the rapid increase in the female electorate as a function of political interests reaching out to women. In the 1964 presidential elections for example, where female turnout increased from 35 percent to 47 percent over 1958, this was precisely the strategy of the Christian Democratic Party. They heavily invested the campaign with a sense of moral urgency, suggesting that women had a considerable stake in the choice between Eduardo Frei's "revolution in liberty" (which would insure stability and maintain the family as the primary social unit) and Salvador Allende's "communist revolution" (which would threaten stability and the home). These tactics may well have at last given many women a rationale for considering voting as a meaningful act.

The emergence of the Christian Democratic Party with its Roman Catholic Church linkages may also have been a sign for women of the increasing relevance of the political arena. Since the Church has played a significant role in much of Latin America in providing access to women for occupational opportunities (Youssef 1973, p. 346) and institutional support for women in general (Nash 1976, p. 8), it is possible that women voted overwhelmingly for the Christian Democrats because that party symbolized salient (and relevant) female interests.

Moreover, between 1964 and 1970 the government made a concerted effort to involve women in popular organizations such as the neighborhood councils and mothers' centers (*Centros de Madres*). By 1969 over 6,000 *Centros de Madres* had been organized with more than 240,000 members (Threlfall 1976, p. 181). About a third of the Mattelarts' rural and urban lower sector female subsample belonged to neighborhood organizations (Mattelart and Mattelart 1968, p. 151). The direct involvement of the Christian Democratic government in the lives of women most certainly helped to make politics more meaningful to them. One radical commentator suggests that organizations such as the *Centros de Madres* did indeed have a significant impact on raising female consciousness (Bambirra 1972, p. 35).

Structural Factors and Variations in Participation. The voting literature has linked socioeconomic and demographic variables such as education, occupational activities, and urbanization to increased female voting (Bealey, et al. 1965, p. 229; DiPalma 1970, p. 134; Duverger 1955, p. 109). Other investigators point to significant variation in female participation according to class status. Some research has found greater gaps in political knowledge among all working class people and a lesser degree of participation among lower-class women (Dowse and Hughes 1971, p. 57; Heiskanen 1971, p. 86). In Chile, on the other hand, Petras suggests that class factors have obviated the latter pattern, creating "a radical political culture which destroys the traditional paternalistic values that have customarily influenced women voters" (1973, p. 246).

As the author indicated above, it appears that the urbanization process has played an important role in politicizing women, particularly in the urban areas where communication networks are strong and where political parties have concentrated on making politics relevant to women. While female participation increased between 1958 and 1970 in all areas of the nation, the rural female vote increased only from 31 percent to 40 percent. The female mining vote jumped from 20 percent in 1958 to 39 percent in 1964 and remained at that level in 1970. In part, these lower than urban level rural and mining turnout figures can be attributed to the fact that men comprise a larger portion of the population in most of the highly rural and mining districts and to lower female literacy rates (a requirement for voting until 1971) in the mining (but not rural) areas.

In examining the aggregate level communal relationships between female voting and several other indices, it appears that employment status of women constitutes an important factor. In both urban and mining communes the relationships between nonagricultural employment and turnout are consistently strong (see table 1). These coefficients suggest that employment opportunities may aid women both in lessening traditional roles and exposing them to political issues. As Baker and Bird suggest in their African study, both urbanization and the opening of occupational roles for women lead to an "increasing variety and diversification of social ends toward which men and women aspire.... [Occupational freedom for women] ... allows a wider range of values with which to justify one's ends" (1959, p. 99). Nadia Youssef points out too, that in Latin America in particular, work has provided a highly effective mechanism for aiding women in breaking away from traditional moral and physical sanctions (1973, pp. 331-33). Finally, women who work may vote in larger numbers simply because they are able to escape the rigid confines of household duties such as child care.

The stable and moderately high correlations between literacy and turnout in rural communes indicate that the ability to read and write may be of some importance in role change and raising political awareness. Too, in areas of relatively low literacy, the effect on turnout may have been pronounced because of the literacy voting requirement. In their study, however, the Mattelarts found that in contrast to men and urban women, the percentage of rural women who failed to register to vote was much higher than the percentage of women who were illiterate (1968, p. 142). Thus, it is likely that, in the rural areas, traditional norms and perceptions of the irrelevance of politics continues to restrain many women even after they become eligible to vote.

The effect of class status on participation is, as has been mentioned, a provocative issue in Chile (Jaquette 1976; Mattelart and Mattelart 1968; Petras 1973; Zeitlin and Petras 1970). Its clearest articulation comes from

James Petras who suggests there has been a dramatic change among Chilean working class women. In his study (with Zeitlin) of the 1958 and 1964 elections, he noted that the distaff vote was not considered because it was disproportionately influenced by nonclass factors (1970, p. 23). However, in the 1970 election analysis he contended that the working-class culture was instrumental in transforming and politicizing working-class women (1973, p. 246).

TABLE 1

PEARSONIAN CORRELATIONS: FEMALE VOTING TURNOUT WITH SELECTED SOCIOECONOMIC INDICATORS

Female Turn-out (as a percentage of the total vote) for:	Economically Active Females in Non-agricultural Occupations	Percentage of Economically Active Population in Industry and Construction	Female Literacy Rate[b]	Mattelart's Index of Socioeconomic Status
Urban Communes (N=33)[a]				
1958	.68**	.10	.04	.34*
1964	.67**	.05	.28	.65**
1970	.84**	−.02	.31*	.61**
Rural Communes (N=41)				
1958			.45**	.27*
1964			.49**	.33*
1970			.54**	.36*
Mining Communes (N=7)[c]				
1958	.71*		−.38	.22
1964	.94**		.06	.78*
1970	.96**		−.07	.66

*p < .05;   **p < .01; others not significant.

[a] The urban communes (N=33) are those with more than 90 percent urban population and those 80 percent urban or greater with a communal population of over 50,000. The rural communes (N=41) include all communes with more than 80 percent of the economically active population in agriculture. The data are from *Mattelart's Atlas Social* (1965). The mining communes (N=12) or districts (some of these units were not listed in Mattelart as communes) were derived from Petras' analysis of voting in mining centers (Petras 1973, p. 245).

[b] The literacy correlations in the urban communes are low because the range of literacy percentages is quite restricted.

[c] Some of the mining voting data used by Petras comes from voting districts which are only a part of a commune. Therefore the correlations are based on only seven cases, those for which we have communal data.

The evidence, however, does not indicate a unique working class district female turnout increase. Instead, the female share of the vote increased between 1958 and 1970 in *all* areas, with the largest growth taking place in the Santiago urban districts with the lowest working class concentration (measured in terms of percentage of economically active population employed in industry and construction). In such areas the average increase in percentage of female voters between 1958 and 1970 was 2 percent more than for communes with more than 40 percent of the population in working-class occupations. Too, while women outnumbered male voters in the working-class districts by about 4 percent in 1970, in the two districts most clearly identifiable as upper-sector bastions, female voters outnumbered men by more than 20 percent. It appears then that in those areas with large working class concentrations the proportional increase in female votes was part of a national trend reflecting changing voting patterns for all women.

Other measures too tend to cast doubt on the thesis concerning increased female class consciousness and participation. Turning again to table 1, one finds virtually no relationship between percentage of working-class population and female turnout, and a significant positive relationship between Mattelart's socioeconomic status index (a rough measure of objective class) and turnout. Finally, the Mattelarts found that, of all urban groups, the lower-sector female felt most positively about leaving political questions to men. Fifty-six percent of this group and 72 percent of the corresponding male subsample (the highest percentage of all groups, rural or urban) indicated that politics was for men (1968, p. 143).

A final caveat to this conclusion is in order, however. All the data except those from the Mattelart's survey provide aggregate measures of objective class and thus should be used only provisionally in evaluating subjective class behavior. Moreover, because of the heterogeneous mix of people in lower-sector districts (including working class, *lumpenproletariat,* and inmigrants), it is possible to make only tentative conclusions linking voting patterns with socioeconomic or political variables such as class consciousness.

Patterns of Support

Voting studies have found consistently that the female vote for "left-wing" parties such as Socialists and Communists has lagged behind the male vote and conversely, that female support for "conservative" or Church-related parties has surpassed that of men. Unflaggingly, these studies have concluded that women, ipso facto, are more conservative than men. Following such logic, it appears that Chile is no exception to this pattern. While the percentage of women voting for Allende did increase nationally in all areas between 1958 and 1970, so did that for the Christian Democrats and the conservative Alessandri (table 2A). By combining the female vote for the Christian Democrats and Alessandri in 1958 and 1970, one notes that only in the mining districts did the percentage increase for Allende surpass that for the "center-right."

TABLE 2
FEMALE VOTING PATTERNS

A. Female Vote for Presidential Candidates, 1958-70 (in median percentages)[a]

Urban Communes	Allende (Left)	Christian Democrat (Center)	Alessandri (Right)	Center-Right Total
1958	28%	24%	28%	52%
1964	35	60	—	60
1970	36	29	35	64
Rural Communes				
1958	17	20	38	58
1964	29	63	—	63
1970	22	34	41	75
Mining Districts				
1958	36	21	14	35
1964	48	43	—	43
1970	53	23	22	45

[a]Other candidates less easily identifiable in terms of ideology were not included in the 1958 and 1964 figures.

B. Sex Indices: Chilean Presidential Elections, 1952-1970[b]

	1952	1958	1964	1970
Left (Allende)				
National	.79	.69	.72	.74
Urban	*	.72	.73	.75
Rural	*	.75	.75	.73
Mining	*	.76	.78	.81
Center (Christian Democrats)				
National	**	1.26	1.29	1.15
Urban	**	1.25	1.38	1.22
Rural	**	1.33	1.21	1.12
Mining	**	1.57	1.36	1.33
Right (Matte [1952] and Alessandri)				
National	1.23	1.13	**	1.22
Urban	*	1.14	**	1.23
Rural	*	1.05	**	1.12
Mining	*	1.10	**	1.44

*Information not available   **No candidate that year

[b]Sex indices were computed in the following manner:

$$\frac{\text{Percentage of female votes for candidate X}}{\text{Percentage of male votes for candidate X}}$$

Too, in comparing male and female support for different candidates, one finds that at the national level the candidate of the left since 1952, Salvador Allende, has consistently received a smaller percentage of female than male votes (table 2B). Conversely, in every election Christian Democrat and conservative candidates (Arturo Matte in 1952 and Alessandri in 1958 and 1970) have drawn larger percentages of female voters. Moreover, the consistency of these ratios over time and comparability in every type of commune indicates a remarkable stability in the aggregate female vote. Women, to 1970, continued to be reluctant to cast their support for "the left" to anywhere near the same extent as men.

It is essential in interpreting these findings to probe the meaning of a vote for the "left," "center," or "right." Does female preference for non-Marxist candidates, for example, indicate that women are inherently more conservative than men or guided by traditional social or religious norms? Or, on the other hand, do the prevailing female voting patterns represent conscious expressions of female interests?

To a certain extent in Chile, the force of traditional values and influence of anti-Marxist church dictums have affected the development of female perspectives. The Mattelarts found this to be the case even among lower-sector women, many of whom are socialized into alien and conservative value systems through employment as domestic servants in middle- and upper-sector homes: A full 40 percent of the female nonagricultural work force in 1970 was in domestic service. Middle- and upper-class values penetrated lower-sector consciousness too through the barrage of the predominantly bourgeois cultural media. Traditionally oriented female publications and radio and television programs stressing dominant class values have had, according to several observers, somewhat of a conservatizing influence on the homebound Chilean woman—of all classes (González 1976, pp. 118-19; Mattelart 1976, pp. 295, 298).

Advancing another perspective, however, it is likely that female voting patterns reflect perceived self-interests as much or more than they do inherent conservatism. For the middle- and upper-sector women, for example, a great deal of the reluctance to support significant political change (such as voting for Allende) was rooted in the implications of such change for existing economic relationships between women of different classes. A paradox of the liberation process for Chilean women has been that in order for them to escape the confines of the home for activities in the marketplace or political arena, these women have had to rely on lower-sector women for domestic assistance. In 1968, for example, 100 percent of the upper-class and 88 percent of the petite-bourgeois women who worked had domestic help (Mattelart 1976, p. 292). Thus, many women have eschewed political reform precisely because of the paradoxical implications of such reform for their own liberation (Chaney 1971, p. 177; Mattelart and Mattelart 1968, pp. 20-21).

Another factor affecting female resistance to radical structural change may have been the perception (by women of all classes) that such change might adversely affect the family, the one social unit in which most women have a power base (Jaquette 1976, p. 228). This may explain the strong female disapproval of divorce found by the Mattelarts, particularly among the most powerless *clase inferior* women (1968, pp. 106, 172). The recognition of the family as the primary female power base may account too for the finding that professional Chilean women usually see their work roles as an extension of familial concerns (Chaney 1973, p. 105). In the home or "extended family" occupational sphere, at least, women at all levels do exercise a certain amount of control. Thus, any threatened shift of this locus of power from the private (family) to the political realm (in the form of collective social policies, for example) where men obviously dominate may have been unacceptable to many women (Jaquette 1976, p. 230).

A third point which questions the concept of the conservatively motivated female vote stems from a redefinition of the significance of the Christian Democratic vote. Considering the role of the Church in furthering women's interests and in providing services for them in Latin America (Youssef 1973, p. 342; Nash 1976, p. 8), it is entirely reasonable to speculate that careful calculation rather than blind conservatism provided much of the impetus for female support of Christian Democrat candidates. It is likely too, that Frei's female oriented policies did much to rally women to the Christian Democratic cause.

A final consideration pertains to the suggestion that the female vote between 1958 and 1970 shifted perceptibly to the left. If one defines the left to include non-Marxist reformist forces, there is some truth to the thesis. By adding the percentage of women voting for Allende and the Christian Democratic candidate for president in 1958 and 1970 (table 2A), one notes that in urban, rural, and mining areas at least 13 percent more women voted for this combination in 1970 than in 1958. Interpreting this increase in terms of a shift to the left (or perhaps better as an indication of the increasing willingness of women to vote reformist) gains more credence when one realizes that in 1970 the Christian Democratic candidate Radomiro Tomic ran a considerably more left oriented campaign, "eschew[ing] the Frei program until the last minutes of the campaign" (Burnett 1970, p. 288).

Another variant of this argument is that increased working class conscious-ness among females led to greater support for the Marxist coalition over time. To test this thesis the author compared the growth of female and male urban support between 1958 and 1970 for Allende and the two others (Alessandri and the Christian Democrats) active in both campaigns (table 3). The first obvious point is that in every type of urban commune (except the mining districts) the growth in male support for the left surpassed that of women. Second, the reason both the left and the other candidates had larger gains in the provincial urban areas was because the Radical Party, which drew its "power from the geographical extremes of the country" (Institute for the Comparative Study 1963, p. 25), did not field viable candidates for the presidency after 1958.

In the central valley, however, the growth of female support for the left was of the same magnitude in all three types of communes. In working class districts, female support for the "other" candidates increased on the average a bit more than it did in the less industrialized areas. Indeed, between 1958 and

TABLE 3
GROWTH OF MALE-FEMALE SUPPORT FOR POLITICAL GROUPS
IN CHILE IN DIFFERENT URBAN AREAS, 1958-1970[a]

	Female		Male	
	Left (Allende)	Other Major Candidates or Parties Running in Both 1958 & 1970 (Christian Democrat and Alessandri)	Left (Allende)	Other Major Candidates (Christian Democrat and Alessandri
Regional Urban Communes				
Northern Communes (N=6)	9.8%	13.7%	10.8%	13.0%
Southern Communes (N=6)	11.2	11.3	11.7	7.8
Central Valley Communes with 30 percent or less employed in Industry and Construction (N=6)	6.8	7.8	8.0	8.0
Communes with 30-39 percent employed in Industry and Construction (N=6)	6.4	9.6	8.8	7.0
Communes with 40 percent employed in Industry and Construction (N=7)	6.9	9.9	8.2	3.6
Mining Districts (N=11)	10.6	8.2	7.6	6.6

[a]Measured in terms of the percentage increase in support for Allende and other candidates or parties ("Other" percentages are summed) running in both 1958 and 1970.

1970, the working-class-district female "other" vote increased nearly ten percent while the corresponding male vote rose only about four percent. Thus, it is clear that in the working-class sectors women did not significantly change their patterns of choice. The growth of the vote for all the candidates was very much like that in non-working-class communes. The disparity in the growth of male-female working-class support for Alessandri might point either to an influx of new female voters (such as older women or inmigrants), the effect of Christian Democratic mobilization of women between 1964 and 1970, or perhaps growing concern with the perceived consequences for women of an Allende presidency.

The only area in the nation where the female vote for the left did outstrip the corresponding male vote was in the mining areas. In these districts, while gross female turnout has been lower than in rural or urban areas, there was a greater willingness among those women who did vote to vote for Allende. In these rather isolated and homogeneous communities, class perceptions may have been strong enough to persuade women to vote for Allende.

The Allende Years: Mobilization Left and Right

In many ways the election of Salvador Allende in 1970 to the Chilean Presidency was a political watershed. Not only did it result in the free election of a Marxist government, but it also signalled the beginning of an unparalleled effort by forces of all hues to mobilize women into the political arena. The results of various elections after 1970 show that these activities were influential both in increasing the total female vote and in moving the female electorate to a greater support of the *Unidad Popular* forces.

In the April 1971 nationwide municipal elections, 50 percent of the votes were cast for the government *Unidad Popular* ticket. Although a sexual breakdown of these votes is not available, there is some evidence pointing to an increased willingness of women to support the government. One author asserted that "for the first time a majority of working class women voted for Allende's coalition" (Morris 1973, p. 151). Moreover, a survey of voters in the Greater Santiago area about the time of the election found no difference in political preference between men and women (Larraín 1973a, p. 44). In a 1972 congressional by-election in Coquimbo, a Communist party woman won that contest carrying a majority of the female vote in seven of the province's 15 communes (Clark 1972, p. 79). In five previous congressional and presidential elections no Marxist candidate or coalition carried more than three communes among women voters.

The 1973 congressional elections seem to indicate a continuation of this trend. In the campaign, in which the opposition hoped to capture two-thirds of the Congress in order to impeach Allende, most preelection polls expected the *Unidad Popular* to garner 40 percent of the total votes (Larraín 1973b, p. 132; Moss 1973, p. 176; Zimbalist and Stallings 1974, p. 132). In the election, however, the government coalition won 43 percent of the vote and 41 percent of the female vote. The female percentage was 14 percent more than in the last Congressional election in 1969 and nearly 11 percent more than in the 1970 Presidential election. Moreover, the gap between male and female support narrowed. In 1973 the female vote for Unidad Popular was 84 percent of that of men in contrast to 74 percent in 1970.

Over 300,000 more women voted in this election than in 1970 and more than 600,000 more than in the previous 1969 Congressional election (before 1973, women turned out less for congressional than presidential elections). By 1973 "women represented 56 percent of the electorate [one assumes that this refers to total registered voters] in Chile," (Chaney 1974, p. 267) a substantial increase over 1970 when women comprised 47 percent of the registered electorate. While Chaney contends that much of the change in female patterns can be attributed to the addition of the newly enfranchised youth and illiterate vote (Chaney 1974, p. 279), there are other indications that this group may not have been as much a force for change as suggested. In the 1971 elections, for example, fewer than 15 percent of the potential new voters, estimated at 700,000, had registered to vote (MacEoin 1974, p. 106). Moreover, Langton and Rappoport found that younger Chileans held political beliefs which were substantially similar to those of their elders (1976, pp. 303-4).

Thus, by 1973 perceptible changes were evident in the female electorate, both in terms of how much they voted and for whom they voted. Although still lagging behind men in total voting rates (49 percent to 51 percent) and in support for the left (41 percent to 49 percent), the female vote seemed to reflect the success of intensive efforts to engage women in the nation's political activities.

The Government Mobilizes Women. Attempts by the Allende government to bring women fully into the governing process were, according to Chaney, of mixed effectiveness. At the highest ministerial levels, activities directed toward women were hampered by narrow sexist orientations and a lack of resources: "Projects to mobilize women invariably were cast in a 'feminine' mold, by Allende himself, and none had materialized after two years of Allende's administration" (Chaney 1974, p. 269).

In spite of the apparent continuing sexual bias and footdragging at upper-level-policy areas, the government did as much, if not more, than previous governments, to convince women, mainly lower sector and intellectuals, of the good intentions of the government. In the first place, Allende frequently reminded his allies of the importance of continual awareness of women's interests and spoke out for programs such as day care centers for working mothers and a ministry of the family. Even if the government did narrowly construe the female role and what constituted women's interests, there was rather consistent evidence of concern. For many women concerned with sexual freedom, it was obvious that only through a rather thoroughgoing social transformation could women finally escape their subordinate and exploited positions at all class levels (Bambirra 1972, p. 34). Certainly the women of *Unidad Popular,* and perhaps others, supported the socialist goal of radical reform in spite of the inadequacies of the government in office.

In the second place, it appears that the government was successful, in spite of some slowness in program implementation and continuing lower sector male sexism (Gissi 1976, p. 35), in reaching lower-sector women through the "resident movement." In lower-sector-residential areas, concerted efforts were mounted, both through official and semiofficial programs to engage and activate groups such as women which had never been organized previously. To a certain extent, the *Unidad Popular* movement built upon existing organizations such as the *Centros de Madres,* neighborhood centers, and sports clubs. While many of these groups, a legacy of the Frei government, continued to be a source through which the opponents maintained influence in the *barrios,* many others became centers of government support (Mattelart 1976, p. 293).

In addition to these activities, which focused largely on recreation and continuing education, the government (and more radical semiofficial youth groups) established an extensive milk distribution program for nursing mothers and young children and set up supply and price committees (JAPS) and people's grocery committees (*Almacenes del Pueblo*) to regulate food distribution and prices in the low-income *poblaciones* and *barrios*. According to several sources, these organizations were of inestimable value in providing "a political education for large sectors who were not involved in other forms of political activities, particularly women" (Threlfall 1976, p. 177; see also Santa Lucia 1976, p. 137). Thus, politics became relevant for many women precisely because the government directly touched and involved them at the level of their greatest concerns, economic necessity and family health.

Lacking electoral data at the communal level, it is impossible to verify the political success of these activities. However, considering the increase in female support for the *Unidad Popular* in 1973 and the corroborating observations of others (Chaney 1977; Morris 1973, p. 151), it is plausible to suggest that these efforts did lead to greater female electoral support for the left than ever before.

The Opposition Organizes Women. The mobilization of women by the foes of the government was much more dramatic, and perhaps in some ways more effective, than that of Allende's coalition. Beginning with the famous pots and pans protest of December and ending with a mass march twelve days before the coup in September of 1973, middle- and upper-class women were instrumental in projecting the erroneous image abroad of a widespread classless female revolt against the government (Garrett-Schesch 1975, pp. 101-3). In this period women continually harassed the police and military for their apparent reluctance to take action against the government, and utilized popular organizations developed by Frei to politically influence lower-sector women (Mattelart 1976, p. 292; Roddick 1976, p. 12).

In large part, mobilization of women by the right, in contrast to that by the government, was directed not at politically empowering women, but at providing an ostensible nonpartisan front for upper-sector interests. For example, 120 editorials appeared in the conservative daily *El Mercurio* between 1970 and 1972 encouraging the women's front and praising it for the sacrifices it had made in the name of Chilean freedom (Mattelart 1976, p. 297). In spite of this element of manipulation, it is hard to deny that one effect may well have been that of raising the political consciousness of these women too, making them aware that the political arena was indeed relevant to their own individual (and collective) interests and concerns. The growth of the registered female electorate from 47 percent to 56 percent between 1970 and 1973, and the increase of over 600,000 female voters from the previous congressional election attests, in all likelihood, to the politicization of all women and not just those in the lower sectors.

Conclusions

While it would be tempting to explain the pre-Allende behavior in terms of traditional female values and role constraints and the post-1970 patterns in terms of the triumph of the class struggle, this paper advances the thesis that the entire process might better be understood in terms of the increasing relevancy of the political process (albeit from different perspectives) to women of all classes. Before 1970, for example, when women voted less than men, they may have felt that the man's game of politics had little meaning for them. When they supported the Marxist left less than men, they may have felt that other parties had done more for them and may have perceived unfavorable consequences of a Marxist regime for their own interests.

After Allende's election the dramatic rise in the total female vote and the shift to the left can be explained in similar terms. Forces representing all interests in the political spectrum made real or symbolic commitments to women and attempted, to a greater extent than before, to involve them directly in political activities. The increase in the female vote attests to the success of both the opposition and the government in sensitizing women to political realities. The increasing female support for the *Unidad Popular* probably is reflective of success by the Allende government (and to some extent, of the previous administration) in mobilizing lower-sector women, a group which before had never really been convinced of the meaningfulness of politics.

Three final points are germane to these concluding observations. First, the changes in women's voting behavior, particularly in the lower sector, took place as much in spite of the attitudes of *Unidad Popular* men as because of changes in those attitudes. To the end of the Allende regime, the evidence suggests that women continued to be stereotyped and relegated to inferior positions within the popular movement (Chaney 1974, pp. 269-70; Bambirra 1972, p. 36; Gissi 1976, p. 44). Second, it is probable that much of the change was a reflection of the involvement of women in activities and organizations which made a difference in their lives, and not of a radical ideological transformation. This is evident in the finding that in 1973 female support for the government slate continued to lag behind that of men. Moreover, in a survey taken in Santiago in mid-1973, women were considerably more critical of both the government and Allende than men (Larraín 1973b, p. 131).

A final point addresses the oft cited assertion that "the hand that rocks the cradle rocked the ship of state of Chile's late Marxist President Salvador Allende until it overturned and sank" (Belnap 1974). In a literal sense the assertion is false. The power of the state never strayed from the hands of male decision makers whether they be Marxist, military, or reformist. Men with impressive ideas attempted to remold the state and men with massive firepower sank the ship of state.

In another sense though, the quote reflects a great deal about the vicissitudes of Chilean politics in the 1970s and about the female role in that process. First and most obviously, upper-sector women did undoubtedly contribute to undermining the Allende government through unrelenting mass activities such as the "empty pot" marches beginning in late 1971. Second, it is plausible to suggest that the "hand that rocked the cradle" did influence the September coup precisely because of the March elections where it became increasingly clear that women could not, in the future, necessarily be expected to provide the margin of victory for non-Marxist candidates. Thus, just as liberation from the traditional homebound role in Chile created among Chilean women a paradoxical bondage to existing class relations, so the liberation of women in the electoral arena may have been an important factor in precipitating the political and psychic bondage of all Chileans.

*Seligson examines the relationship between economic develop-
ment and political participation. He finds that, contrary to
expectation, participation is higher in the poorer regions of
Costa Rica than it is in the wealthier ones. He concludes that
poor people get involved in politics to satisfy basic human needs
which are taken for granted by individuals living in wealthier
regions.*

9.
Development and Participation
in Costa Rica: The Impact of Context

MITCHELL A. SELIGSON

Studies of political participation have stressed the impact on participation of
the characteristics of individuals, thereby greatly shortchanging the role of
context. Despite the abundance of research on the socioeconomic, demographic, and attitudinal correlates of political participation, and despite the
large number of hypotheses thoroughly tested and well-substantiated (Milbrath and Goel 1977), emerging research on contextual correlates suggests
that context plays a major role in determining both the nature and degree of
political participation. Thus, for example, Verba and Nie (1972, pp. 229–47)
have discovered a relationship between the size and "boundedness" of
communities on the one hand and participation on the other. Seligson and
Booth (forthcoming-a) and Booth (1975a, 1975b) have explored the relationship between urbanization and political participation in Costa Rica; and Tullis
(1970) has shown that peasant activism varies with community type. Seligson
and Salazar X. (1977) have shown that levels of interpersonal trust and trust in
government vary with community type, and Seligson (1972a; 1972b) has
compared participatory behavior in urban and rural settings.

Economic development forms the contextual variable of this paper. Research on the relationship between economic development (usually defined in
terms of industrialization and development of infrastructure) and participation
frequently confirms the hypothesis that underdevelopment inhibits participation. Evidence for the confirmation usually derives from cross-national
studies. Milbrath and Goel (1977, p. 94) cite several studies which lead to the
conclusion that "countries with higher economic development have higher

The research for this project was made possible by grants from the Social Science Research
Council and the Danforth Foundation. I would like to thank John A. Booth, Michael Sullivan, and
Edward J. Williams for helpful comments on an earlier draft of this paper.

absolute rates of participation than countries at lower levels of development."
The validity of this conclusion must be questioned, however, for cross-national
studies typically fail to isolate the effect of development from the larger
sociopolitical context. That is to say, one does not know if the lower
participation rate in poor countries is a result of the contextual factor of
economic development or of other factors, such as regime type or political
culture. Since most of the lesser developed countries (LDC's) of the world are
ruled by authoritarian regimes, and most of the more developed countries
(MDC's) have democratic rule, it is difficult to hold constant regime type and
have enough cases for meaningful comparative analysis. Indeed, interpretation
of participation rates is itself problematical since in some regimes certain forms
of participation may be prohibited (e.g., campaigning) while others may be
required (e.g., voting).

More convincing evidence of the relationship between economic development and participation has come from studies of single nations. Such studies do
not have to concern themselves with regime type or political culture since these
factors are held constant. Contrary to what cross-national investigations seem
to demonstrate, these studies provide some evidence that underdevelopment
may actually *stimulate* participation rather than inhibit it. Evidence for the
positive association between underdevelopment and participation comes from
Cornelius (1975), for example. Cornelius has compared six urban communities in Mexico City and has found that demand-making (in the form of citizen-
initiated contacts with government officials) was higher in the squatter
settlements than in the housing projects. Unfortunately, it is not possible to
attribute higher participation levels to the lower level of development alone
because the communities that Cornelius studied were selected not only on the
basis of their relative development, but also on their age and the manner in
which they were originally established. Consequently, it is not clear which of
these factors is responsible for the variation in participation rates in the
Cornelius study.

Method

For many years the analysis of contextual effects on behavior followed the
model established by Blau (1960) in which contingency tables were used. In
the late 1960s, however, it became clear that the Blau model was inadequate.
The more powerful technique of analysis of variance (and covariance) was
shown to produce much more convincing results (Fennessey 1968; Schuessler
1969; Hauser 1970).

In this paper the relationship between economic development and participation is analyzed through the use of analysis of variance. The results will be
displayed by means of multiple classification analysis. Variables which are
known to have a significant impact on participation are held constant, with the
exception of level of economic development, through sample design and

through covariance analysis. The hypothesis to be tested is that mean participation scores at each level of development do vary significantly from the grand mean when other participation related variables are held constant.

The Data

Of the variables known to be related to participation,[1] occupation is perhaps the most difficult to control for statistically as a result of segregated housing patterns. Occupationally high status respondents are typically found in the more economically developed sample segments, and most occupationally low status respondents are located in the less developed sample segments. Given such samples, statistical control is extremely difficult since the effect of occupation cannot be partialled out of the equation.

In order to overcome the problem of controlling for occupation, the present sample was designed to be occupationally relatively homogeneous. Homogeneity in occupation also helps to minimize differences in income and education among respondents.

The data analyzed were gathered by the author in Costa Rica in late 1972 and early 1973 (see Seligson 1974, 1975, forthcoming-a). All 531 respondents in the survey (oral interviews) are male peasants.[2] Hence, the impact of occupation and sex are held constant throughout the sample design. The sample design minimized but did not eliminate variation in income and education. The mean of the total family income of the households surveyed was 199 colones (the equivalent of $23 weekly), which, when subjected to a log transformation (in order to reduce the impact of extreme values) resulted in a mean of 4.87 and a standard deviation of .78. Education averaged 2.87 years with a standard deviation of 2.12 years. Variation in income and education is partialled out statistically through the use of covariance analysis.

Economic development is operationalized in this study through the use of an index of industrialization and infrastructure development.[3] Two measures are used to divide the sample into groups according to similarity of infrastructure development. The first of these is the quality of sanitary facilities available in the county (i.e., *cantón*). The 1973 national census figures (Dirección General 1975) provide data on the number of dwelling units with indoor plumbing, as opposed to those with latrines, and to those with no sanitary facility at all. An index, created out of the census data, gives three points for each dwelling unit with indoor plumbing, two points for units with latrines and one point for units with no facilities. The second measure of infrastructure development measures the level of development of public educational facilities. However, since primary education is mandatory and universal in Costa Rica, little regional variation is found in this variable. High school (*colegio*) education, in contrast, is optional and there is considerable variation on this variable. The number of high school students per capita is used to measure the development of the education infrastructure. These figures come from the Ministry of Education of

Costa Rica. The measure of industrialization comes from the 1973 census report of the percent of economically active individuals working in industrially related jobs. A combined overall development index based on sanitary facilities, education, and industrialization was created by first standardizing the variables and then summing them.

The sample was subdivided into four groups based on the overall development index. The level of economic development of the four groups of peasants varies greatly. The poorest areas constitute one extreme in which 30 percent of the population has no sanitary facility, only 1 percent of the population is enrolled in high school and less than 1 percent of the economically active population has industrial jobs. At the other extreme are the most highly developed areas, in which only 1 percent of the residents has no sanitary facility, 16 percent is enrolled in high school, and up to one-third has industrial jobs. The poorest areas generally exhibit quite primitive living conditions. Homes rarely have electricity, floors are frequently earthen, and cooking is done over an open hearth wood-burning *fogón*. The communities enjoy few governmental services (e.g., post offices, police protection, hospitals), although, as everywhere throughout Costa Rica, even the poorest village will have a primary school of at least three grades. The more developed communities present quite a different picture. The homes there have electricity, polished wood or mosaic tile floors, and gas or electric stoves. Such developed villages also enjoy paved roads, post offices and police stations, rural health stations (*unidades sanitarias*), agricultural extension agencies, and community development offices.

It should be emphasized that the data on which the economic development level is based are not taken from the survey but from the other sources. Most contextual analyses rely upon data drawn from the survey itself (by aggregating individual characteristics so as to provide an index of the context). Such a procedure, while the only alternative when no other data are available, introduces a number of problems into the analysis. First, the aggregation of individual characteristics builds in a certain amount of autocorrelation between the characteristics of individuals and the characteristics of the contextual unit of analysis. Second, biases in sample design may render the contextual information unreliable. Third, responses to the questionnaire items which establish the context index may be contaminated by responses to prior questions in the survey. The use of census data in this study eliminates all of these problems. Fortunately, the Costa Rican Census Bureau and Ministry of Education are widely recognized as being among the most professional in Latin America and consequently the reliability of the data is quite high (Collever 1965, pp. 94-102).

Political participation, actions influencing or intended to influence the distribution of public goods (Booth and Seligson, chapter 1), is conceptualized as multidimensional, following Verba, Nie, and company (Verba, et al. 1971; Verba and Nie 1972). Elsewhere (Booth 1975a, 1976; Booth and

Seligson 1976; Seligson and Booth 1976; Seligson 1977c) the different modes of political participation found in Costa Rica are described in detail. The modes were isolated using factor analysis (see Boni and Seligson 1973) and verified by a comparison with another study of participation conducted in Costa Rica (Booth, et al. 1973). The four modes include organizational activism, communal project participation, contact with local government, and voting. Organizational activism measures the involvement of the individual in local community organizations, such as the parent-teacher association (*patronato escolar*), community welfare committee, and other organizations. A combined index reflects the frequency of attendance at these communal meetings. Community project participation refers to the involvement of the individual in projects such as nutrition center construction and road building. The index is based on the number of projects in which a respondent reports involvement. Contact with local government is measured by the individual's attendance at the town council meetings (*municipalidad*); and voting is measured by the respondent's answer to a question regarding his participation in the last election prior to the survey. Table 1 provides frequency distribution information regarding these four modes of political participation.

TABLE 1
THE MODES OF PARTICIPATION

Mode	Variable	Percent active
1. Voting	Voted in previous presidential election	79.8%
2. Contact with Local Gov't	a. Attended meeting of the town council (*municipalidad*) in the last year	22.0
	b. Percent of town councilmen named correctly Mean Percent	16.3
3. Organizational Activism	Attendance at meetings of the PTA (*patronato escolar*), school board (*junta de educación*), church committee (*junta de la iglesia*) and the progressive committee (*junta progresista*). Codes: (4) almost always (3) once in a while (2) almost never (1) never. Overall score is a summated index weighted by frequency of reported participation. Percentage figures refer to proportion of respondents who reported some level of participation. Organizations not present in a particular village are treated as missing data.	
	a. PTA	44.3
	b. School Board	37.4
	c. Church committee	34.9
	d. Progressive Committee	21.2
4. Communal Project Participation	Reported making an effort to solve one or two respondent-identified communal problems.	44.3

Findings

The results of the multiple classification analysis for the four modes of political participation are presented in figures 1-4. The multiple R and level of significance of the main effects for the analysis of variance are indicated on each figure. In each of these figures the index for each participation mode has been standardized so that deviations above and below the mean can be compared among the measures. Each respondent's score is corrected for his income and education through inclusion of these two variables as covariates. In addition, the scores are corrected for "remoteness," by including as a covariate the distance, in kilometers, of the respondent's dwelling unit from San José, the capital of Costa Rica. Finally, the respondent's length of residence in the community is included as a covariate, since political participation is somewhat affected by this variable.

The inclusion of these four covariates corrects the participation scores for each of the four modes so that the effect of these variables will not influence the relationship between development and participation. In effect, the inclusion of the covariates "partials out" the impact of these variables. Other covariates were added to the analysis (such as alternative indicators of respondent SES) but these made no substantive difference in the analysis of variance results and therefore are not included here.

All of the four modes of political participation (organizational activism, voting, community project participation, and contact with local government) exhibit patterns directly contradicting the hypothesis that economic development leads to higher participation levels. Figures 1-4 show a trend in the opposite direction. In each case, peasants living in the least developed areas exhibit the highest levels of participation and peasants living in the most developed areas exhibit the lowest participation levels. In figures 1, 2, and 4 the relationship holds across all levels of development, while in figure 3 there is a slight deviation at the intermediate levels.

Discussion

Why do individuals participate politically? While there is obviously a wide range of motivations, according to Chaffee (1977; forthcoming), Booth (1975a; 1977b; chapter 6) and others, much participation is motivated by rational, instrumental considerations on the part of the individual. People participate in politics, at least in part, in order to obtain something from the system. In Chaffee's terms, participation is motivated by a desire to share in public goods. For example, parents contact local government officials when they wish to build a school house, or people join nutrition center committees in order to help assure better health for their children.

If, in fact, participation is motivated by instrumental considerations then we have a clue as to why peasants living in less developed areas participate to a greater extent than those living in more developed areas. In areas where the

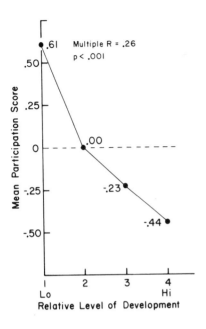

FIGURE 1.
Organizational Activism

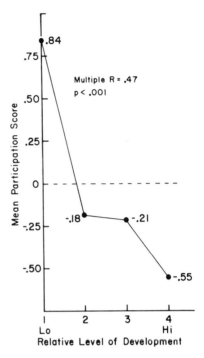

FIGURE 2.
Contact with Local Government

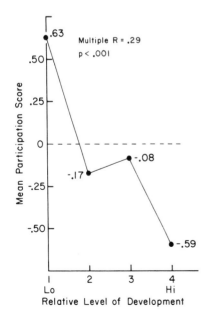

FIGURE 3.
Community Project Participation

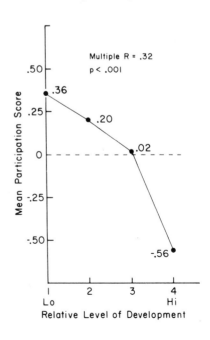

FIGURE 4.
Voting Participation

infrastructure is poorly developed and government services are minimal, individuals are compelled to participate politically if they hope to see some improvement. Schools, roads, bridges, and the like are not built unless they are demanded, especially in Latin America where capital resources are scarce. Even when demanded, such projects often are delayed for years. In contrast, in areas which already have acceptable roads, sufficient schools and school teachers, and adequate health services, individuals do not feel as intensely in need of services and consequently are less strongly compelled to participate (see Booth 1975b).

Important qualifications must, of course, be made to the above explanation of the relationship between participation and development. Not all individuals in less developed areas participate, and well-developed areas are by no means characterized by nonparticipation.

The important point is that instrumental motivation is indeed quite rational. Therefore, where need is greatest, participation will be highest. Second, it should be recalled that participation levels are correlated with other factors (such as income, education, remoteness and length of residence). Higher levels of participation in less well developed areas can be found even after the effects of such variables are partialled out through covariance analysis. Finally, exogenous factors such as systematic suppression of participation by landlords, politicians, police, or other powerful forces can significantly lower levels of participation.

Conclusion

Economic underdevelopment has a stimulating effect on political participation. It would be inappropriate at this point to generalize beyond the peasant population of Costa Rica. Further research among different occupational groups and different political settings needs to be conducted. Nevertheless, given the findings presented here, the supposed linkage between development and participation needs to be reexamined. The statement that participation is "a sort of luxury which cannot be 'afforded' by those who are struggling to fulfill their subsistence needs" (Milbrath and Goel 1977, p. 98) should be questioned in light of the data presented here. Conceptualizing participation as the response of an individual to his social needs calls into question the assertion that participation is a luxury for the poor and for those living in underdeveloped areas. They have many immediate, pressing needs which may be resolvable only through recourse to politics. For the poor, participation may be a necessity rather than a luxury.

Notes

1. Milbrath and Goel (1977, p. 102) report that "persons of higher occupational status are more likely to participate in politics."

2. Peasants are defined here following Landsberger and Hewitt (1970, p. 560): "any rural cultivator who is low in economic and political status." This definition encompasses landed and landless peasant alike and therefore, the sample is only relatively homogeneous, since there are in fact differences among peasants based on access to land and other factors (see Seligson 1977b). However, for the purposes of this article the fact that all of the respondents earned their living from land which they directly cultivated, whether owned or not, imposed a homogeneity of occupation on the sample far greater than obtained in the typical cross section sample.

3. Some details regarding Costa Rica's industrialization in relation to the Central American Common Market are found in Seligson (1973).

III
Participation and the State

This chapter compares the relationship of participation to social security policymaking in Latin America. Increased participation in this area has led to an "atomization" of distributable public resources. The result has been a negative relationship between participation and the ability to use social security programs to promote and broaden social equity. Successful efforts to reform these inequities have come about with the imposition of authoritarian regimes that have repressed participation in social security policy.

10.
Indirect Participation Versus Social Equity in the Evolution of Latin American Social Security Policy

MARK B. ROSENBERG and JAMES M. MALLOY

The question of citizen participation in political activity has received much scholarly attention during the past five years. Indeed there has been an increasing sophistication in the analysis of participation. What was once regarded as a simple unidimensional phenomenon has been revealed to be the complex and multidimensional process that it really is.

Accordingly, there has been a renewed effort to deal with this question in cross-national settings, especially in Latin America. Among others, Seligson and Booth (1976) have attempted to point out the weakness of the participation research and to suggest an agenda for research that will help us to better explore this complex process in the Latin American context.

Seligson and Booth suggest that "misconceptions" about citizen political activity have tended to obscure a great deal of politically relevant citizen participation. No doubt they are right, as other analysts theoretically and empirically suggest in this volume. One of the principal methodological vehicles that Seligson and Booth propose, to clarify the participation issue, is analysis along its "several distinct aspects, or modes" (1976, p. 96). Through its modal manifestations, Seligson and Booth hope to prove that there has been a gross underestimation of participation in Latin America.

The strategy of investigating participation along its various modes is only one useful approach that may be employed to gain insight into the participation question. Another useful strategy is to investigate the question of participation along various issue areas.

The purpose of this study is to analyze the role of participation in the issue area of social policy development in Latin America. We are particularly concerned with the constellation of social policies which come under the general designation of social security, or *previsión social*. All Latin American countries, as well as most countries of the world, have social security programs. These programs range from workman's compensation to social insurance providing old age, invalidity, and retirement pensions, and to health care benefits.

The scope of social security coverage in most Latin American countries is variable depending on a number of factors (Aaron 1967; Stone 1975; Collier and Messick 1975).[1] What is relevant for this study is the fact that social security policy making provides another arena in which citizens can participate in the making of decisions which directly affect them.

This investigation of the development of social security in Latin America will confront the multiple themes suggested by the new concern for the understanding of participation. First, an analysis of the politics of social security falls within the scope of the definition of political participation suggested by one recent analysis: "Political participation involves activity influencing or designed to influence the distribution of public goods."[2]

Social security policy is first and foremost a policy of the distribution of goods, both public and private. Social security in Latin America constitutes a public good in two ways. First, social security programs are legally mandated, subject to executive and legislative adjustment, and enforced juridically. Second, most social security programs are intimately linked to the financial capacity of the state. The private element of social security is constituted by the legally mandated supportive contributions paid by the citizens who are obligatorily or voluntarily enrolled in social security. The nexus of the public and private can be found in the particular distributional relationship of funds, which is mandated by the state. It is at this juncture that the political struggle over social security usually ensues: Who contributes what and how much? What are the qualifications for benefit eligibility? And, what is the scope of available benefits? Obviously, participation in the decision-making processes surrounding these questions can be a key factor in determining who gets what, and who does not get what.

A second theme which has been suggested by the new approach to participation relates to the impact of the context of participation (see Seligson, chapter 9). In particular, two questions are relevant: the context provided by the regime type, and that provided by the geosocial environment (i.e., the spatial location of the population under study). This essay will suggest that participation is influenced by contextual factors, especially those concerning the type of regime. Further, the geosocial environment does make a difference with regard to participation in social security. This has been true historically and in the present situation. Finally the logic of the types of programs themselves also has affected participation. These three factors help account for the variable patterns of participation in the social security programs of Latin America.

A third theme suggested in the analysis of participation concerns its relationship to the payoffs of participation. Because social security programs are, in the final analysis, state-sponsored policies of distribution, the payoffs of participation can be extremely high, especially in an environment of scarcity and limited social welfare.

The main thesis of this chapter is that where there have been high degrees of participation in social security policy making, the resulting levels of equality of specific social security systems have been low. More participation in the making of social security policy has resulted in less overall socioeconomic equality in the system. To use Seligson and Booth's terminology, participation in social security policy making has led to an "atomization of distributable public resources" (1976, p. 105). Participation in social security policy making has also encouraged short-range, particularistic intergroup conflict in Latin America. Thus, there has been a negative relationship between participation in this issue area and the ability to use social security programs to promote and broaden social equity.

In this first section we will examine the historical evolution of social security programs from the perspectives of participation and equity. We will then examine recent developments in social security policy as played out around concerted attempts in most nations of the region to "reform" their respective social security programs in the name of the goals of administrative rationality and social equity. To date, competitive democratic regimes have been incapable of reforming their social security systems. The three at least partially successful cases of social security reform have taken place in the context of authoritarian regimes. In all three, reforms designed to promote administrative rationality and social equity have taken place at the expense of previous patterns of participation in social security policy making.

Participation and Social Security: The Issue Defined

Social security policy in Latin America evolved as an attempt by political elites in various countries to cope with social problems created by capitalist economic growth, and to adapt to the political reality of an emerging working class. Historically, the policy was linked to the expansion of the functional power of the state as a central regulating force in society.

Since at least the 1930s the state has developed policies such as social security to override the market as the primary mechanism determining the distribution of wealth and power among social groups in Latin America. Particularly in the more economically developed countries (which were the first to adopt social security programs), group relations in the modern sector in many crucial respects have been "administered politically." Social security programs, for example, were used to maintain income and health levels among groups of workers despite the vicissitudes of the market. In addition, these programs, along with others, were political acts that increased the bargaining power of key groups such as organized white-collar workers in the urban sector.

The adoption of social security programs in Latin America theoretically opened a new and important arena for mass participation. However, the actual structural configurations of the social security programs did not promote either broad-based or direct participation. It is true that many social security programs in Latin America were established as a direct response to mass pressures for their creation (Mesa-Lago, forthcoming). However, the history of the early social security programs (those established prior to 1940 in Latin America)[3] reveals a particularistic, piecemeal approach. For the most part, these early programs were organized around "funds" that granted protection to designated social sectors usually identified and defined in terms of economic function and/or occupational criteria. These multiple fund systems grew incrementally as new funds were created for newly recognized groups: the general pattern was to move from military and civil public employees, to those employed in critical infrastructure activities, to those in critical urban services, to those in industrial activities, and only more recently to the urban self-employed and to rural workers. As late as the 1960s only a small proportion of the economically active populations were actually covered: for example, countries such as Brazil, Colombia, Guatemala, and Mexico provided coverage for less than 30 percent of their economically active populations, while on the other extreme, Cuba provides total coverage, and Chile about 70 percent coverage (see Rosenberg, forthcoming).

In addition, the main questions concerning participation did not center on direct citizen participation per se. Rather, the main issues have been concerned with the representation of classes or types of citizen interests. Thus, debates over who should properly participate in social security policy making have usually been concerned with the question of which groups had the legal, juridicial right to participate in the decision-making process. From the point of view of the individual, participation was seen less as a way of influencing policy than as a means of "acquiring concrete monetary and occupational benefits, status rewards, social contacts, and other psychic and emotional gratifications" (Baylis, chapter 2).

As they were originally conceived in Latin America, social security programs were not granted on the basis of a citizen "right" but rather on the basis of a group-specific contractual obligation. Recipients of social security coverage were to be those who played a productive role in the nation's modern sector: those who were directly susceptible to the growing fluctuations of international political economy. Thus, social security was not intended as a mass-based program. Following Baylis, it is clear that social security was originally created for "workers" and not just "citizens." Therefore, even at its outset, social security was neither mass based nor egalitarian in Latin America. It was limited to those who were privileged with employment in the modern sector.

The question of the role of the masses in initiating programs is an important one. Our evidence indicates that the major role in initiating and defining the content of social security policy was preempted by reformist wings of established elite groups. Organizations representing the masses (and especially working groups) were able to call attention to the need for state intervention in the "social question." But, it does not appear that they were strong enough to make their definitions of the problem the basis for social policy or to define the contents of policies such as social security. Social security programs in such countries as Brazil, Chile, Argentina, Uruguay, and Peru were not designed to embrace the masses as a whole. They developed by accretion as government granted specific programs to specific working groups who were perceived to have the actual or potential power to threaten the system.[4] This approach in turn fostered a particularistic orientation among sectors of the organized working class. Instead of using their power to press classwide demands, these sectors tended to bargain for group-specific benefit schemes and advantages. Thus, banking employees in Argentina, Brazil, Chile, Cuba, and Uruguay received "privileged" social security protection; and railway workers in Argentina, Bolivia, Brazil, Chile, Paraguay, and Mexico were similarly treated (Mesa-Lago, forthcoming; Malloy 1976; Mallet 1970). The much-discussed phenomenon of the creation of "working-class aristocracies" is quite clear in the development of social security programs.

The particularistic, piecemeal approach to the granting of social security coverage was compounded by the actual structural arrangements for the participation of groups in social security policymaking. Because social security in most Latin American countries was conceived as a tripartite financial arrangement between employers, employees, and the state, each of these groups was provided with de jure representational rights on the legally constituted governing boards of the respective funds. They were legally organized into a corporatist structure of representation by officially recognized (often created) "interest associations." The rationale behind this corporate mode of representation has been that since each of the aforementioned groups was obviously affected by the operation of a given social security program, each should have a structured input into the decisions that would collectively affect their interests.

The representation of group interests in social security policymaking bodies has been one of the most widely accepted means of participation in the development and implementation of social security policy. This was the case in both competitive democratic systems such as Chile[5] and authoritarian systems such as Brazil[6] under Getulio Vargas. However, the points of participatory access were much more complex in competitive democratic political systems in Latin America due to the willingness, if not necessity, of legislatures to respond to a broader range of particularistic group demands for a greater share of the pie. This was especially the case in Chile and Uruguay;

but functional representation was a universal characteristic of social security programs in the region.

Whichever the case, it appears that the patterns of social security participation which emerged between 1930 and the present have had adverse consequences from the point of view of social equity and administrative efficiency. First, group representatives have tended to reflect narrow group interests. Therefore, to the extent that there has been an interest in maximizing the participation of given groups, it has been in the direction of short-run strategies of benefit and privilege maximization (Mesa-Lago, forthcoming; Malloy 1976). And the more powerful the group in terms of its vocational and sectoral location, the more successful that group has been, as Mesa Lago has empirically illustrated in his recent research.

In addition, the social insurance funds became an important political resource to be deployed in the more general arena of political competition due to the fact that they provided critical services and a large cache of public jobs. In many cases the funds have been "captured" by particularistic groups, such as organized labor, who have used them to enhance their own political bargaining power. This piecemeal cooptation—from below—of the social security funds has been part of a larger process evident in the region wherein particularistic groups have "colonized" a large part of the state apparatus leading to the now familiar phenomenon of the existence of large and formally powerful state structures which in practice are internally disarticulated and quite weak (Kenworthy 1970).

The structure of social security participation has also been linked to a number of other structural weaknesses which have plagued most of the states in the region: chronic inflation (Wolfe 1968, p. 160), bloated governmental bureaucracies (Soares 1969; Weinstein 1975, p. 67), and a general immobilism manifested specifically in the inability of civilist regimes to launch reform projects in the area of social policy. In railing against the situation in Chile, President Eduardo Frei caught the flavor of the situation in most of the nations of the region:

> The multiplicity, disparity, privileges, omissions and injustices of the present social security laws not only constitute a permanent source of insecurity and unrest, but also a paralyzing obstacle to the carrying out of the plans of economic development and social reform in which we are embarked. The proliferation of laws has reached incredible extremes, with legislation in favor of very small groups and sometimes of a single person, contradicting the whole spirit of universality that inspires modern social security (quoted in Wolfe 1968, p. 161).

In large part, the victims have been the unorganized masses, those on the periphery of the distribution of goods and services.[7]

In essence, social security programs became the means by which groups could establish and maintain their privileged socioeconomic and political status through de jure, legally sanctioned means. The pattern of representation as well as the strategic location of these various groups meant that they could hold the state as a virtual prisoner in this policy domain, with the costs being shifted downward to those who had progressively less access. In effect, the multiple provision of social security benefits by groups has meant that, in countries like Brazil, Chile, Argentina, and Uruguay, there has been no generalized "public interest" or even "class interest" articulated by the state, but only a variety of variously competing state sanctioned group interests. Thus, the pattern of participation and group representation in the making of social security policy in Latin America has resulted in greater overall social and economic inequality rather than equality as has been mistakenly conceived.[8]

The inequities arising from existing social security programs have not only come about through the interaction of organized group interests with the state. There has also been an administrative, institutional logic to the functioning of social security (Mishra 1973) in Latin America. The administrative logic reinforced the tendency to cover only certain types of groups, especially those employed by public and private organizations which could provide employee and employer contributions, and which could be easily policed. Once in place, the pattern of program growth reflected the reinforcing convergence of group pressure and administrative logic; the programs sought out concentrated clienteles that were readily identifiable and financially strong. They would thus be easier to administer. This administrative logic reinforced the tendency to cover organized workers in the modern market sector. The great mass of urban marginals (domestics, self-employed, subemployed) and rural folk were excluded, both because they lacked political clout and because they were not administratively "attractive." In sum, the structural imperative of the programs and the political context initially converged to create highly inequitable social security systems. Privileged groups used their capacity to particpate in the funds as a source of power to perpetuate the situation.

Participation and Social Security Reform

We have suggested that the structured inequalities of early social security programs were largely the result of internal (i.e., national) political, organizational, and administrative dynamics. In short, the pattern of group participation in conjunction with the organizational imperatives of the particular issue combined in such a way to guarantee differential access to the distribution of social security goods and services.

At the same time that these patterns were becoming institutionalized in most Latin American countries, there was another development which would play an important role in the nature of social security participation. Parallel to the development of most Latin American social security systems was the emergence and development of an international organization which was deeply concerned with national programs of social security. From its inception in 1919 the International Labor Organization has been particularly concerned with the establishment of social protection schemes for the working class (Johnston 1970, pp. 195-207; ILO 1936). In 1936, the ILO sponsored the "First Conference of American States Members of the ILO" which declared that social legislation in every country should provide for obligatory social insurance (Mallet 1970, p. 81). Following the ILO's relocation from Geneva to Montreal in the early 1940s, the organization became particularly active in social security matters in the Americas[9] (ILO 1942; ILO 1944; ILO 1945): it provided skilled actuaries to various Latin American countries which were organizing local social insurance programs; and it sponsored social security conferences where country delegations discussed common social security problems.

Evidence suggests that the ILO experts played an instrumental role in the shaping of the social security programs of those Latin American countries that began to develop social insurance systems in the early 1940s. ILO representatives were consulted during the earlier stages in the development of programs in Venezuela (Uzcategui 1966, p. 17), Costa Rica (Rosenberg, forthcoming), Mexico (Garcia Cruz, 1972, p. 74; Spalding 1977), Bolivia, and others (ILO 1945, p. 7).

Equally important was a growing international debate over questions related to social security, in part stimulated by the Beveridge Report of 1944. In particular, ILO-sponsored regional conferences (in 1942 and 1946) became important focal points for the discussion of questions of social security organization and reform. As a result, an international pool of social security experts emerged who were largely divorced from national political contexts and increasingly oriented to a common internationally sanctioned approach to the question of social security in the Western world.

From these discussions came a general social insurance doctrine which incorporated a number of important postulates. First, there was a call for the extension of the scope of obligatory social insurance to include agricultural workers, domestic servants, and the self-employed (Chamberlain 1942). Second, diversified social insurance systems should be unified into an integral, highly centralized system (ILO 1945, pp. 2-3; ILO 1972, p. 306; Mallet 1970, p. 82). Third, countries were urged to adopt systems based on a single uniform plan of benefits and financing. Finally, "social solidarity" in social security organization was suggested. This principal called for a basic plan of benefits for all citizens ("universalization" of coverage), with the more affluent contributing a higher percentage of their income to finance the benefits of those who could pay little or nothing to finance their protection. This principle obviously implied a rather significant redistribution of income.

It is no accident that as the locus of the debate over social security shifted upward, the potential for providing coverage for the previously unprotected masses increased. Thus, once the debate was shifted to an international forum, bureaucrats and *técnicos* began to conceive of social security for all citizens, not just for the privileged working groups.

The emerging social security doctrine was seen as a way to simplify, rationalize, and equalize the administration and impact of social insurance policy in Latin America. Clearly this doctrine was aimed at wiping away the particularistic gains that groups had made as a result of their participation in social security decision making arenas. Moreover, as these plans were formulated by an international cadre of social security experts, they clearly implied that social security policy was basically a technical problem best left to homegrown experts responsive to internationally defined criteria.

As the concept of an international arena of social security expertise spread through the region, local social security administrators and *técnicos* were less and less responsive to local (i.e., national) groups and political interests, and more responsive to internationally formulated principles of organizational efficiency and social equity.[10] In the process a key goal became that of achieving social equity on a mass basis through a unified and centralized administration of social security policy and a greatly expanded clientele. This concept of reform clearly clashed with the preexisting reality of multiple funds and corporate representation of interest groups in the administration of decentralized social security agencies. Essentially the root dilemma has been this: Should particularistic interests continue to dominate social security policy making? Or should their participation be restricted by transferring social security decision making to an "apolitical" group of national and international *técnicos* operating with internationally derived standards of efficiency and equity? In Latin America this dilemma has led to an intense political struggle which has persisted from the 1940s to the present.

Social Security Reform: Experience

The actual debate over social security reform in Latin America has been a prolonged one, especially in those countries with the older, more diversified systems (Mallet 1970, p. 81; Mesa-Lago, forthcoming; Malloy 1976, 1977b). Throughout, the key national groups consistently pushing for reform based on the internationally defined doctrine of the 1940s have been the publicly employed social security technocrats.

In large part, the social security reform effort has been unsuccessful in most Latin American countries. Governments have been unable to override the particularistic group interests which have combatted reform. And, in those cases (Argentina, Brazil, Chile, Uruguay) where a large and complex set of institutions has been fashioned to administer the benefits, and where the clientele groups are in strategic vocational locations, the issue of reform has been particularly difficult.

In general, we have found that it has been almost impossible for civilist-democratic regimes to reform their social security systems, owing to the legal and electoral limits placed on such regimes. This has been particularly true of "populist" type regimes which have been dependent on the support of urban labor groups to gain and secure their governmental power.

Democratic regimes have attempted various kinds of "reforms" such as the extension of benefits to previously excluded groups. However, even when expansion of coverage has taken place, concessions have been made to the privileged groups such that patterns of social security stratification and inequality have been maintained or exacerbated (Mesa-Lago, forthcoming). In most cases, expansion of coverage has meant the addition of new administrative entities alongside the complexity of established institutes. From a political point of view, the main weakness of these regimes has been their inability to reorganize the systems administratively around the concepts of unification and centralization. In a real sense the battle over social security reform has boiled down to a conflict between the principle of corporatist representation and consequent particularistic privileges versus the principles of the dominance of technological administrative rationality and generalized social equity.

Ironically, the most "successful" reforms from the point of view of the social security doctrine defined in the 1940s have taken place under the military-dominated, authoritarian regimes which emerged in the 1960s. These regimes carried out reforms which have expanded coverage and rescheduled benefits in such a way as to increase general social equity; but by no means have they promoted generalized equality or a massive redistribution of income. In addition, these regimes have reorganized their systems in such a way as to diminish if not eliminate particularistic group participation in the administration of the systems. While promoting equity, rationalization, and efficiency the reforms have increased the power of administrative technocratic elites and the general regulatory power of the state over society.

Concrete efforts aimed at social security reform in Latin America have been described elsewhere (Mesa-Lago, forthcoming; Malloy 1976; Rosenberg and Malloy 1976; and Mallet 1970). However, specific instances of social security reform deserve brief mention.

Chile presents the clearest case of the failure of social security reform in Latin America. Indeed, Chile is the best example of a country with particularistic, unequal social security schemes covering privileged workers, the official recognition of this inequality, and the state's inability to do anything about it—at least until late 1973 (Parrish and Tapia Videla 1970; Mesa-Lago, forthcoming; Wolfe 1968; Davis 1964).

Throughout the 1950s and 1960s there was a recognition at the highest executive levels of the inequitable arrangement of social security schemes in Chile. Both presidents Alessandri and Frei attempted social security reforms along lines suggested by the internationally derived standards. They were unsuccessful. And despite the fact that he was committed to a program of increasing social and economic equality, President Allende, fearful of alienating his main support groups, did not pursue social security reform at all. In fact, Allende's activities during his presidency appeared as a "regressive" trend in the matter of social security reform (Mesa-Lago, forthcoming). It is interesting to note that while it has yet to act, the Pinochet regime has announced its intention to reform and unify the social security system.

The democratic political context combined with the established and institutionalized de jure patterns of participation in both decision making and distributional questions in Chile resulted in a deadlock over the question of reform. The inability to resolve the social security question was symbolic of the larger ongoing crisis of Chilean society, which has been partly, if brutally, resolved since the 1973 coup.

The history of social security reform efforts in at least three other Latin American countries (Argentina, Peru, Brazil) closely resembles the struggle over reform in Chile. However, as we suggested earlier, a change of regime type has made an important difference in these three cases. Authoritarian governments in Argentina (1967-73), Peru (1968-74), and Brazil (1964-present) have decisively moved to reform social security following the internationally derived standards described earlier. And, in all three countries there has been a substantial effort to standardize benefits and to unify disparate funds. The cost has been great in terms of the central issue of this study: participation.

In the first place, previously autonomous, decentralized decision making boards were either eliminated or intervened in each country. Whereas policy guidelines and fund priorities were previously a question to be decided on an ad hoc, particularistic basis, they are now decided at the highest decision making levels by social security *técnicos* interested in implementing internationally derived standards within elite formulated national development plans. Thus, the content and impact of participation by groups on the decision making boards has been severely altered, if not eliminated. This is consonant with the larger efforts at state centralization and control over public policy which are characteristic of post-1964 modernizing authoritarian rule in Latin America. Second, the impact of the reorganization of social security has meant that particularistic group inequalities with respect to the concrete payoffs of participation have been substantially diminished.

In all three cases many of the most glaring inequalities of the previous systems have been diminished. The most extensive reform has taken place in Brazil (Malloy 1976, 1977b). Coverage has been extended to rural workers, domestics, and the self-employed. Coverage in the rural and urban sectors is different, but in both, the plans are standardized; and both programs are controlled by a new Minister of Social Security. Reform in Argentina and Peru has been less profound but nonetheless extensive. In Argentina a multiplicity of funds—thirteen (Diéguez and Petrecolla, 1974)—were partially unified into three funds providing standardized benefits for public employees, private sector employees, and the self-employed, respectively. The three funds are controlled by an office of the Ministry of Social Welfare (Mesa-Lago, forthcoming; *International Social Security Review* 1974). In Peru separate funds for blue- and white-collar workers have been unified into a single system with a standardized schedule of benefits (Mesa-Lago, forthcoming; *International Social Security Review* 1973). The fund is controlled by the Ministry of Labor. It should be pointed out, however, that in all three cases the regimes have maintained separate and superior programs for the military.

Conclusion

Direct citizen participation has never been an issue or a real possibility in the area of social security policy in Latin America. The issue has been one of the "representation" of "classes" or "groups" of interests, defined vocationally, before the state by organizations officially empowered (by recognition) to articulate such interests. This question, especially among the earlier adopters, was approached within a corporatist framework of representation which operated at two levels. Coverage as a rule was not extended to citizens as such or to broad classes of citizens; rather, wage and salary earners were divided (fragmented) into discrete occupational groupings for purposes of social security coverage. Second, the administrative boards of the funds provided for the inclusion of groups representing the specific insured group, employer associations, and the state.

Social security coverage in general evolved on a piecemeal, group-by-group basis. The usual sequence in the evolution was: the military and public functionaries; workers in critical infrastructure activities; workers in important urban services; and industrial workers. By and large, the quality of coverage was positively correlated with the sequence of coverage. Both the sequence and quality of coverage were determined by the power of groups to pose a threat to the existing sociopolitical systems and the administrative logic of the contractual type of social insurance schemes developed within the region. As a result, the great mass of rural workers and urban marginals were either ignored or received coverage of an inferior quality. The upshot was the incremental evolution of social security systems that were both highly fragmented and unequally stratified in terms of the quality of programs. Even among late adopters, which had more unified administrative structures, coverage was extended on a piecemeal and unequal group-by-group basis.

The corporatist structures of "representational participation" were an important factor accounting for the fragmentation and inequality of the social security systems. These structures, which were often a part of a general corporatist approach to labor relations, reflected the goal of established elites to undercut the emergence of a broad, class-conscious movement of workers. In the social security area these structures both encouraged and permitted discrete groupings to pursue their own particularistic advantage at the expense of other groups. Once in place, the structure of representation provided privileged groups with the means to protect their advantages from various internationally derived schemes of reform defined in terms of unification, standardization, and universalization.

The issue of reform pitted organized interests embedded in the system against emergent cadres of social security technocrats identified with the international models of reform. In all cases civilist regimes operating in a democratic framework, despite rhetorical commitments, have been incapable of achieving reform in the image of the technocratically defined models of administrative rationality and social equity. At best they have been able to extend coverage to new groups, but only at the price of increasing the benefits of established groups. When reform has come it has been in the context of authoritarian regimes in which the military has provided both the will and the muscle to impose the reforms counseled by the social security technocrats.

The evolution of social security policy has been symptomatic of the general pattern of development in the structures of political economy evident in the Latin American region. As Anderson (1967) among others has pointed out, elites in the region were able to maintain essential structural continuity in the systems of political economy through the segmental incorporation of new "power contenders," such as organized labor, into the extant political game. This process led to an increase in the level of demands pressed on the state and to a weakening of the state owing to the fact that it was "colonized" internally by incorporated groups. These twin processes were most evident in the respective social security systems of the region.

By the mid-1960s a general crisis of political economy plagued most of the nations of the region. Underlying the crisis was a growing imbalance between the demands pressed on the systems and the resources available to the systems due to the exhaustion of the import substitution models of growth followed by most countries since the 1940s. The clearest manifestations of the general crisis were hyperinflation and political immobilism (Malloy 1977b). The social security systems, wracked by financial insolvency and the unsuccessful reform efforts, illustrate the general crisis.

As O'Donnell (1973) has argued, the crisis was perceived by established elites as a crisis of "participation" created by the previous policies of controlled segmental incorporation of new power contenders, especially organized labor. In many cases this perception led to the emergence of military-backed, authoritarian regimes oriented to reorganizing state-society relations in order to spur a new process of state-guided, capitalist development. Key to this developmental effort has been the imposition of the costs of development on organized labor as well as urban marginals and the rural masses. Hence, these regimes have sought to exclude, by force if necessary, groups such as organized labor from the political game.

To achieve this exclusionary goal, modernizing authoritarian regimes have sought to undercut the organizational basis of labor's power in the system. One such base was the social security funds. Hence, these regimes (Argentina, Brazil, and Peru) set out to reform the social security systems in ways that would reduce or eliminate the ability of organized labor to use them as an autonomous power base. The three reforms came about as a result of a convergence in the goals of modernizing military elites and cadres of social security technocrats. The latter saw in the military regimes a source of power to impose their technocratic image of reform long frustrated by the policy immobility of democratic regimes. The military elites saw social security reform as a means of emasculating organized labor and as a means of alleviating at least some of the effects of their regressive wage policies. In addition, reform aided the primary goal of increasing the autonomy and functional power of the state over society. The three cases of social security reform illustrate, in one policy area at least, the much discussed military-technocratic alliance upon which the new modernizing authoritarian regimes have been based.

Again the process has been carried the furthest in Brazil. In Argentina the process has been frustrated by a mélange of large and sophisticated labor organizations that have proved most difficult to control and dislodge. Owing to its early reformist and mobilization policies, Peru might appear to diverge from the general pattern. However, from the first the regime clearly sought to control the process of mobilization from above through state-created organizations such as SINAMOS (National System in Support of Social Mobilization) (See Woy, chapter 12). Moreover, since 1975 the regime has clearly shifted toward the more common pattern of state-enforced demobilization and control.

Historically the question of participation in social security policy has been a most complex phenomenon. It can be argued that the patterns of "representational participation" in this policy area contributed significantly to situations that "provoked" the emergence of modernizing authoritarian regimes formed around soldiers and civilian technocrats. In any event, the three cases of social security reform examined here contributed directly to a decline in the capacity of organized labor to "participate" in the formation of public policy, and a general rise in the power and control of a technocratically oriented state apparatus.

Notes

1.   Other general studies of social security in Latin America worth consulting are Wolfe (1968), Mallet (1970), ECLA (1968), ILO (1972), and Roemer (1973). Useful general discussions of social security can be found in Rimlinger (1971), Rys (1966), Aaron (1967), Arroba (1969), LuBove (1968), and Heclo (1974).

2.   This definition has been suggested by Booth and Seligson (chapter 1). Their definitional approach is influenced by Chaffee's recent analysis (1976).

3.   Mallet (1970) provides an excellent summary of social security development in Latin America.

4.   The first generalized social security program was introduced by Chancellor Bismarck in Germany in the 1880s. While the program had economic and social purposes, it was specifically introduced as part of Bismarck's more general strategy to coopt labor and insure social and political peace (Rimlinger 1971).

5.   For instance, the governing body of the Caja de Seguro Obligatorio in Chile (which provided health and pension social insurance to blue-collar workers) represented the multiple group interests of the government, employers, and the medical profession (ILO, 1945, p. 19). The latter group, fearful that unchecked state intrusion into the health-care field might destroy the

private practice of medicine, was able to penetrate the governing body so as to protect its professional, medical interests. The Caja de Seguro Obligatorio was later reorganized into the Servicio Nacional de Salud in 1952 (Mesa-Lago, forthcoming, chap. 2). The administrative regulations for the directing board of this agency provided for fifteen members: The Minister of Public Health, the Director General of the Social Security System, the Director of the Health Care System, a representative of the president of the country, three advising representatives from employers' organizations (to be designated by the employers' organizations which had been legally sanctioned), three workers' representatives (designated by legally sanctioned employees' organizations), the Director General of the Social Welfare System, two representatives from the Senate, and two from the House of Deputies (Gaete Berrios 1952, p. 72-73; Parrish and Tapia Videla 1970). To make the system of representation even more elaborate and complex, provincial and subprovincial directing boards were established which contained a representative directly appointed by the country's president, two employers' representatives (directly appointed by those regional employers' organizations which were legally recognized), and two workers' representatives (elected by direct vote of the members of the regional unions which were legally sanctioned) (Gaete Berrios 1952, pp. 78-79).

6. In Brazil, the first Caixas de Aposentadoria e Pensoes were governed by representatives of the owners of the companies affected and representatives of the employees. During the 1930s under Vargas, newly streamlined and rationalized social security institutes were still collegially governed under the general supervision of the Ministry of Labor (Malloy 1976).

7. An examination of the type and degree of state sponsored social protection offered to the marginal and popular sectors is very revealing. Mass rural protection is only a very recent and isolated phenomenon (Malloy 1976; Leal de Araujo 1973; Wolfe 1968). And the low-skilled, low-income, urban workers in Latin America who actually are covered by social security receive decidedly inferior benefits (Mesa-Lago, forthcoming; Roemer 1964, 1973; Teller 1972).

8. Mesa-Lago (forthcoming) convincingly demonstrates that the actual distribution of social security benefits has functioned to maintain, if not exacerbate, overall social and economic inequalities in four Latin American countries (Chile, Uruguay, Peru, and Argentina).

9. For a review of the ILO's current approach to social policy questions, see ILO (1976).

10. Cox and Jacobsen (1973, p. 18) suggest the strong possibility of alliances between "elements in the international and national bureaucracies on the basis of common views." Certainly our findings would seem to confirm that this possibility is indeed a reality in the social security issue area. Others, such as Lawrence Juda (1977) attempt to deal with this phenomenon in terms of transnationalism and transgovernmental relations.

*Genuine reform has resulted from the Peruvian military govern-
ment's attempts since 1968 to restructure the mechanisms by
which citizens become involved in politics. Forms of cooperative
and community enterprises have multiplied dramatically, particularly in the agricultural and industrial sectors. However, the
government's ideology of participation has outstripped its capacity for implementation, and a plethora of bureaucratic
agencies, often with overlapping and changing responsibilities,
has invited confusion. As a result, citizens already in relatively
privileged strata not only have new opportunities for participation but also find that "old" structures and procedures continue. But for the rest of the population, the net effect of the
changes to date has probably been adverse.*

11.
Citizen Participation Under Innovative Military Corporatism in Peru

HENRY A. DIETZ and DAVID SCOTT PALMER

The argument that military government and genuine citizen participation are inherently incompatible is both a pervasive and a persuasive one. Few exceptions exist historically. Even those which at first glance appear to have fostered citizen involvement in the decision-making process, such as Turkey under Kemal Ataturk (Rustow 1963), Pakistan under Ayub Kahn (Sayeed 1967), or Egypt under Nasser (Perlmutter 1974), upon closer examination more prove than disprove the general rule (Hammond and Alexander 1972). Recent reviews of military-regime literature suggest no dramatic changes currently underway which might alter the basic argument (Schmitter 1973; Jackman 1976). Huntington's dictum that military regimes "shrink from the role of political organizer" still holds sway (1968, p. 243).

Nevertheless, one can observe in Latin America over the last decade a proliferation of military governments, several of which have proclaimed their

The authors are grateful for assistance provided for the preparation of this paper: Dietz to the
Institute of Latin American Studies, University of Texas at Austin, and to the American Philosophical Society; Palmer to the Bowdoin College Faculty Research Fund and to his student
assistant, David Ruccio.

172

intention of bringing about fundamental structural reforms, including important changes in the relationship of the citizen to the political system. The Brazilian military has organized a two-party system in which one party is supposed to play the role of permanent loyal opposition. During the administration of General Juan José Torres (1970-71), Bolivia briefly experienced a National People's Congress organized along sectoral lines. The Panamanian National Guard under General Omar Torrijos is committed to the establishment of rural and urban cooperatives. The military government of Ecuador is carrying out a constitutional convention under its auspices which may someday transform civilian politics in that country.

While these experiments have met with varying degrees of success, they suggest that the Latin American military's perception of its role as ruler may be changing. Under certain circumstances, Huntington's generalization may be transcended by militaries who see part of the solution to the host of problems facing their countries resting on the establishment of new forms of political organizations for citizen participation. Nowhere in Latin America, however, has the commitment of a military regime to organizing politics been more profound than in Peru.

Not surprisingly, therefore, worldwide attention has focused on Peru's self-titled "Revolutionary Military Government" since it assumed power by *golpe* in October 1968, and began proclaiming its intention of establishing a "fully participatory social democracy." Selected titles of studies of post-1968 Peru suggest the difficulties close observers of Peru have had in categorizing the present regime: "Military Populism in Peru . . ." (Cotler 1969), "Peru's Peculiar Revolution" (Hobsbawm 1971), "Peru: Revolution or Modernization?" (La Porte and Petras 1971), "The Myth of Military Revolution" (Letts 1971), "Nationalism and Capitalism in Peru" (Quijano 1971), "State Capitalism in Peru . . ." (Quijano 1972), "Revolution from Within . . ." (Einaudi 1973), "Revolution from Above . . ." (Palmer 1973), "Peru's Ambiguous Revolution" (Lowenthal 1975), "The Peruvian Experiment . . ." (Lowenthal 1975), ". . . A Corporatist Revolution" (Chaplin 1976).

Our own categorization, "innovative military corporatism," suggests hierarchy, sectoral organization, central direction by the military, and a willingness to experiment. Such a categorization, however, is not intended to infer fixed and immutable elements, but rather, characteristic tendencies which may themselves ebb and flow as conditions change. Recent circumstances have been anything but favorable: the appearance of military unity has been shattered publicly, wildly optimistic economic projections have proven hopelessly awry, and many citizens at all levels of Peruvian society have demonstrated clearly their capacity to reap many of the benefits made available since 1968 without being incorporated into the system on terms dictated by the center.

Whatever the difficulties in categorizing the Peruvian military government, several core observations can be made before we proceed to the body of our paper. First of all, this regime has been quintessentially reformist. That is to say, the major initiatives for increasing citizen involvement in the decisions which affect their lives[1] depend on distributing increments to the basic national resource stock, not on redistributing existing stock (Palmer 1974a). While economic growth was rapid, there were sufficient new resources generated to support initiatives in citizen participation. When growth slows or stops, as it has in Peru since 1974, so do the initiatives, and emphasis turns to consolidation and control.

Secondly, a reformist orientation which evolves from national security considerations has, by definition, limited parameters. A development imperative born of national security concerns both promotes and constraints citizen participation. The "corporatist solution," most actively promoted in Peru between 1971 and 1975, attempted to involve the populace on the central government's terms (hierarchically, by economic sector, and emphasizing classless base organizations at the local level), while at the same time discrediting but not proscribing preexisting organizations, such as political parties and unions. The corporatist solution contributed to the proliferation and consequent overlapping of citizen organizations and provoked increased competition among them for official resources which became scarcer over time.

Thirdly, one very important outgrowth of the "national security equals development" imperative, including the paradox of wanting to stimulate citizen participation while simultaneously controlling it, has been the rapid expansion of the state. This growth involves a series of important implications for citizen participation. Because the state expands first and most effectively into those areas most accessible to it, those objects of reform closest to the centers of state initiative receive most of the benefits. The military government's national security concern complements this tendency by trying to reincorporate on the military's terms those elements of the population which had greatest access under prior regimes. But since these citizens are, by and large, those with the most experience in dealing with government, they are therefore most able to make demands on government. The result is disproportionate benefits to "the most privileged of the less privileged" (Webb and Figueroa 1975).

The rapid expansion of the Peruvian state into numerous areas simultaneously has also resulted in a certain degree of bureaucratic slippage because of overlapping jurisdictions, new employees who are often inexperienced, and uncertainties in resource allocations (Cleaves and Scurrah 1976). Policy implementation often appears to be disjointed and haphazard. From the perspective of citizens and groups, such bureaucratic slippage gives those with organizational capacity and experience greater room to maneuver and manipulate the system for their own ends, whatever the goals of central government (Palmer and Rodríguez 1972). This also means that government in practice is much more open and flexible than the decree-law or the organizational chart would make it appear. A further implication, however, is that the bulk of new resources (or public goods) are absorbed close to the center and do not reach the periphery where objective needs are greater (Roberts 1975).

Our major objectives are to examine both the principal innovations undertaken by the Peruvian military regime since 1968 toward realizing its stated objective of a "fully participatory social democracy," and the popular responses to these innovations. What explains the commitment of a military government to provide opportunities for its citizens to participate in the political system? What are the parameters of this commitment, how have they changed over time, and what are their implications for citizen, ruler, and system alike?

The Military As Political Organizer and Citizen Response

The citizen participation policies of the Peruvian military government since 1968 progress in overlapping fashion through six main stages.

Rhetorical commitment. The military government, from the very first days after the *golpe,* proclaimed its commitment to a new political order. This rhetorical commitment to full citizen participation has continued, but during the government's first year or so was of particular importance as a regime-legitimating device. However, the specific content of the evolving ideology of a fully participatory social democracy has been continually subject to refinement and even to redefinition. This suggests not only the degree to which rhetoric and ideology have been shaped by citizen response to concrete policy initiatives, but also the continuing tension among government officials and agencies over those policies.

Furthermore, official pronouncements regarding participation have sometimes been counterproductive, for they have often raised popular expectations beyond the point of the regime's capacity or willingness to meet them. Some popular sectors may then avail themselves of the more traditional methods (e.g., strikes, marches, use of political parties, etc.) that the government is trying to do away with to achieve their goals; in practice, such strategies have often succeeded. One example occurred in the North Coast sugar cooperatives in 1972. Members, with the assistance of strong APRA[2] unions, succeeded through work stoppages and protest marches in eliminating some of the most onerous central government imposed restrictions on their participation within each cooperative. The urban poor, especially those in the *pueblos jóvenes* (squatter settlements) of Peru's major cities, have likewise resorted to demonstrative measures to make their demands; one group suddenly produced large posters when President Juan Velasco Alvarado passed in review during an Independence Day parade. Citizens' ability to utilize alternative routes to satisfy demands which official rhetoric helped stimulate in the first place has often relieved the pressure which had built up between citizen and system over participation issues.

"Spontaneous" versus "Coordinated" citizen participation. During 1969 and 1970, some government officials and media spokesmen encouraged the formation and registration of Committees for the Defense of the Revolution (CDR) (Palmer 1973, pp. 85-88). These grass roots organizations, totaling more than 600 at their peak, originated in a burst of popular enthusiasm following the 24 June 1969 Agrarian Reform Law and simultaneous expropriation of North Coast sugar estates. When it appeared by mid-1970 that some CDR's were being "taken over" by traditional political parties, the government dropped the project. This example illustrated the continuing ambivalence of the military government towards participation initiatives organized by the citizens themselves, even when those "bottom up" efforts were intended to support administration policies. Such ambivalence is based on the military's tendency to identify such participation with the "old style" civilian partisan politics. Many officers blamed the elitism, the bargaining processes, and the checks and balances of Peru's limited multiparty constitutional democracy with undermining ordered development. This represented to them a threat to national security. The threat could be overcome only by, among other things, replacing "old style" politics with a new structure of citizen participation which would be carefully cultivated and channeled by some official agency.

Various government organizations have played this role. The National Cooperative Office (ONDECOOP) had primary responsibility from 1969 through 1971 for the establishment of cooperatives under the Agrarian Reform, while the National Young Towns Office (ONDEPJOV) performed a similar coordinating role in the squatter settlements. After 1972 these and most other government agencies involved with citizen participation were combined into a single entity, the National System for the Support of Social Mobilization (SINAMOS). In 1975 another new entity, the National Social Property System (SNPS), became for a brief time the cutting edge of central government initiatives for organizing the citizen.

Whatever the government's wishes and intent, however, participation not orchestrated or controlled from the center has continued apace, sometimes with dramatic effect on government policy. The 1971 mass squatter invasion of Pamplona in Lima, carefully organized by thousands of Lima's so-called "marginal residents," forced the government to make a huge tract of state land available to the poor, a step it had not contemplated until the invasion. Marches on the capital at various times by miners and coastal agricultural workers, sometimes spontaneous, sometimes organized by APRA or communist unions, occasionally provoked repression, but more often an adjustment in government policy in their favor. Opposition to various government policies in 1974 crystallized in a series of demonstrations around the country and the sacking or burning of SINAMOS offices in various provincial capitals. One result was an official reappraisal of the assumptions underlying SINAMOS' role as vanguard of the mass participation movement and its repotting in a more subordinate position.

Such examples suggest the limitations in the capacity of a reformist military government, one which was normally not prepared to use either systematic repression or proscription, to build a "fully participatory social democracy" from the top down without a good deal of "spontaneous" participation seepage.

Cooperatives. The cooperative movement in Peru, active since receiving important Church support in the late 1950s and a major program of the immediately preceding civilian government, expanded markedly under the military (Bourque and Palmer 1975). Close to 200 cooperatives per year were established during the first five years of President Velasco's administration (1968-75), compared with an average of approximately 140 per year during Fernando Belaúnde Terry's government (1963-68).

The 1969 Agrarian Reform Law provided major incentives for the cooperative organization of the Peruvian countryside. Among the most important collective forms of property ownership and management under the law were the Agrarian Production Cooperative (CAP) and the Agrarian Social Interest Society (SAIS). By mid-1975, 50 SAIS's and 424 CAP's had been established, and another 336 collective enterprises provisionally adjudicated. Cooperative farms accounted for 97 percent of the land turned over to farmers under the agrarian reform and more than 92 percent of the farmers receiving land were themselves included in such cooperatives (Bayer 1975, p. 19).

The rate of expansion of single-unit cooperative farms slackened markedly after 1973, however, as the government experimented with alternative arrangements for ensuring better distribution of surpluses across the entire agricultural sector rather than simply within a single productive unit. Experiments with Integral Development Projects (PID), intended to transfer some surplus from the more prosperous farmers to those less fortunate within geographical regions, met with very limited success. Members of the more wealthy cooperatives (e.g., the sugar cooperatives of the North Coast) have usually availed themselves of the vote in their cooperative assemblies to thwart the government's wishes along these lines.

However, steadily declining productivity and profitability in the sugar cooperatives, in part the result of memberships' decisions to distribute profits as personal income increases instead of reinvestment, led to requests by several cooperative assemblies for formal government intervention, which occurred in March 1977. In the case of the sugar cooperatives, effective local participation dramatically increased individual benefits in the short run, but at considerable cost to the collectivity and to the nation within a few years.

In principle, the expanding rural cooperative infrastructure has provided marked increases in opportunities for local participation by those citizens who became members. In practice there has been wide variation. In a variety of non-sugar-producing cooperative enterprises in North Coastal valleys and in the more prosperous central *sierra* around Huancayo, McClintock (1976a, 1976b) found marked increases in levels and effectiveness of participation, if not in support for the government. Here most members had participated in various kinds of organizations prior to the establishment of cooperatives, were on relatively fertile land which usually produced a surplus, and received substantial assistance from government agency technicians and promoters.

In the sugar cooperatives, participation increased but support for the government decreased (Horton 1974; Roca 1975). Here, too, most had participated in the new regime created organizations, but at the same time were members of pre-1968 party and union organizations basically opposed to the military government. Both the APRA background and the production of sugar, important to exports and the economy, led the government to devote massive resources here to try to control participation.

In the more marginal *sierra* (e.g., Ayacucho), participation and support remained very low (Palmer 1973; Palmer and Middlebrook 1976). Here government had the power to take lands from the *hacendados* and distribute them to the peasants, but not the capacity to provide technical assistance or support to the new cooperatives. Most beneficiaries did not have prior organizational experience and most of the land expropriated did not provide a surplus. Where objective needs were greatest, government for several years was least capable of providing assistance.

In 1972 the government established a new national farm organization, the National Agrarian Confederation (CNA), to articulate the interests of this sector at the national level. Since becoming operative in 1974, the CNA has at times assumed a much more vigorous role in defending the interests of the members than almost anyone expected. Intermittent government efforts to make CNA more submissive, including the arrest of numerous local leaders in 1975 and manipulated elections for national leaders in 1976, have largely failed. CNA, on balance, appears to be one clearly corporatist creation of the central government which has assumed an independent life of its own and which can on occasion influence government policies in the agricultural sector at both national and local levels.

While the government has spent much more time and money in its agrarian programs than in urban reform, the poor in Peru's cities have received some attention. The majority has gone to the *pobladores* or inhabitants of the squatter settlements, who are the most readily identified, and the easiest to organize. ONDEPJOV and then SINAMOS devoted much energy to distributing land titles to the pobladores, a good which satisfied a strongly felt need and which involved minimal cost to the government.

But, as in the rural areas of the country, participation and support were unevenly distributed. The pobladores, by and large, constitute the urban working poor, and as such are not the "hard-core" poor. The unemployed and unemployable, the truly marginal and destitute of the cities, inhabit the *callejones* and *corralones* and *tugurios* of the central city. These rental slum areas, which probably contain at least a million people (as do the pueblos jóvenes), comprise the city's major social and economic problems, and they are virtually untouched by the Revolutionary Government. No urban reform law has yet attempted in a comprehensive fashion to control real estate speculation, overdevelopment through tract lots and housing, rents, landlord abuses, multiple ownership of dwellings, or the maintenance of basic services in the slums. Compared with the slum dwellers, the pobladores are far easier to identify, coerce, control, and assist. The slums present enormous difficulties socially, economically, and occupationally, and almost nothing has been done.

Among the pobladores, the insistence that the squatter settlements organize themselves according to SINAMOS directives has aroused opposition. Most pueblos jóvenes had reasonably strong and frequently democratic local associations prior to 1968, and saw no compelling reason to reorganize. However, the government generally made reorganization a requisite for receiving land titles or other assistance, and has in more than one instance defaulted on its promises to deliver titles following such restructuring. In addition, the tendency of SINAMOS to penetrate ever more deeply into poblador life, coupled with more frequent political activities and insistence upon attending them, has produced demands upon the pobladores' time and energies, both of which are scarce. These broadened requirements create an imposition upon the poor, who have little spare time for what they view as time-consuming or fruitless exercises.

In some areas, it appeared at first that the Revolutionary Government's efforts had been successful; Villa el Salvador, the immense low-income planned settlement which resulted from the Pamplona land invasion already mentioned, was organized by SINAMOS into hundreds of local committees in an attempt to create a "self-managing urban community" (*comunidad urbana autogestionaria*). However, Villa el Salvador as a showcase has itself encountered problems of its own. In April of 1976, some 10,000 pobladores from this area began a march on downtown Lima to support a list of demands that had been ignored by the government. The march was forcibly broken up by the police on the highway, thereby providing a classic case of organizational-participatory capacity outstripping the ability to deliver promised goods.

Industrial Communities. About a year after the Agrarian Reform Law began the cooperativization of much of Peru's farm sector, the landmark Industrial Law was promulgated. Contained in the August-September 1970 statute were provisions to establish industrial communities in all private manufacturing enterprises above a certain size. A community would be made up of all employees of the firm, would hold seats on the board of directors of the company, and would gradually increase its ownership of the enterprise to a 51 percent majority through the purchase of stock from a certain portion of the profits. As of early 1975, 3,533 industrial communities had been established, encompassing about 200,000 workers (4.3 percent of the 1973 economically active population of Peru), with an average enterprise ownership of about 13 percent (Santisteban 1975, pp. 6-8).

During 1971 the government extended the community concept to the mining, fishing, and telecommunications sectors, encompassing perhaps 100,000 additional workers. The extension contained the important addition of an overarching compensation community for each sector to redistribute profits slightly from the more to the less profitable enterprises. Subsequently the government's temporary nationalization of the fishing sector and partial nationalization of the mining and telecommunications sectors effectively negated the community concept in terms of workers' management and ownership. This turnabout resulted from the law's provision that enterprises with 25 percent or more state control do not qualify for progressive worker ownership.

Representatives of the Industrial Communities established CONACI (National Commission of Industrial Communities) in 1973 as an organization independent of the SNI (National Industrial Society) over the strenuous objections of most ministry-level military officials. Key support by some middle-level government people combined with the determination of most workers in this new sector to protect and even enhance the benefits they obtained under the 1970 Industries Law. The result was a national organization forged from one of the most innovative of the military government's reforms which was largely autonomous from that regime. CONACI's leadership had few qualms about regularly speaking out against the government, even at the risk of occasional arrests and deportations and a substantial but ultimately unsuccessful effort by SINAMOS to break them up. (Santisteban 1975).

Social Property. The last in the series of government initiatives regarding popular participation was the Social Property Law of April 1974 (Knight 1975). This law, promulgated after the unusual procedure of advance public circulation of a draft statute for comment and criticism, was designed to overcome the multiple problems associated with private ownership or co-operative/collective/community ownership at the level of the single unit. Ownership in social property was to be neither individual, nor vested in the single unit, nor in the hands of the state, but a truly collective endeavor of all the workers in the entire sector. Social property, which the government at one time stated would eventually be predominant in Peru, was to be made up primarily of entirely new enterprises, although some preexisting entities (public enterprises, cooperatives, and industrial communities) might eventually qualify (de las Casas Grieve 1975). The economic and political crises of 1975 and 1976 effectively scuttled plans for the rapid expansion of this initiative.

Consolidation. Official retrenchment on social property exemplifies the government's citizen participation policies since the replacement of General Velasco as President by General Francisco Morales Bermúdez in August 1975. Rather than inititate new participation enterprises, the military regime shifted its emphasis to trying to improve those already in existence. Beginning in 1976, the number of government officials (from the Ministry of Agriculture-Agrarian Reform, the Ministry of Food, and SINAMOS) in the field to assist the various types of agricultural cooperatives already established, particularly in more marginal areas, increased markedly.[3] In early 1977 a new law cut back on the levels and rates of worker participation possible in the Industrial Communities in order to stimulate long stagnant private investment in the manufacturing sector. Social property was reduced to a small experimental program from the original commitment to make it the predominant sector. Finally, another development was General Morales Bermúdez's commitment in his 1977 New Year message to hold municipal and national elections by 1980.

While the military government was by no means signaling the failure of the Revolution, the consolidation phase clearly indicated the military's recognition that the successful implementation of its many reforms was far more difficult than originally believed. A series of economic crises knocked out the cornerstone of continuing rapid increases in economic resources on which the reforms were to be built. Agriculture and fishmeal production declined precipitously, adversely affecting the balance of payments. The very optimistic early projections of probable oil reserves, which had stimulated decisions from 1971 to 1973 to advance reforms on all fronts and to borrow heavily in international lending markets, proved wildly exaggerated. A tenfold increase in the rate of inflation further eroded public confidence in the regime and its policies.

Economic difficulties reinforced and generated political opposition and discontent. Strikes, marches, and antigovernment demonstrations increased; official promises of compromise and accommodation became less and less convincing. The depth of popular dissatisfaction was made evident to all in February 1975, when thousands of Peruvians took to the streets of Lima to pillage and burn after the National Police had not only refused to obey the government's orders but had also taken up arms against their erstwhile military colleagues. For the first time army tanks fired on fellow Peruvians to restore order. Scores were killed. This tragic event made clear to the military leadership that the first phase of the Peruvian "revolution" had ended. The combination of economic difficulties and determined popular opposition signaled the necessity for the regime to pursue another course. The bloodless coup of August 1975, followed by consolidation and the decision to turn formal power back over to civilians and political parties, were the results.

Toward Explaining the Military's Role As Political Organizer

With all of its problems and pitfalls, the military since 1968 has remained committed to the role of political organizer. To explain this role requires consideration of several factors which combined over time to change most officers' perceptions of the military's responsibilities in society. The most important of these are the various forces which caused the Peruvian military to identify national security with social and economic development (Einaudi and Stepan 1971; García 1974).

The Center for Higher Military Studies (CAEM), founded in 1951, quite early on developed a specialized year-long course for promising career officers emphasizing matters of national social, economic, and political development (Villanueva 1972). By the early 1960s CAEM graduates figured disproportionately in promotions to general. The first months of the inter-regnum military government of 1962-63 were marked by considerable official emphasis on national development matters. Military publications of the period reflected an increasing concern for development issues (North 1966).

The Civic Action programs of the 1960s, largely U.S. supported, put large numbers of Peruvian officers into day-to-day contact with basic national realities through literacy, road building, and school construction programs (Valdez Pallete 1971). The successfully conducted brief guerrilla war of 1965 both increased the military's self-confidence as an institution and made many officers realize that a failure to stimulate internal development could provoke internal war, a most unpalatable alternative (Villaneuva 1969).

The result of these various elements was to forge among the officer corps, especially in the army, a unity of purpose for the military as an institution. This unity was based on the identification of national security with internal development. At first the military was perfectly willing to have civilians carry out these goals. However, the reformist civilian administration of Belaúnde faltered in its development program for a number of reasons: timidity of leadership, opposition political party machinations, U.S. foreign aid and assistance holdups, and an unacceptable International Petroleum Company nationalization agreement. The military took over as an institution to rekindle national development and thus ensure national security. The alleged failure of civilian institutions disqualified them in the minds of most military people from any formal role in the new administration. The military's disdain for traditional parties and structures as mechanisms for promoting development contributed to their concern for establishing alternative means for citizen participation.

To contribute to national security and national development, however, the military felt that it should retain control of such alternative participation structures. Therefore, the military government itself would decide what kind of participation was permissible and what was not. The result in principle was, on the one hand, a top-down corporatist framework which emphasized hier-archy and local-level participation organizations within economic sectors. Additionally, potential challenges were to be "imaginatively subverted" by official downgrading of political parties, by setting up competing unions, and by placing restrictions on union membership and participation.

The identification of national development with national security gave the military its reformist orientation, but at the same time it set quite limited parameters within which the reforms were to be carried out. In the Peruvian case, national security concerns both promoted and constrained development initiatives in principle. In practice, the government's efforts to create new opportunities for participation actually increased alternatives for a segment of the population, intensified political conflict with those who felt left out, and contributed directly to the series of crises which eventually forced the regime to drastically modify its participation strategy and policy.

The Parameters and Implications of the Commitment to Participation

Commitment to workplace participation. The government's search for alternatives to what many military officials considered corrupt "old style" civilian party politics led it to the important innovation of workplace participation. The local participation units of agricultural cooperative, industrial community, and social property structures were designed explicitly to increase the opportunity of the worker, individually and collectively, to be involved in decisions which affected his/her daily life and routine.

Roughly 600,000 workers, who account for some 3,000,000 Peruvians (including their families),[4] were incorporated into these units between 1969 and 1976. This represents about 13 percent of the economically active population, and over 21 percent of the total population of Peru. The limited evidence available to date for evaluating the performance of the agricultural cooperatives and industrial communities suggests wide variation, as we have noted. In terms of citizen participation, however, it seems evident that most cooperative governing units, the administrative and vigilance committees, do in fact function, however perversely at times, and that in many industrial communities worker representatives on the boards of directors, though a minority in virtually all cases, effectively voice the concerns of the rank and file.

Thus an alternative mode of participation has been proposed and implemented. Workplace participation represents real expansion of citizens' involvement in decisions affecting their daily lives and routines along a dimension which had received little central government initiative heretofore. However, the prior modes of party, union, marches, and strikes have not been eliminated. The net result for an important minority of citizens is an expansion in the number of participation alternatives open to them at the local level. In terms of citizen participation, this may well be the most important outcome of long-term reformist military rule in Peru.

The limited impact of participation reforms. While the government's citizen participation reforms were real enough, their impact has been felt most markedly by the most privileged segments of Peruvian labor: namely, the full-time agricultural and manufacturing workers in the larger, more productive enterprises. Opportunities for participation thus have increased for those segments of the population which were already the most prosperous and the most socially mobilized. The participation alternatives have thus increased only for those citizens who were better off in the first place, while the situation of the majority has not materially changed. Indeed, for the period that the government discouraged more "traditional" participation mechanisms, their situation most likely deteriorated.

Commitment to a corporatist solution for aggregating citizen demands. Until after the 1975 *golpe,* the military leadership of Peru was unwilling to consider any solution to popular participation at the national level which included the established political parties—APRA in particular. Official policy emphasized local or workplace participation alternatives instead. With the simultaneous undermining of parties and unions, the one established transmission belt for citizen demands to the national government was being cut off just as the potential for such demands was being stimulated at the local level.

The government addressed the problem of aggregating citizen interests above the local level by decreeing a series of laws in 1971 and 1972 which either established or reorganized, on paper at least, a series of national federations by economic sector, including the National Agrarian Confederation (CNA), the National Industrial Society (SNI), the Mining Compensation Community, and the Fishing Community. Many local, regional, and national delegates were to be elected by the principle of democratic centralism, and these were to be vested with limited interest aggregation responsibilities. During the same period the government created the National System of Social Mobilization Support (SINAMOS) as the official agency entrusted with responsibility for both stimulating and channeling popular participation (see Woy, chapter 12).

Though practice was to diverge markedly, the clear intent of the regime during this period was to build a new system of popular participation along corporatist lines which would eventually replace the old transmission-belt mechanism based on party. However, the vicissitudes of the implementation process, including divergent official views, personal rivalries, financial difficulties, and the need to deal with individuals and groups which had their own ideas regarding participation, kept the corporatist solution from becoming reality in any systematic fashion. As we have indicated, some elements did become established in some areas, such as CNA and CONACI, but even here not along the lines originally envisioned by the regime.

With consolidation and the relegitimation of political parties after 1975, the "map" of popular participation mechanisms in Peru now resembles an overlapping mosaic of old and new structures, within which participation alternatives for citizens who are plugged into the system appear to have increased. Even though the Peruvian military has now apparently resolved the dilemma facing all military regimes of how to transfer national power back to civilians—through the traditional political party system—our prediction is that the elements of the corporatist solution which were actually established—

the local participation units, CNA, and CONACI—will remain. This is because these elements deal effectively with genuine perceived needs of citizens and because they are in practice largely controlled by members themselves.

The paradox of citizen participation with central control. The Peruvian military regime's commitment to political organization stemmed in large measure from its identification of national development with national security. This implied that any political organization initiatives had to be closely scrutinized and controlled from the center. Government leaders assumed that they knew best the country's needs and how to satisfy them, and thus policies were announced and implemented with little encouragement of public debate. But policy makers usually failed to elicit the needs and desires of those who were going to be affected by the reforms, and instead assumed that the goals of the reforms were in fact congruent with the people's most salient needs.

As a result, the government was on numerous occasions rudely and belatedly awakened to the intensity of citizen concerns. Until some 25,000 people demonstrated with the 1971 Pamplona invasion that the urban poor had no alternative open to them to get homes but to occupy land forcibly and illegally, the regime had made no effort to assist. To its credit, once alerted, the government shifted priorities and made available some 50,000 lots and provided rudimentary facilities. Within four years more than 200,000 people had settled in Villa el Salvador.

Likewise in the rural area, it took massive worker protests and a series of work stoppages in the North Coast sugar cooperatives in 1971 and 1972 to eliminate the worst of the restrictions placed by the government, in the name of increased productivity, on citizen participation in these cooperatives. The initial government policy of changing recognized Indian Communities over into Lima's conception of proper cooperative enterprises with cooperative statutes was eventually abandoned in the face of large-scale resistance and a constant flow of peasant delegations into the Ministry of Agriculture to request withdrawal as official communities.

The regime has generally had better success when it has responded imaginatively to citizen demands and initiatives rather than when it has tried to impose its own solutions. Many of the difficulties the Peruvian military government experienced in its citizen participation policies resulted from trying to impose too much control from the center rather than to facilitate and assist citizen initiatives. Fortunately, in actual practice the limits of the state to impose its will, particularly among the most marginally poor segments of society, has permitted greater diversity in local solutions than official perceptions and policy formulations would lead one to predict. Such limits, along with occasional imaginative official responses and accomodating if belated adjustments to reality, have encouraged the development of citizen participation organizations. The consolidation phase, itself in large measure a reactive response to citizen actions demonstrating the loss of legitimacy of policy formulation in a vacuum, may well turn out to be more satisfactory to all, since official policy under the consolidation phase is much less presumptuous about what the state can reasonably accomplish.

Conclusions

The Peruvian military government has since 1968 transcended Huntington's generalization that the military shrinks from the role of political organizer. A number of factors explain why this is the case for Peru. Internal changes within the Peruvian military over a fifteen-year period led the institution to redefine its raison d'être by coming to identify national development with national security. The establishment of well-institutionalized structures to channel citizen participation came to be a major objective within the military's new perception of its mission. At the same time, the military as an institution insisted upon the implementation of this objective without bloodshed. CAEM was instrumental in the redefinition of the military's basic purpose. The concern for nonrepressive implementation is largely explained by the strong ties of many leading officers to the Catholic Church by way of the progressive archbishop who himself had close family and personal relationships with many officials. He organized intensive *cursillos* on the social obligations of the Catholic layperson which were attended by most high-ranking officers, and which are believed to have had a profound effect on many (Adizes 1971).

Social and political factors external to the military also played an important role. Levels of social mobilization in Peru were among the lowest in Latin America (Palmer 1974b), and the major political parties were very much oriented around "establishment," nonradical concerns. Thus the organized capacity of citizens prior to 1968 was relatively low, and the major political actors who channeled this capacity tended to be more interested in keeping their options open than in galvanizing the masses around radical causes.

Thus intramilitary factors led to the military's predisposition to organize the citizenry in nonrepressive ways, and societal factors gave the military the "political space" to do so without feeling that national security consider-ations—e.g., a serious guerrilla threat—required implementation by force.

One result was a series of reforms which did provide new opportunities for participation, largely at the local or workplace level. Most of the reforms were originally imposed from the top within a corporatist framework, as the military attempted to avoid channeling citizen participation through traditional politi-cal parties, which were blamed for threatening national security by not providing for national development. However, these potentially authoritarian implementation procedures were attenuated by a number of factors.

(1) The military government almost invariably adjusted its reforms rather than respond with repression when citizens who were the objects of reform applied strong pressure. This obeyed in part the military's commitment to "nonviolent reform," and also reflected the tolerance for a diversity of views

within the top echelons of the military government. The outcome was greater responsiveness in practice to citizen views than there appeared to be in principle.

(2) The proliferation of government agencies dealing with citizen participation concerns in one form or another was part of the rapid expansion of the state which occurred between 1968 and 1976. Government employees doubled, as did the state's share of the GNP (Fitzgerald 1976). Overlapping and often changing jurisdictions of these agencies created opportunities to expand clientelist relationships with government officials who might be able to help them with their own concerns, whatever the ostensible objective of the government representative.

(3) Whatever the government's intentions and however rapidly the state did expand and state agencies proliferate, there were very real limits in the ability of the state to implement policies. Bureaucratic politics played a role, as did the difficulties in building up government programs, especially in peripheral areas, and the differences in official perceptions as to the best way to proceed. Since it was often easier to adjust that portion of the implementation process most within their power to change, the regime tended to build up governmental superstructure (i.e., facilities, equipment, and office personnel) rather than to use new resources to assist the objects of reform. Furthermore, the capacity of government itself was affected by such structural constraints as the quality of the preexisting bureaucracy, availability of new economic resources, and the quality of new employees.

These factors often meant that the military regime could not fully implement the policies to which it was committed. As a result citizens often had more leeway in practice to organize and operate in terms of their own perceptions of their basic needs and interests (cf. Dietz 1977a). Those citizens with greater experience in organizing and participating were often able to take advantage of the limits of state control. For the marginal sectors, however, urban and rural alike, the limits in government capacity meant that they could not depend on the system to deliver basic services which had been promised to improve their marginal situation. Only now, in the consolidation phase, does this seem to be changing, at least in some marginal areas.

In sum, the triple paradox of citizen participation under military government is resolved for the Peruvian case.

(1) The apparent contradiction in terms of citizen participation under military rule is resolved in part by the evolution of the doctrine of national security equals national development.

(2) The policy formulation paradox of promoting citizen participation in order to control it is overcome in large measure due to the unwillingness of the military government in most circumstances to use force to impose its policies.

(3) The policy implementation paradox of actually increasing citizen participation alternatives while attempting to reduce them is explained by the combination of the limits in government capacity in practice and the unanticipated strength of citizen response.

With the prospect of turnover of government to the political parties once again in sight, an increase in citizen participation alternatives, new and old, must be further legitimized and institutionalized. The civilian regime will face the same problems as the military, however: how to find resources to satisfy citizen demands emanating from existing organizations, and at the same time to try to extend greater assistance to the more needy marginal areas. One can hope that the political parties will develop a responsiveness to popular concerns and demands at the grass roots, thus permitting the civilian regime to carry out its governance with greater success than its military conterpart. Nevertheless, the record shows quite clearly that in many ways the military's citizen participation policies succeeded in spite of themselves.

Notes

1.   Such participation may also be defined, as Wilber Chaffee has done (1976) and as adopted by Booth and Seligson in the introductory chapter of this volume, as "activity influencing, or designed to influence the distribution of public goods." Our purpose in adopting the definition we have, after Pateman (1970) and others, is to highlight the importance of considering a broad rather than a narrow concept of political participation: that is, to include in the definition such activities as citizen involvement in local neighborhood organizations and in their workplace. Such activities may influence the distribution of public goods, as in obtaining or maintaining legislation favorable to certain citizens' situations. Then again, they may not, as in gaining nongovernmental financing for neighborhood projects or in receiving a share of the profits from private enterprises which permits the strengthening of workplace organizations. In our judgment, the Peruvian case in particular illustrates the importance of using this broad definition of political participation.

2.   The American Popular Revolutionary Alliance, founded in 1924 by Victor Raúl Haya de la Torre, remains to 1977 under his leadership. APRA is generally acknowledged to be one of the few long-standing, mass-based political parties in Latin America. The party is historically reformist, anti-Communist, and antimilitary, with its strongest support in the North of Peru, and has dominated the country's union movement. In recent years, the party has been more concerned with achieving national political power—particularly the presidency—than with reform. Its obstructionist actions as leader of the congressional opposition majority to the reform attempts of President Belaúnde and his party, AP (Popular Action), between 1963 and 1968, were major factors in bringing about the 1968 military *golpe* (Jaquette 1971). Nevertheless, its remarkable organizational resiliency makes APRA again a leading (perhaps *the* leading) contender in the new civilian order now scheduled to emerge around 1980.

3.   Based on Palmer's field notes of interviews in the Department of Ayacucho in March 1977. The increase in SINAMOS, Agrarian Reform, and Food Ministry field workers, called *promotores* and *sectoristas,* over a two-year period in this agrarian reform zone was truly remarkable: from a total of approximately 25-30 to some 180-200!

4.   The calculation of five members per worker family is one made by the Ministry of Agriculture in 1969 in its estimate of the number of potential beneficiaries of the agrarian reform.

From 1968 to 1975, the Peruvian Revolutionary Armed Forces under General Juan Velasco Alvarado established an innovative system of participation aimed at providing an alternative to the traditional elitist political structures and "imported" ideologies. The system was SINAMOS (National System for the Support of Social Mobilization), which Woy investigates in its role as social mobilizer and promoter of grassroots organizations. She evaluates the government's intent, investigates the functions and characteristics of the key agents of social mobilization, and, in a brief case study, looks at those individuals who participate in SINAMOS.

12.
Infrastructure of Participation in Peru: SINAMOS

SANDRA L. WOY

In 1971 the Revolutionary Armed Forces of Peru sought to establish an innovative and comprehensive "infrastructure of participation" that would (1) structurally alter the political system to allow the accomodation, integration and reconciliation of the demands of disparate social groups; (2) provide a viable alternative to the institutional and organizational schemes of alien ideologies; and (3) build a major bulwark of support for the government. To achieve these ends, the military government created SINAMOS (National System for the Support of Social Mobilization). SINAMOS has been attacked from all sides; some labeled it a "communist-inspired" means of channeling all participation through cadre groups, while others denounced the agency for its "corporatist, fascist, and anti-classist" tendencies. Yet, it is the government's political arm; the only legitimate channels of participation and access to governmental decision making are through the base organizations established by SINAMOS.

Frequently in political science literature there is a distinction made between "real" or democratic participation and "support" or ceremonial participation found in many developing or mobilizing political systems.[1] Unfortunately, the implication of such a definitional distinction is that in developing or mobilizing regimes "participation" does not exist. Too readily, the authoritarian institutional patterns and structures in these systems are accepted as evidence that the citizens do not really participate. In this manner important insights into participation as a concept are lost. If participation is "activity aimed at influencing [causing to happen that which otherwise would not have happened] the distribution of public goods" (Booth and Seligson, chapter 1), then real participation may take place in all regimes though the form may differ. The important theoretical question to be addressed here is: to what extent do citizens who take part in governmental organizations, which are authoritarian and manipulative, actually influence the political system by their activity in these sponsored groups?

The purpose of SINAMOS is to promote social mobilization and to organize grassroots groups which are system supportive and at the same time participatory. Hesitant to call these objectives contradictory, this paper will investigate their compatibility. Why, how, and to what extent do citizens participate, that is, influence the distribution of public goods in system-supportive and system-dominated organizations? In seeking some preliminary answers to that question, this chapter will outline the process by which the Peruvian government has structured political participation. First we shall look at the government's intent and the organizational model chosen to create their "infrastructure of participation." Second, we shall investigate the functions and the characteristics of the *promotores* of the agency who, as the actual point of contact between the government and the population, are the key agents of social mobilization. Finally, we shall concentrate upon one sector of the participant, or organized, public—the students—and ask why do they participate (what demands do they have), how do they participate (through what type of activities), and with what effect do they participate?

Political Participation

At this point it is necessary to expand upon what is meant by participation. Recognizing its multifaceted character, the quality of which may be expected to vary according to context, the concept of political participation is best understood by analyzing its most important aspects. Following the guidelines of work done by Verba and Nie (1972) and Myron Weiner (Binder, et al. 1971, pp. 159-204), these aspects can be identified as voluntarism, choice, and action.

The degree of voluntarism involved is one means of distinguishing the difference between what has been labeled "support" and "real" participation. When membership in organizations, attendance at mass rallies, and turnout for elections are the result of governmental connivance and coercion, participation is involuntary and undemocratic. But cultural biases must not obscure the fact that many people join the government-supported labor confederation, vote for the *oficialista* candidate, or demonstrate out of preference and not simply or solely because of political manipulation. To follow the prescribed course is not necessarily to act involuntarily. If, however, the scope of legal activity is so narrowly defined that all action is predetermined, or if the modes of persuasion make alternatives meaningless, the degree of voluntarism is nil.

The point is that the *impetus,* not the activity itself, differentiates "real" from "support" participation. In this regard we must explore the advantages and disadvantages present in the Peruvian system for affiliation with official groups and for adherence to alternate or opposition groups.

The second fundamental aspect is that of choice. Participation assumes a partaking in decision making where alternatives are presented and the probability of adoption of each is less than one hundred percent. In other words, to participate is to have an influence upon a decision, the outcome of which is not known or determined in advance. This aspect of participation refers to the extent to which decisions are the product of a deliberative process. We must determine whether or not those organizations created by the Peruvian military with the express purpose of facilitating popular participation actually provide freedom of choice both in regard to the election of leaders and policy formation.

The third element of participation is action. Attitudes toward and feelings about the political system do not represent participation unless they are manifested through activity. The types of activities that have been used as indices of participation vary. Past discussions were almost exclusively concerned with electoral acts and behavior and closely followed Lester Milbrath's "hierarchy of political involvement" (1965, p. 18). More recently, however, Verba and Nie have suggested that participatory activities, while correlated, do not relate in a hierarchical pattern but can be analytically separated into four categories or "modes": voting, campaign activity, particularized contacts, and cooperative, group, or communal activities (1972, pp. 56-81). Cross-national studies have produced similar modes of participation based on factor analyses of survey data (Verba, Nie, and Kim 1971, pp. 1-80; Biles, chapter 5; Seligson and Booth, forthcoming-c). A further study of data from Yugoslavia indicated that individual acts fell into the voting and particularized contact modes, but that activities distinguished as campaign or communal formed one mode and activities within the functional self-management bodies formed a separate mode (Verba and Shabad 1975). In short, any study of how citizens participate in a particular regime must take into account distinctive ways in which citizens *may* be active politically. Thus our third consideration in describing the character of contemporary political participation in Peru will be to delineate the parameters of accepted activities. This is not to deny the importance of illegal forms of participation, but the emphasis of this study is upon the quality and nature of legitimate participation afforded by a bureaucracy dedicated to participatory activities.

SINAMOS: Infrastructure of Participation

On July 28, 1974, the Comité de Asesoramiento de la Presidencia de la República (COAP) published the *Plan Inca,* the manifesto which had guided the military junta for the previous six years. Popular participation ranked number 25 of the 31 specific objectives and actions deemed significant enough to be included. From the military's viewpoint the partisan competition of the traditional electoral system was divisive, corrupt, and a threat to their goals of national development, national integration, and national security. They believed that citizen support would be generated by their populist and redistributive reforms. Their conception of popular input into the revolutionary process was participation in productive units—unions, cooperatives, collectives, neighborhood councils—oriented toward national development. The junta postulated that the emphasis on economic participation (e.g., profit sharing and self-management) or social participation (e.g., self-help and youth groups) would substitute for political participation in the partisan sense because the supposed objectives of these groups were collective, not competitive.

Despite the efforts of the military to realize a national commitment to Peruvian solidarity and to stifle the raison d'être of partisan affiliation by limiting elections to local organizations and undercutting all patronage benefits, the political parties in Peru survived. These groups and their rural liaisons served as an important linkage in the communication system. They acted as intermediaries between the bewildered provincial farmers and the bewildering capital bureaucracy. From the first elections held in the local productive units, it became obvious to the military that the candidate slates were but thinly disguised partisan lists. Those most able to benefit from the new associational forms offered to the population were those groups which were already organized—the traditional parties and their affiliated unions. This development helped pressure the military into considering a means of mobilizing support for the "revolutionary process." They realized that as their ability to redistribute resources and provide new services diminished they would need loyal, sustaining supporters. Thus, the junta finally conceded that a more formal political organization was necessary to channel the spontaneous support generated by the reforms and to provide the assurance that associational groups spawned by these reforms were truly dedicated to the revolution's objectives.

Until recently political scientists have stressed the reluctance of military leaders to organize politically. Such involvement can threaten the military as an institution, and it most assuredly compromises the stance of the military as being "above politics." Samuel Huntington characterizes the dilemma of military juntas as being "caught between their subjective preferences and values and the objective and institutional needs of their society" (Huntington 1968, p. 244).

After considerable internal debate and influential civilian input, the Peruvian military confronted this dilemma with the creation of SINAMOS in June 1971. The theoretical and organizational framework of SINAMOS seeks to incorporate the population within institutions that provide "social democracy with full participation" and at the same time to further the military's developmental and security goals.

SINAMOS is admittedly a political entity. In fact, former Minister of

Energy and Mines, Jorge Fernando Maldonado, called it "one of the most creative of the ideological and political arms of the Peruvian Revolution . . ." (Pequeño and Fudrini 1973, p. 75). But the aim of SINAMOS is not the same as a traditional political party and the creation of *political* institutions per se has never been its objective.

The stated goal of the Peruvian "revolutionary process" is to effect the structural transformation of the institutional mechanisms of power. Decision-making power is to be transferred from small, closed groups of privileged and interrelated elites to the masses organized into "authentically participationist" institutions. The most comprehensive, thoughtful, and influential articulation of the theory of participation in Peru has been made by Dr. Carlos Delgado Olivera.[2] His ideas are particularly important as he was a member of the civilian advisory group and the first director of SINAMOS. According to Delgado, a "prerequisite to genuinely representative institutions at the national level" is the creation of a vast "network of participatory infrastructure" throughout the country. Related generally to the citizen's associative activities, he feels these organizations should be "completely autonomous, nonmanipulated and nonmanipulable . . . subject only to the decisions of their members." Delgado is convinced that the experience gained at the local level "will indicate the best ways of building a system of ascending interrelationships of national scope." The national entity would then "coordinate the decisions that rise from the bases of society itself into coherent policies." He believes these policies would be "authentically democratic," as the mechanisms would provide "genuine popular representativeness" (Delgado 1973, p. 250).

The most important characteristics of SINAMOS, as a theoretical construct, are that (1) it is nonpartisan and nonclassist, and (2) it does not intend to be a permanent institution, only to be a support agency to aid in the creation of permanent institutions.

In Decreto Ley 18896, SINAMOS was charged with three general objectives: (1) the capacitation (training), orientation, and organization of the national population; (2) the development of entities of social interest; (3) the communication and particularly a dialogue between the government and the population.

Of these, the first is most essential because it facilitates the others. As its full name—the National System for the Support of Social Mobilization—straightforwardly declares, SINAMOS' mission is the mobilization of the Peruvian population. Perhaps the most crucial aspect of mobilization is "capacitation." Although usually translated as "training," capacitation is an accepted English word, meaning a more general state of enabling, making fit, or making one more qualified (American Heritage Dictionary 1970, p. 199); it provides the best rendering of the Peruvian meaning and will be used throughout this paper.

If the Peruvian revolutionary ideals are to be taken seriously, capacitation is the key element in the process. In order for power to be transferred to the popularly organized groups, the population must be prepared to receive and to exercise this power and to encourage the continuation of this transfer beyond the initial reformist stages. The people must be informed about the process, instructed in the requisite skills, and included in the planning. It is this task that SINAMOS is to perform.

Organizationally, SINAMOS is composed of three major levels. The first is the *Oficina Nacional de Apoyo a la Movilización Social* (ONAMS), the National Organization for the Support of Social Mobilization. The national office is responsible for delineating national policy and for providing support to the 10 regional (ORAMS) and the more than 70 zonal (OZAMS) offices.[3] This support is provided in five areas of service: capacitation, publicity, infrastructure support, financial support, and legal and administrative support. These services are provided directly to the grassroots organizations.

These organizations form the base of the participatory system. Theoretically, they have a high degree of operational autonomy, defining their needs, implementing their own programs, and appealing to the governmental offices at the ORAMS and ONAMS levels only as they require external support services listed above. It is important to note, however, that these groups exist in the first place because their organization has been promoted by the officials or *promotores* of SINAMOS. In pursuing their aim of creating an organized, participant population, the Velasco government directed its efforts toward those sectors deemed strategic for the social and economic development of the country. These sectors represent either an important economic group or groups that have experienced a high level of social conflict (i.e., the traditionally deprived majority sectors of the population). Within SINAMOS, these areas have been defined operationally as: labor, campesino groups, the marginal urban population living in *pueblos jóvenes* (squatter settlements) and other underdeveloped urban areas, the rural proletariat, the youth, and those cultural and professional groups whose talents have often been ignored because of their folkloric orientation to literature, music, and art.

Capacitation of the Population

In regard to capacitation, the specific duties of the Dirección de Capacitación (ONAMS) are to rationalize and make more efficient use of resources, and to systematize and standardize the ideopolitical, technical, and organizational aspects of capacitation. After testing and evaluating methods, the ONAMS office publishes and distributes the materials used for capacitation throughout the system (Dirección de Capacitación 1974, p. 19).

The major charge at the ORAMS level is that of "orienting and coordinating" the zonal activities through budgetary and administrative controls. At the national level the operational and functional areas are viewed as distinct entities. At the regional level, however, capacitation is just one of many tasks to be performed in the overall process of creating base organizations. Activities and resources are to be integrated and shared by a "team" called the

Organism for the Promotion of Organizations (OPO). Their purpose is to "facilitate the formation of grassroots associations whose form and content are most conducive to permitting the local population to participate and to exercise social, economic and political power" (Dirección de Capacitación 1974, pp. 12-13).

At the OZAMS level, that closest to the population, the capacitation teams have three missions: (1) to capacitate the directors and leaders of the grassroots organizations, generating in them a militant position; (2) to capacitate the *promotores* of the System who are the key bridge between the government and the people; (3) to coordinate the activities of capacitation with other sectors in which SINAMOS is charged with the ideological content (Dirección de Capacitación 1974, p. 14).

The content of the capacitation course changes in slight but important ways according to its constituents. Capacitation of the population is concerned with analyzing the local situation in its social, economic, and political spheres and raising the peoples' consciousness of their circumstances. Its emphasis is on stimulating local developments which necessitate communal organization and an identification with collective goals. The capacitation of the administrative workers in SINAMOS and other government bureaucracies is concerned with making them aware and tolerant of, if not militantly in favor of, the revolutionary process. In the bureaucracies, perhaps the hardest group to reach, capacitation is accomplished by passing out pamphlets, articles, reprints, and books, and then holding mandatory office seminars to discuss the materials.[4]

The capacitation of the *promotores* merits special attention. They should be the dynamic element of the process; they should be cadres of committed individuals who are skilled in organizing. Thus, their preparation is crucial. The National Plan for Capacitation suggested that top priority be given to imbuing in the OZAMS personnel a clear comprehension of the importance of the political goals outlined by the System; then to developing a realistic view of the zone's problems in relation to the entire country; and finally to mastering a technical skill (ONAMS 1973).

The *Promotores*

The criteria for permanent *promotores* were set by the national office. Their standards were: (1) university study or technical training; (2) working knowledge of the economic, social, and political problems of the region; (3) experience in field work, particularly in capacitation activities; (4) aptitude for group work; and (5) residing in the region not less than one year (SINAMOS 1974).

These criteria are the ideals, but SINAMOS unfortunately has never been able to maintain such a quality core of *promotores*. The first problem is that there has been no uniform procedure for hiring. Each ORAMS office operates under its own set of standards. In some cases the *promotores* are hired according to the results of a competitive examination that involves theoretical concepts and practical testing. In other cases there is only a personal interview. In many ORAMS, *promotores* are "chosen" by the zonal directors on the recommendation of local leaders.

Not only is there a great variation in the method of recruitment, but there is also a noticeable difference in salaries and educational standards. The median income for *promotores* in 1973 was 6,000-6,999 *soles* per month ($133-55). Yet, in Puno and Iquitos, 76.5 percent and 68 percent of the functionaries, respectively, made less, while in Piura and Arequipa, 40 percent and 22 percent received wages of 10,000-10,999 soles ($222-44). The educational qualifications of the *promotores* ranged from illiterates working in the Cuzco office, to the staff at Arequipa where 80 percent were professionals. Of the 1,184 *promotores* in the system in 1973, 41 percent had professional degrees. While this is a respectable percentage, the distribution was far from even. More than 50 percent of those who had such training were working for the Huancayo or Chiclayo ORAMS. After Lima, these are the largest regions in terms of population, and they have the largest number of *promotores* even including the Lima area.

The importance of the *promotores* as the link between the government and the population cannot be exaggerated, and the quality of this link is a vital component of the government's chance for success. All *promotores* take a capacitation course which covers three major themes. The first is the ideo-political dimension which is composed of three subtopics: (1) world social-political phenomena and alternatives to capitalism, (2) Peruvian prerevol-tionary reality, and (3) the "revolutionary process," which involves the evolution of the armed forces and the significance of their relationship to national development. The second major theme, popular promotion, is concerned with the problems of field work, work procedures, and some sociological and anthropological background. Designed to help the *promotores* analyze objective conditions in their region, this topic also emphasizes the concepts, methods, and techniques of grassroots planning. The third area of study is social mobilization. The aim here is to provide the *promotores* with a better understanding of the national policies for mobilization and the organization of SINAMOS. In addition, there are intensive courses covering the same topics in greater detail, along with specialized courses emphasizing methodology, communication, and other auxiliary skills (ONAMS 1973).

Examinations were administered on the materials covered in the twenty-two courses offered during 1973. ONAMS was greatly disappointed by the results.[5] Relatively low scores on the ideopolitical parts were interpreted by the national office to mean that a great majority of the *promotores* were coming in contact with certain ideas for the first time and that others were still adherents to "alien" ideologies or to traditional political parties (SINAMOS 1974).

This "evidence" of lack of training gave some credence to the claims made by both the government's supporters and its critics, that saboteurs easily infiltrated SINAMOS. A concern for this fundamental deficiency led the national office to increase the quality and quantity of ideopolitical instruction in the capacitation courses and to establish a "basic library for the promotor" which included the significant documents of the sectoral reforms, Plan Inca, the collected speeches of President Velasco, the ideological writings of Carlos Delgado, etc. It was hoped that subsidized printing and liberal distribution of these materials would lead to a standard understanding of the "revolutionary process."

Although ONAMS was disturbed by the lack of knowledge of the process itself, of perhaps greater import are the even lower mean scores for the area of popular promotion and grassroots planning—the two major missions of the *promotores*.[6] Only the functionaries in the *pueblos jóvenes* of Lima scored substantially higher than the system mean of 67.0. Their ranking of 95.0 most likely reflects the availability of trained social workers in that metropolitan area and the fact that this program is to a great extent a continuation, although admittedly on a much broader scale, of previous community development projects.

The national office was concerned not only with the low level of tested knowledge, but also with what they perceived to be a low degree of commitment to the revolution. There were two causes for this: On the one hand, a portion of the *promotores* had strong traditional political ties. It was noted that the partisan background of many *promotores* provoked a "distorted" view of the government's political position (SINAMOS 1974). Some were able to read into the theoretical guidelines what they wanted, and tried to conduct their activities for SINAMOS in a partisan mode. On the other hand, many of the *promotores* at the OZAMS level said they had never considered their work political. Their low commitment was the result of an apathetic attitude toward the political content of such public work. Each of these individuals had a different vision as to what the revolution really meant. This discordance of opinion between the various regional and zonal directors and the *promotores* led to hostile and often arbitrary firing of promotional units or large-scale resignations of frustrated *promotores*. The turnover rate in the first two years for field workers was more than 60 percent. ONAMS responded to this by suggesting that in the ideopolitical courses it must be emphasized that "while there is pluralism of ideology outside SINAMOS, there must be militant unity within" (SINAMOS 1974).

Thus, for ONAMS the problem is twofold: the *promotores* must understand the political nature of their work and they must differentiate between the traditional partisan approach to politics and the direction envisioned by the military government. Most of their evaluations emphasize the necessity of capacitating good *promotores,* those whose knowledge and attitudes are appropriate to their task, and who have successfully served a two-month probationary period under supervision. The second major concern is to develop a "methodology" of techniques and work procedures with the population "that will fulfill the institutional objectives, adjusted to the political circumstances" (SINAMOS 1974).

The idea that such a "methodology" is necessary is indicative of the ONAMS' interest in centralization and control of the most fundamental connection to the population—the *promotores'* organizing and capacitating mission. The ideologues in Lima are preoccupied with the goal of a truly innovative revolutionary process, but they are aware of the fact that the *promotor* works in a very conventional manner, stimulating developmental projects and dealing with traditional social-political leaders even in rural communities. The *promotor* and his labor projects are the target of attacks by the politicized *campesino* groups and all those opposed to the revolution. Given the strength of the power groups that seek to obstruct the work of the government's functionaries, all the grassroots organizations they create need extensive material, financial, and psychological support; but the *promotor* is often not in a position to provide such support unless the national office will do so. A direct connection from ONAMS to the *promotores,* however, is ideologically suspect and administratively circuitous.

The dilemma of mobilizing the population to participate in the revolution is not merely a matter of training competent and committed individuals to do the field work. It also entails an organizational and administrative structure that encourages such mobilization.

Obstacles to Success

SINAMOS has faced two major obstacles to carrying out its mission; one relates to the external system, the other to its own organization. The first and most fundamental obstacle has been the military government's ambiguity in supporting SINAMOS.[7] At its creation, SINAMOS was given an important role by the military; its director, General Leonidas Rodríguez Figueroa, was a good friend of President Juan Alvarado Velasco and a member of the planning group for the October 3rd Revolution. With a sizeable budget, a large bureaucracy (4,000), and a nonvoting cabinet position for its director, SINAMOS was in the limelight. Its goal of establishing popular participatory organizations and of incorporating many leftist civilian leaders provided a dimension of widespread interest if not acceptance. It was not long, however, before the military's theoretical expectations and the civilian administration diverged. Political support for the work of SINAMOS was often weak and sometimes contradictory. Sensitive to public criticism, the military allowed SINAMOS to bear the brunt of regime opposition. It was a visible target because of its nationwide mobilization activities; a frequent target because of its inability to immediately satisfy expectations; and it was a logical target because its work was "*oficialista*" and support oriented. Rather than strengthening the resources of SINAMOS in the face of sometimes hostile and bitter opposition, the government retreated. In several instances the military supported other governmental agencies in jurisdictional conflicts with SINAMOS, and they have transfered the capacitation functions for the labor communities and the industrial communities outside of the purview of SINAMOS. Not the least of the reasons for this posture toward SINAMOS is the feeling that a stronger SINAMOS would ultimately mean a weaker military.

The second stumbling block for SINAMOS was the internal conflict between the technical and political missions that was exacerbated by the decentralized administrative structure. At an ONAMS conference in 1974, *promotores* complained that OZAM administrators directed their activities in a "vertical and authoritarian" manner. Rather than being consulted on zonal activities, they found themselves at the base of a dual hierarchical structure, receiving uncoordinated orders and directives from the OZAMS and ORAMS. The *promotores* maintained that an emphasis on the mere promoting of organizations had relegated political and technical capacitation to a minor role. Evidence of this was noted in delays of information, pamphlets, resource materials, etc., from the national external support areas. ONAMS interpreted this to "show the traditional negative conception of popular mobilization" (SINAMOS 1974). The ORAMS and OZAMS are operated generally by bureaucrats with prerevolutionary training whose inclination is to move forward with the modernization and developmental projects but to dally with ideological programs.

Major problems have arisen as the *promotores,* not being well integrated, circumvent the zonal and regional offices and depend upon ONAMS for resources and action guidelines. The results of this relationship were that (1) the functionaries were isolated and alienated from the policy formation in operational areas, (2) capacitation was nonexistent, sporadic, or in some cases, duplicated by other state agencies, and (3) many capacitation courses were programmed from Lima by officials in the Civic Center office with no communication to the regional or zonal officials.[8] This situation undermines the theoretical and administrative decentralization of the System and is deplored by those committed to the stated goals of the System. In addition, it bypasses the conservative regional power groups to give direct access to the more liberal groups at the national level. This adds fuel to the critics' claim that SINAMOS is a centralized, manipulative, political organization, which then gives the military a reason, through the regional and zonal officials, to remove the "bad" or partisan *promotores.* With the System divided against itself, unclear in the armed forces' commitment to achieve its stated objectives, it is no wonder that SINAMOS as a political support agency has fallen short.

In April 1975, a reorganization of SINAMOS was announced. The immediate impetus for the change was the apparent failure of SINAMOS in establishing grassroots political support for the "revolution." During the disturbances in February in Lima there was little evidence of pro-regime solidarity among the city's masses. Most observers agree, however, that the rioting and looting were not the result of political discontent, although certain factions encouraged and utilized the opportunity. Immediately after these events, the clamor for an institutionalized political movement took on a greater stridency than at any time since the Committees for the Defense of the Revolution were dissolved by the formation of SINAMOS. Editorials, mimeographed handbills, and magazine articles made it clear to the government that its supporters wanted a means of participating in a frankly political manner and that SINAMOS, as previously constituted, had not provided such a means.

Despite "reorganization," the fall of Velasco, a rapid turnover in directors (three since January 1975), and the judgment of some observers that SINAMOS has been discarded to the "scrapheap of the revolution" (*Latin America*, June 6, 1976), its experiences are instructive and its impact will not be merely transitory.

The Participants

One especially notable impact of SINAMOS is the government's attempt to organize youth movements. The *Dirección de Areas Juveniles* of ONAMS has been charged with promoting and development student and youth organizations. These organizations have been divided into the youth of the *pueblos jóvenes*, the rural youth, and urban youth. In the urban areas there is a further division into primary and secondary school youth groups, student work and production centers, volunteer groups and university students. Given the priorities of the government, the rural groups and the *pueblos jóvenes* were the first to be organized.

One of the goals of SINAMOS during 1974 was the formation of a national organization for university students. The role of the university student in the revolutionary process is an essential one. If there is to be a transfer of power to organized popular groups, the students are sure to be one of those groups; not only because of their propensity for social criticism and activism, but also because of their potential as qualified professionals and technicians. Traditionally the students are café critics of all regimes, more concerned with guarding their political autonomy than with committing themselves to concrete action on behalf of the government. Yet, their humanitarian and altruistic spirits can be kindled by voluntary social work programs. Beginning in 1964 with *Cooperación Popular*—a local self-help plan—Peruvian students have participated in government-sponsored development projects. Through the Youth Organizations office in ONAMS, a nationwide voluntary movement, *Trabajo Popular Voluntario,* was initiated in 1972. In 1974 a subdivision of this group was formed—*Trabajo Popular Universitario* (TPU).

The students consistently picture themselves as being revolutionaries, and SINAMOS appealed to this self-image with advertisements and radio and television spots exhorting: "*Si eres revolucionario, demuéstralo en el campo. Hazte voluntario!*" (If you are a revolutionary, prove it in the countryside. Become a volunteer!) The *promotores* who were to organize the university students dealt heavily with the theme of the university's failure to fulfill its social function. They also lamented the fact that there were virtually no channels of communication between the government and the students. The *promotores* insisted that the dialogue did not mean the individual was pro-military, but pro-Peruvian.

The objectives of *Trabajo Popular Universitario* were worked out by students and *promotores* at a meeting in Ancón, a coastal government retreat near Lima, in June 1974, six months before the first national meeting of TPU. They were:

1. To strengthen student contact with national reality through concrete actions of T.P.U. in the campesino and rural communities.
2. To support the organization of a broad voluntary movement of students to support the revolutionary process.
3. To channel the technical-scientific support and social motivation the students can offer for national development.
4. To forge a worker-peasant solidarity through participation in local community projects. (TPU 1974, p. 3)

From the government's point of view, such groups provided relatively inexpensive, skilled work forces that could assist in local infrastructure construction, thus gaining support for the revolution from the communities that benefitted and at the same time integrating future professionals into the process by arousing in them a commitment to national development and a social consciousness. The *promotores* at ONAMS wanted to form "brigades" of students from the universities or the specialized institutes. They envisioned field work in three areas: (1) technical support, (2) assistance to the grassroots organizations administration, and (3) physical labor. This work was to be "permanent." That is, enough time was to be spent in the area initially, at least two months, to get the project well underway. Thereafter, vacations and some weekends were to be spent continuing the work. Not only were the *campesinos* to benefit immediately from the project; they would also, through this experience, become more receptive to technicians, government officials, and other outsiders. At the same time the students would learn about Peru and add a practical dimension to their college learning.[9]

The ideopolitical aspects of student participation were, of course, equally important. The focus of student capacitation was to increase their understanding of "national reality," especially the conditions of "domination and dependence" which characterize a developing country such as Peru. ONAMS felt this was necessary to "overcome the orientation and faults of earlier voluntary work, which responded to foreign objectives" (TPU 1974, p. 4). In other words, TPU was not to be equivalent to Belaunde Terry's *Cooperación Popular,* which in their eyes was little more than a Peruvian Peace Corps. (It was more than coincidence that the U.S. Peace Corps was sent home the same month of the first national meeting of TPU.)

TPU was defined as "the voluntary, autonomous force, organized by university youth, supported by SINAMOS to service the structural changes and the popular organizations of the Revolution" (TPU 1974, p. 2). The students felt that this definition identified their activities with a revolutionary process and not a "mere modernizing change of the social structure." They state that theirs is a "new concept of voluntary work that is particularly questioning of the status quo"; one which makes them a part of the community rather than an "assistant" in the formal, paternalistic sense (TPU 1974, p. 5).

To this end, the second major portion of the capacitation courses was devoted to learning about the actual legal-administrative regimen. The students were expected to become thoroughly conversant with the various reform laws and their application. Actual student participation was to be coordinated by the OZAMS, whether it be giving support to research groups, holding organizational meetings, doing physical work, or planning an irrigation system.

The implementation of this plan produced mixed results. The first dilemma was how to attract the university students. In one year the *pueblos jóvenes* had youth groups totaling 50,000 members; TPU could count only 750 (ONAMS 1973, p. 13). The usual way of organizing political groups in the universities is to start *circulos de estudio* (study circles) on contemporary issues of interest. Yet, antigovernment sentiment ran so high among students, that attendance in such circles diminished rapidly as soon as they were identified as "sinamistas" by other students.[10] More successful were the lecture programs, especially those given by Héctor Béjar who, because of his renowned guerrilla activities in 1965, remained somewhat of a folk hero with the students. Although many saw his position as the director of Youth Organizations for SINAMOS as a "sellout" to the reformists, others were still fascinated by his presence; moreover, his articulation of the goals of the revolution was inspiring. The most successful stimulant to interest on the college campus, however, was the organization of voluntary work in the countryside.

The students who responded and enrolled in the capacitation courses in April, June, and August of 1974 numbered in the hundreds each time. Between fifty and sixty persons actually showed up for the courses given in August, September, and October. Attendance declined as the courses got underway, and the number that eventually participated in a "salida" or working trip to the Sierra or the Amazon area, were approximately 34, 24, and 19 for each of these months.

The reasons the students enrolled were varied.[11] Some were genuinely altruistic and wanted to "help" people less fortunate than themselves. Others were mere joiners who wanted to meet people or sought the benefits offered— lunches provided during capacitation, transportation, food, and facilities for two months out of Lima. Some were frankly after jobs. The social science student has few options for employment. The government is the greatest employer, followed by private research groups and private colleges. SINAMOS had become, in two years, a "good" job for the sociologists and anthropologists who were almost unemployable elsewhere.[12] Several persons with a firm political persuasion joined to "find out" what the government was thinking, to challenge the *promotores,* or to convert the students to their own convictions.

Those with a leftist posture were often surprised to find the *promotores* as much, if not more, "radical" philosophically than themselves. Even so, those given to strong partisan political expression, from the left or the right, generally dropped out or became discouraged by numerous "problems" connected with their departure on a working trip.

The capacitation course was given on weekends and lasted all day Saturday and Sunday. The format of the meeting was to have a lecture or presentation in the morning, followed by discussion groups and an evaluation of the specific topic. After lunch there might be a movie, a panel discussion, another group evaluation which would be written up and mimeographed for comparison with the larger body's evaluation, and often there would be an examination on the materials covered. The participants had the feeling that the content of the course expanded and grew as things happened, but with little real long-range planning. The work groups organized in Lima could not go to the Sierra until there was a community ready to receive such visitors. The first groups went to the SAIS Tupac Amaru, which is the most modern and technically advanced cooperative in the Sierra. Later groups assisted with elections on the coast and with the process of legally recognizing the grassroots organizations that were to form an Agrarian League in the Department of Lima. In October 1974, the groups did relief work in the aftermath of the October 3rd earthquake.

This last activity provides a good example of the relationship between SINAMOS and the popular organizations it sponsors. The municipality of Lima had acquired land in the area of Zarate on which they planned to build modern multifamily dwellings. Approximately five hundred families were to be moved to this area from downtown Lima because the two square blocks of Jirón Amazonas and Jirón Lampa where they lived had been condemned. The October 3rd *temblor* destroyed most of this decayed section and it became necessary to move these people immediately. The Civil Defense office of the municipal government coordinated the transfer. Each family and its belongings were loaded into army trucks and carried to the Urbanización Azcarrunz where they were dumped on a "lot" marked with lime. When they arrived at their plot of dirt the government supplied the head of each family with six *esteras* (straw mats), four poles, and a packet of nails. They were to construct a temporary dwelling until the modern homes were erected. As many of the families consisted of women and children, the university volunteers of TPU assisted with this construction process. Three- or four-person teams built four to five straw houses a day.

On the first day all went well as the dignitaries were present to inaugurate the community and the press was there to take the requisite publicity pictures. It was reported that city services of street lighting, water, and sewage were to be installed "shortly" and that the National Office for Nutritional Support (ONAA) would furnish three meals a day from funds donated by the International Red Cross, CARITAS, and the municipality of Lima (*La Prensa,* October 14, 1974).

For the first three days, transportation to the *urbanización* was provided for the students; thereafter, they took regular microbuses. By the fourth day there were no more nails and *esteras* were hard to come by; in fact the demand created by building such accomodations for 492 families (many of whom had purchased more on their own to enlarge their dwellings) had caused the price to more than double in five days. The project had been all but forgotten by officialdom at the end of the first week. Food and water trucks arrived until the *ambulantes* (street vendors) were allowed in with their wares; dark light poles dotted the tract; and the problem of sewage disposal was being met with typhoid inoculations.

The forty to fifty students who had worked diligently from dawn to dusk for more than two weeks, however, had begun to develop that tie to the people that was theoretically their purpose. Their physical labor had helped produce housing; their organizational skills had been tested by administering a health questionnaire and by providing entertainment and sports for the youth in the area. Their commitment to continue volunteer work in this community was quickening when ORAMS decided that another project now had priority. The neighborhood development programs in Azcarrunz were to be placed under the jurisdiction of a different OZAMS. Although some of the students were ready to move on to another area, at least a few felt let down by the bureaucracy. They had no qualms about being a mobile work force, assisting when and where the need was most immediate, but they openly questioned their own autonomy, their ability to participate in deciding with the ORAMS and OZAMS youth units where their energies were to be applied.

Based on my experience as a participant in three capacitation courses and several work projects from July to December 1974, I can make several observations about the type of student who joined this official, government-sponsored organization during the school year 1974.

Perhaps not surprisingly, the overwhelming majority of the students who participated in the "salidas" to the countryside were male. This is not to say that the female portion of the student population is uninterested. The inscription in the capacitation courses was roughly equivalent male to female, but cultural and familial prohibitions on the type of work and living conditions in the countryside generally reduced female participation to one-fifth of the group.

A more interesting observation was the participant's hometown. Almost twice as many of the members of the TPU Brigada "Tupac Amaru" came from the provinces as came from Lima. In other words, a majority of those students whom the *promotores* were helping to gain a better understanding of Peruvian reality by sending them from the urban center to the *selva,* sierra, or the coast, were those who already had intimate knowledge of the stark geographic, economic, and social conditions of the country outside of Lima. For this very reason they were probably more concerned with the call to help in such areas in the first place.

Perhaps connected to their origins, the *compañeros* of TPU were studying many nontraditional subjects. Of eighteen members in one course, there were only two medical students and one law student. On the other hand, five persons were pursuing degrees in administration, two in engineering, two in oceanography (fishing), two in sociology, and one each studied economics, business, and psychology. It may be speculated that such occupational goals lend themselves to a greater concern for the practical application that work in SINAMOS promised.

Finally, in that particular capacitation course, 80 percent of the students attended the smaller, private universities or institutes. In general terms this indicates an educational atmosphere that is more likely to be academic than political, and an orientation that is more likely to be conservative than radical. For many students, belonging to a SINAMOS group was not something they discussed at school, and several avoided having their pictures taken at Azcarrunz to spare unwanted confrontations with campus activists. The majority of the "core" workers for TPU was in most respects nonpartisan. This is not to say, however, that they were nonpolitical.

Conclusions

Returning to the questions posed at the beginning of this chapter and relating them to the specific case study, we should now ask—to what extent did the students of TPU "participate"? There is no doubt that those who joined did so voluntarily. There were alternatives available to the activities of TPU, and the benefits were not of a nature that there was subtle pressure to become a member; in fact, if anything, peer opinion inhibited the growth of this group. For the most part, TPU attracted students who wanted to work, who wanted to make concrete social contributions. SINAMOS had the resources to mobilize and sponsor such activities.

The "freedom of choice" allowed TPU in regard to the election of leaders and policy formation varied. Their choice of leaders within a *brigada* (formed from those who participated in the same capacitation course or *salida*) was completely democratic, decided upon by the members. Some possible candidates, of course, are "selected out" early by their unwillingness to adhere to norms established by the organizing agency. In terms of policy formulation and action, it must be noted that TPU was an official group. The broad guideline to action was that it be system supportive, i.e., fostering national development in a nonpartisan, noncompetitive manner. Which specific activities fell into this category were determined by the participants only with the concurrence of the government's liaison. At least initially, decisions as to work projects originated with the ONAMS or ORAMS bureaucracy. This was to be expected as the groups had little experience. But, as they grew to form a unit that had lived together in the countryside, worked side by side on the outskirts of Lima, organized jointly in the schools, or traveled as a group to Cuba, they increased their skills and their demands. As they believed in the participatory nature of their organization, it was not surprising that the leaders of the TPU *brigadas* of Lima were in the forefront as a competitive political force at the *II Encuentro Nacional de Voluntarios* (Second National Volunteers' Encounter) when the national organization created the *Comité Coordinador de la Juventud Revolucionaria*. This coordinating committee was concerned with the support of the revolution and therefore formed units of the *Juventud de la Revolución Peruana* (Youth for the Peruvian Revolution—JRP), which since spring 1975 has backed the call to establish a broadly based political movement dedicated to the ideals set forth during the Velasco administration, or the "first phase" of the Peruvian Revolution.[13]

The civilian ideologues of the first phase had attempted to separate the revolutionary process from traditional politics. For eight years they sought to avoid having their goals reduced to yet another partisan position on the already crowded Peruvian political spectrum. Thus, their dogmatic pursuit of nondogmatic solutions and their eclectic search for nonideological and non-foreign alternatives led to the creation of an innovative participatory network stimulated by SINAMOS. But the government's denial of its political potential was both hypocritical and shortsighted. When civilian *promotores* played an overtly political role (partisan for the revolutionary process), the organization was criticized based on the military's interpretation of its nonpartisan stance. On the other hand, not to use the grassroots organizations in a partisan (prorevolutionary) manner deprived the process of a significant popular base.

This is perhaps the crux of a very complex matter. SINAMOS, with its revolutionary ideals, its grassroots structure, and its participationist opportunities and experiences, could have developed its political potential into a dynamic movement that the military could not control. This possibility was foreshadowed by the inauguration of the National Agrarian Confederation (CNA) in 1974 which brought together more than 16,000 grassroots organizations that had been grouped into 120 regional leagues and then into 18 departmental federations. This confederation and the others to follow were to be the capstones of the process initiated by SINAMOS. According to the Plan Inca they were the entities to which power would be transfered as the revolution progressed, replacing elections based on party politics and the de facto military rule.

Far from being as easily controlled as the base units, the CNA proved to be strong enough to have its demands heeded by military decision makers. Philosophical splits became evident in the military leadership, however, as other popular organizations took their ideopolitical capacitation seriously and began to demand the same progressive development to participation in decision making at the national level. Since the Morales government took over in August 1975, it has deemphasized the economic participation reforms of the Velasco government in the labor and industrial communities, while re-emphasizing the private property sector of the economy. The stated goal of transferring political power to the *organized* populace has become less important in the "second phase" of the revolution. The CNA and the JRP, along with the other mass groups,[14] now find they are no longer the official channels of participation *in* the political system, but rather that they are in competition with pre-1968 political groups for influence *upon* the political system.

It might be said that the atrophy of SINAMOS' promotional activities has been due as much to its success as to its failure. The grassroots organizations have been system supportive, but at least a part of the military seems unsure if that "system" includes the military administration, or is limited to the ideals of the revolutionary process as expounded by the *promotores* of SINAMOS.

From this discussion we might draw some tentative conclusions about the quality of participation in government-sponsored organizations. First, the government's intent is rarely to create a mere mechanism for participation. Some outcome is expected, whether it be system stability, adherence to constitutional principles, dedication to national development, etc. Thus, the greater the congruence of the definition of goals between these groups and the national decision makers, the greater will be their satisfaction, participation in, and influence upon the national leadership. That is, the greater will be their ability to select leaders, formulate policies, and implement decisions regarding the activities of their own groups' interests. Participation is most meaningful when national goals are agreed upon and official channels for participation are theoretically and actually important.

If, however, the national leadership is ambiguous in its definition of goals, the quality of participation by official groups diminishes. The government makes loyalty to itself the highest value. Factions compete for control of such groups as instruments in a power struggle, forcing ideological ridgity. Or, competition among groups may neutralize all their possibilities of influence. Participation in this situation is manipulated, frustrated, or ineffective.

Finally, when official groups are more attracted to the promises of the regime than the personnel, and critically evaluate performance, they may find their official status suspended or at least challenged. While the parameters for action are limited for the sponsored group, their access to resources is a considerable incentive to remain in favor. Yet, the more successful the initial politicization and mobilization of the population, the more resources, time, and effort spent on training, education, and consciousness-raising, the more self-sufficient these organizations become. Once they are willing to jeopardize their status for their principles, the harder it is for the government to eliminate their impact upon the political system, even though their activities may no longer have legitimate sanction. Many an administration has found itself the "victim" of the consequences of the participatory process it promoted.

Notes

1.   Verba and Nie (1972, p. 2) make the distinction that "support" or "ceremonial" participation is actually a means of coopting the participants for the benefit of the regime, whereas "democratic" participation works the other way, the regime responding to the influence that has surged upwards. I believe this distinction is not so clear-cut in practice.

2.   Delgado's role as theoretician was so visible that after the announcement of his appointment to be Superior Director of SINAMOS, the daily *Ultima Hora* declared that he actually wrote all the speeches for Velasco and that the ideology and plans of the revolution were not the collective efforts of COAP, but rather the work of Delgado alone. President Velasco vehemently denied this insinuation (Pease and Verme 1974, pp. 287-88, II).

3.   There were 10 regions and more than 40 zones in 1972; in 1974 there were 11 regions and 52 zones; by 1976 there were more than 70 zones in 10 regions once again as two ORAMS in Lima were combined.

4.   Office seminars were mandatory, attendance would be taken even for international civil servants working in Peruvian agencies.

5.   The mean scores for the 1,184 *promotores* on the ideopolitical parts of the examination were: World Social-Political Phenomena—78.0, Peruvian Reality—80.6, Revolutionary Process—74.1, SINAMOS Policy—78.8 (SINAMOS 1974).

6.   The mean score for Popular Promotion was 72.9 and for Grassroots Planning it was 67.0 (SINAMOS 1974).

7.   See Joost Kuitenbrouwer (1973) for an excellent discussion of the ambivalent attitude the military adopted toward the revolutionary process. He notes their position first in the nature of a military government and secondly from strategic and practical considerations. Only from their perspective that the "people were the objects of their good intentions" is it possible to understand how the military could initiate radical economic changes yet be bewildered by ensuing social and political transformations.

8.   Interview with government functionary, Dirección de Capacitación, ONAMS, December 6, 1974.

9.   Interview with government functionary, Dirección de Areas Juveniles, ONAMS, September 18, 1974.

10.   Interview with government functionary, Oficina de Areas Juveniles, OZAMS IV, May 28, 1974.

11.   This information was gathered from students informally from August to December 1974. As I was participant in many TPU projects, I had first-hand knowledge of some individuals' attitudes and opinions. My observations were unable to be verified scientifically, however, as the use of questionnaires and foreigners doing contemporary research were looked upon with suspicion during these months.

12.   Interview with a student at San Marcos University who now works for the National Office for Statistics and Censuses, November 23, 1974.

13.   The first phase of the process roughly coincides with Velasco's administration and is marked by seven years of revolutionary initiatives in the political, social, and economic systems of Peru. When Francisco Morales Bermúdez took over in August 1975, he promised to continue the revolution. Gradually, however, differences emerged as the Velasco appointees were made to feel uncomfortable, retired early, resigned, were purged or eventually exiled. Dedication to establishing the social property sector of the economy was slowed down and then eliminated. The promise of elections signaled the revival of the traditional political parties and politicians instead of a transfer of power to the organized populace. The differences had become so obvious by 1976 that a practical division had to be made in the process even if symbolic continuity was necessary. The ideologues of the "first phase," adherents of the Plan Inca are now called subversive as they label the "second phase's" Plan Tupac Amaru a reversal of the revolution.

14.   The other mass organizations formed in the first phase of the process were: Central de Trabajadores de la Revolución (CTRP), the Associación Nacional de Trabajadores del Arte (ANTA), the Central de Profesionales de la Revolución Peruana (CPRP), and the Sindicato de Educadores de la Revolución Peruana (SERP).

Collected Bibliography

AARON, HENRY
 1967 "Social Security: International Comparisons." In Otto Eckstein, ed., *Studies in the Economics of Income Maintenance*. Washington, D.C.: Brookings Institution.

ADAMS, RICHARD NEWBOLD
 1959 *A Community in the Andes: Problems and Progress in Muquiyauyo*. Seattle: University of Washington Press.

 1967a "Political Power and Social Structures." In Claudio Veliz, ed., *The Politics of Conformity in Latin America*. New York: Oxford University Press.

 1967b *The Second Sowing: Power and Secondary Development in Latin America*. San Francisco: Chandler.

 1970 *Crucifixion by Power: Essays on Guatemalan National Social Structure, 1944-1966*. Austin: University of Texas Press.

 forth- "The Structure of Participation: A Commentary." In Mitchell A.
 coming Seligson and John A. Booth, eds., *Political Participation in Latin America*, volume 2: *Politics and the Poor*. New York: Holmes and Meier Publishers.

ADAMS, ROBERT M.
 1976 "Ancient Incas and Modern Revolution." *The New York Review of Books* 23 (March 18): 43-47.

ADIE, ROBERT F., AND GUY E. POITRAS
 1974 *Latin America: The Politics of Immobility*. Englewood Cliffs, N.J.: Prentice-Hall.

ADIZES, ICHAK
 1971 *Industrial Democracy: Yugoslav Style*. New York: Free Press.

ALEXANDER, ROBERT J.
 1964 "The Emergence of Modern Political Parties in Latin America." In J. Maier and R. W. Weatherhead, eds., *Politics of Change in Latin America*. New York: Praeger.

 1969 *The Communist Party of Venezuela*. Stanford: Hoover Institution Press.

ALMOND, GABRIEL A., AND G. BINGHAM POWELL, JR.
 1966 *Comparative Politics: A Developmental Approach*. Boston: Little, Brown.

ALMOND, GABRIEL A., AND SIDNEY VERBA
1965   *The Civic Culture: Political Attitudes and Democracy in Five Nations.* Boston: Little, Brown.

ANDERSON, CHARLES W.
1967   *Politics and Economic Change in Latin America: The Governing of Restless Nations.* Princeton: Van Nostrand.

ANDERSON, THOMAS P.
1971   *Matanza: El Salvador's Communist Revolt of 1932.* Lincoln: University of Nebraska Press.

ARENDT, HANNAH
1969   *On Violence.* New York: Harcourt, Brace and World.

ARISTOTLE
1962   *Politics (Aristotle's Politics).* Oxford: Clarendon Press.

ARROBA, GONZALO
1969   "Social Security Schemes and the National Economy in the Developing Countries." *International Social Security Review* 22 (no. 1): 28-60.

BACHRACH, PETER
1966   *The Theory of Democratic Elitism: A Critique.* Boston: Little, Brown.

BACHRACH, PETER, AND MORTON S. BARATZ
1963   "Decisions and Non-Decisions: An Analytical Framework." *American Political Science Review* 57 (September): 632-642.

BAILEY, NORMAN A.
1967   *"La Violencia* in Colombia." *Journal of Inter-American Studies and World Affairs* 9 (October): 561-575.

BAKER, TANYA, AND MARY BIRD
1959   "Urbanisation and the Position of Women." *Sociological Review* 7 (new series, July): 99-122.

BALOYRA, ENRIQUE A., AND JOHN D. MARTZ
1976a   "Classical Participation in Venezuela: Campaigning and Voting in 1973." Paper presented to the Seminar on the Faces of Participation in Latin America: A New Look at Citizen Action in Society, San Antonio, Texas, (November 12-13).
1976b   *Political Attitudes in Venezuela, A Report to the National Science Foundation.* Chapel Hill, N.C.

BAMBIRRA, VANIA
1972   "The Chilean Woman . . ." In *New Chile,* prepared by the North American Congress on Latin America. Berkeley: NACLA.

BARRY, BRIAN
1970   *Sociologists, Economists and Democracy.* London: Collier-Macmillan.

BAYER, DAVID L.
1975   *Reforma agraria peruana: descapitalización del minifundio y formación de la burguesía rural.* Lima: Universidad Nacional Agraria La Molina, Centro de Investigaciones Socio-Económicas.

BAYLIS, THOMAS A.
1976a   "Participation without Conflict: Socialist Democracy in the German Democratic Republic." *East Central Europe* 3 (no. 1): 30-43.
1976b   "Socialist Democracy in the Workplace: The Orthodox and Self-Management Models." In Andrew Janos, ed., *Authoritarian Politics in Communist Europe*. Berkeley: Institute of International Studies.

BEALEY, FRANK, J. BLONDEL AND W. P. MCCANN
1965   *Constituency Politics: A Study of Newcastle-Under-Lyme*. London: Faber and Faber.

BELL, JOHN PATRICK
1971   *Crisis in Costa Rica: The 1948 Revolution*. Austin: University of Texas Press.

BELNAP, DAVID
1974   "Women Played Big Role in Allende Fall: Pressure Both Subtle and Obvious Forced Military's Hand." *The Capitol Times* (February 4).

BENGELSDORPF, CAROLEE
1976   "A Large School of Government." *Cuba Review* 6 (September): 3-18.

BENNETT, STEPHEN E.
1973   "Consistency Among the Public's Social Welfare Policy Attitudes in the 1960's." *American Journal of Political Science* 17 (August): 544-570.

BERELSON, BERNARD R., PAUL F. LAZARSFELD AND WILLIAM N. MCPHEE
1954   *Voting: A Study of Opinion Formation in a Presidential Campaign*. Chicago: University of Chicago Press.

1966   *Voting: A Study of Opinion Formation in a Presidential Campaign*. Phoenix Edition. Chicago: University of Chicago Press.

BERGER, PETER L.
1976   *Pyramids of Sacrifice, Political Ethics and Social Change*. Garden City: Anchor Books.

BERNS, WALTER
1968   "A Critique of Berelson, Lazarsfeld and McPhee's *Voting*." In Norman R. Luttbeg, ed., *Public Opinion and Public Policy: Models of Political Linkage*. Homewood, Illinois: Dorsey Press.

BILES, ROBERT E.
1972   "Patronage Politics: Electoral Behavior in Uruguay." Baltimore: Ph.D. dissertation, Johns Hopkins University.

1975   "Social Class and Political Behavior in Latin America: An Uruguayan Case Study." Paper presented at the annual meeting of the Southwestern Political Science Association, San Antonio, Texas (March).

1976a   "Modes of Political Participation in Uruguay." Paper presented at the national meeting of the Latin American Studies Association, Atlanta (March).

1976b   "Political Involvement and Political Behavior in Uruguay." Paper presented at the annual meeting of the Southwestern Political Science Association, Dallas, Texas (April).

1976c   "Political Participation in Uruguay: Structure, Extent, and Sources." Paper presented at the Seminar on the Faces of Participation in Latin America: A New Look at Citizen Action in Society, San Antonio, Texas (November 12-13).

1977   "The Semi-Liberated Women: Female Political Behavior in Uruguay." Paper presented at the annual meeting of the Southwestern Political Science Association, Dallas, Texas (April).

BINDER, LEONARD, ET AL.
1971   *Crises and Sequences in Political Development.* Princeton: Princeton University Press.

BLAISIER, COLE
1967   "Studies of Social Revolution: Origins in Mexico, Bolivia and Cuba." *Latin American Research Review* 2 (summer): 28-64.

BLAU, PETER
1960   "Structural Effects." *American Sociological Review* 25 (April): 178-93.

BLOOM, REYNOLD
1976   "The Chilean *Campesinado*—The Political Implications of Socio-Economic Diversity." Paper presented at the Seminar on the Faces of Participation in Latin America: A New Look at Citizen Action in Society, San Antonio, Texas (November 12-13).

BLUM, FRED H.
1968   *Work and Community: The Scott Bader Commonwealth and the Quest for a New Social Order.* London: Routledge and Kegan Paul.

BLUMBERG, PAUL
1969   *Industrial Democracy: The Sociology of Participation.* New York: Schocken.

BLUTSTEIN, HOWARD I., ET AL.
1971   *Area Handbook for Cuba.* Washington, D.C.: Government Printing Office.

BONACHEA, RAMÓN L., AND MARTA SAN MARTÍN
1974   *The Cuban Insurrection, 1952-1959.* New Brunswick: Transaction.

BONI, FELIX G., AND MITCHELL A. SELIGSON
1973   "Applying Quantitative Techniques to Quantitative History: The Case of Mexico." *Latin American Research Review* 8 (summer): 105-110.

BONILLA, FRANK
1964   "The Urban Worker." In John J. Johnson, ed., *Continuity and Change in Latin America.* Stanford: Stanford University Press.

BOOTH, JOHN A.
1974   "Rural Violence in Colombia: 1958-1963." *Western Political Quarterly* 27 (December): 657-679.

1975a   "Democracy and Citizen Action in Costa Rica: The Modes and Correlates of Popular Participation in Politics." Austin: Ph.D. dissertation, The University of Texas at Austin.

1975b   "Organizational Processes in the Growing Community: Strategies for Development." *Journal of the Community Development Society* 6 (spring): 13-26.

1976   "A Replication: Modes of Political Participation in Costa Rica." *Western Political Quarterly* 29 (December): 627-633.

1977a   "Political Participation in Latin America: Levels, Structure, Concentration, and Rationality." Paper presented at the Latin American Studies Association Meeting, Houston, Texas (November).

1977b   "Reason, Political Activism and Democracy: A Test of Participant Rationality in Costa Rica." Paper presented at the Southwestern Political Science Association Meeting, Dallas, Texas (April).

BOOTH, JOHN A., MIGUEL MONDOL VELÁSQUEZ AND
ALVARO HERNÁNDEZ CARVAJAL
1973   *Tipología de comunidades, Tomo II: Estudio para una tipología de comunidades.* San José, Costa Rica: Dirección Nacional de Desarrollo de la Comunidad-Acción Internacional Técnica.

BOOTH, JOHN A., AND MITCHELL A. SELIGSON
1976   "Peasant Political Participation: An Analysis Using Two Costa Rican Samples." Paper presented to the Seminar on the Faces of Participation in Latin America: A New Look at Citizen Action in Society, San Antonio, Texas (November 12-13).

BORÓN, ATILIO ALBERTO
1975   "The Popular Classes and the Politics of Change in Latin America." In Joseph Tulchin, ed., *Latin America in the Year 2000.* Reading, Mass.: Addison-Wesley.

BORRICAUD, FRANCOIS
1964   "Lima en la vida política peruana." *América Latina* 7 (October-December): 89-96.

BOURNE, RICHARD
1970   *Political Leaders of Latin America.* New York: Alfred A. Knopf.

BOURQUE, SUSAN C., AND DAVID SCOTT PALMER
1975   "Transforming the Rural Sector: Government Policy and Peasant Response." In Abraham F. Lowenthal, ed., *The Peruvian Experiment: Change under Military Rule.* Princeton, N.J.: Princeton University Press.

BOURQUE, SUSAN C., AND KAY B. WARREN
forth-   "Female Participation, Perception and Power: An Examination of
coming   Two Andean Communities." In Mitchell A. Seligson and John A. Booth, ed., *Political Participation in Latin America,* volume 2: *Politics and the Poor.* New York: Holmes and Meier Publishers.

BROEKMEYER, M. J.,ED.
1970   *Yugoslav Workers' Self Management.* Boston: Reidel Publishing Company.

BROWN, STEVEN R. AND RICHARD W. TAYLOR
    1973   "Frames of Reference and the Observation of Behavior." *Social Science Quarterly* 54 (June): 29-40.

BURNETT, BEN G.
    1970   *Political Groups in Chile: The Dialogue between Order and Change.* Austin: The University of Texas Press.

BWY, DOUGLAS P.
    1968   "Political Instability in Latin America: The Cross-Cultural Test of a Causal Model." *Latin American Research Review* 3 (spring): 17-89.

BYARS, ROBERT S.
    1973   "Culture, Politics and the Urban Factory Worker in Brazil: The Case of Zé Maria." In Robert E. Scott, ed., *Latin American Modernization Problems.* Urbana: University of Illinois Press.

CAMPBELL, ANGUS
    1962   "The Passive Citizen." *Acta Sociologica* 6:9-21.

CAMPBELL, ANGUS, PHILIP E. CONVERSE, WARREN E. MILLER AND DONALD S. STOKES
    1960   *The American Voter.* New York: Wiley.
    1964   *The American Voter: An Abridgement.* New York: Wiley.

CAMPBELL, ANGUS, GERALD GURIN AND WARREN E. MILLER
    1954   *The Voter Decides.* Evanston, Illinois: Row, Peterson.

CASALS, LOURDES
    1975   "On Popular Power: The Organization of the Cuban State during the Period of Transition." *Latin American Perspectives* 2 (no. 4): 78-88.

CASTILLO, HERNÁN
    1964   "Chaquicocha: Community in Progress." Ithaca, N.Y.: (Socio-economic Development of Andean Communities, Report No. 5) Department of Anthropology, Cornell University.

CASTRO, FIDEL
    1970a   "Speech on the 10th Anniversary of the FMC." *Granma Weekly Review* (August 30): 1-6.
    1970b   "Speech on the 10th Anniversary of the CDR." *Granma Weekly Review* (October 4): 2-4.
    1976   "Report of the Central Committee of the Communist Party of Cuba to the First Congress." In *First Congress of the Communist Party of Cuba.* Moscow: Progress Publishers.

CASTRO, RAÚL
    1974   "Speech on the 15th Anniversary of the Triumph of the Revolution." *Granma Weekly Review* (January 13): 2-3.

CENTRO LATINOAMERICANO DE ECONOMÍA HUMANA (CLEH)
    1963   *Situación económica y social del Uruguay rural.* Montevideo: Ministerio de Ganadería y Agricultura.

CHAFFEE, WILBER A., JR.
    1975   "A Theoretical Look at Revolutions with Case Studies from Latin

America." Austin: Ph.D. dissertation, The University of Texas at Austin.

1976   "Entrepreneurs and Economic Behavior: A New Approach to the Study of Latin American Politics." *Latin American Research Review* 11 (no. 3): 55-68.

1977   "A Rational Choice Model of Mass Participation in Politics." Paper presented to the Southwestern Political Science Association Meeting, Dallas, Texas (April).

forth-   "Let Jorge Do It: A Rational Choice Model of Political Partici-
coming   pation." Mitchell A. Seligson and John A. Booth, eds., *Political Participation in Latin America,* volume 2: *Politics and the Poor.* New York: Holmes and Meier Publishers.

CHALMERS, DOUGLAS A.
1974-75   "Partidos políticos y sociedad en América Latina." *Estudios Andinos* 10 (no. 1): 39-83.

CHAMBERLAIN, J. P.
1942   *The First Inter-American Conference on Social Security, Santiago de Chile, September 10-16, 1942.* New York: Carnegie.

CHANEY, ELSA M.
1971   "Women in Latin American Politics: The Case of Peru and Chile." Madison: Ph.D. dissertation, The University of Wisconsin.

1973   "Women in Latin American Politics: The Case of Peru and Chile." In Ann Pescatello, ed., *Female and Male in Latin America.* Pittsburgh: The University of Pittsburgh Press.

1974   "The Mobilization of Women in Allende's Chile." In Jane S. Jaquette, ed., *Women in Politics.* New York: John Wiley and Sons.

1977   Personal correspondence with Dr. Chaney.

CHAPLIN, DAVID, ED.
1976   *Peruvian Nationalism: A Corporatist Revolution.* New Brunswick, N.J.: Transaction.

CHAPMAN, PHILLIP C., AND LAWRENCE A. SCAFF
1976   "The Use and Abuse of Politics." *Polity* 8 (summer): 529-557.

CHONCHOL, JACQUES
1965   "Land Tenure and Development in Latin America." In Claudio Veliz, ed., *Obstacles to Change in Latin America.* New York: Oxford University Press.

CIRIA, ALBERTO
1974   *Parties and Power in Modern Argentina (1930-1946).* Albany: SUNY Press.

CLARK, KATE
1972   *Reality and Prospects of Popular Unity.* London: Lawrence and Wishart.

CLARK, ROBERT P., JR.
1974   *Development and Instability.* Hinsdale, Ill.: Dryden Press.

CLARKE, JAMES W.
1973   "Race and Political Behavior." In Kent S. Miller and Ralph M. Dreger, eds., *Blacks and Whites in the United States.* New York: Seminar Press.

CLEAVES, PETER S., AND MARTIN J. SCURRAH
1976   "State-Society Relations and Bureaucratic Behavior in Peru." SICA Series No. 6, Hayward, Cal.: California State University.

COBB, ROGER W.
1973   "The Belief-System Perspective: An Assessment of a Framework." *Journal of Politics* 35 (February): 121-153.

COBB, ROGER W., AND CHARLES D. ELDER
1972   *Participation in American Politics: The Dynamics of Agenda Building.* Boston: Allyn and Bacon.

COHEN, CARL
1973   *Democracy.* New York: The Free Press.

COLEMAN, JAMES S.
1971   "The Development Syndrome: Differentiation-Equality-Capacity." In Leonard Binder, et al., *Crises and Sequences in Political Development.* Princeton: Princeton University Press.

COLLEVER, O. ANDREW
1965   *Birth Rates in Latin America: New Estimates of Historical Trends and Fluctuations.* Berkeley: University of California Institute of International Studies.

COLLIER, DAVID, AND ROBERT MESSICK
1975   "Prerequisites versus Diffusion: Testing Alternative Explanations of Social Security Adoption." *American Political Science Review* 69 (December): 1299-1315.

COMERCIO EXTERIOR
1975   "Peru: Abortive Attempt at Insurrection; Recent Economic Evolution." (March): 97-99.

COMITÉ DE ASESORAMIENTO DE LA PRESIDENCIA DE LA REPÚBLICA (COAP)
1974   *La Revolución Nacional Peruana: Manifiesto, Plan, Estatuto del Gobierno Revolucionario de la Fuerza Armada.* Lima.

CONFEDERACIÓN DE TRABAJADORES DE CUBA (CTC)
1973   "Theses of the 13th Congress of the CTC." *Granma Weekly Review* (September 2): 7-12.

CONSTITUTION OF THE ORGANS OF PEOPLE'S POWER
1975   *Constitution of the Organs of People's Power.* New York: Center for Cuban Studies.

CONVERSE, PHILIP E.
1968   "The Nature of Belief Systems in Mass Publics." In Norman R. Luttbeg, ed., *Public Opinion and Public Policy: Models of Political Linkage.* Homewood, Ill.: Dorsey Press.

CORNELIUS, WAYNE A.
1971   "The Political Sociology of Cityward Migration in Latin America: Toward Empirical Theory." In Francine F. Rabinovitz and Felicity M. Trueblood, eds., *Latin American Urban Research, Volume I.* Beverly Hills: Sage.

1974 "Urbanization and Political Demand-Making: Political Participation among the Migrant Poor in Latin American Cities." *American Political Science Review* 68 (September): 1125-1146.

1975 *Politics and the Migrant Poor in Mexico City.* Stanford: Stanford University Press.

CORNELIUS, WAYNE A., AND HENRY A. DIETZ
1976 "Urbanización, formulación de demandas y sobrecarga del sistema político." *Revista Latinoamericana de Estudios Urbano Regionales (EURE)* 5 (June): 9-46.

COTLER, JULIO
1969 "Crisis política y populismo militar en el Perú." Lima: Instituto de Estudios Peruanos.

COX, ROBERT W., AND HAROLD K. JACOBSON, EDS.
1973 *The Anatomy of Influence: Decision Making in International Organizations.* New Haven: Yale University Press.

CRICK, BERNARD
1964 *In Defense of Politics.* Baltimore: Penguin Books.

CUBA SOCIALISTA
1962 *Cuba Socialista* 9 (May): 129-132.

CURRELL, MELVILLE
1974 *Political Woman.* London: Croom Helm.

CZUDNOWSKI, MOSHE M.
1968 "A Salience Dimension of Politics for the Study of Political Culture." *American Political Science Review* 62 (September): 878-888.

1976 *Comparing Political Behavior.* Beverly Hills: Sage Publications.
DAHL, ROBERT A.
1956 *A Preface to Democratic Theory.* Chicago: University of Chicago Press.

1970 "Power to the Workers?" *New York Review of Books* 15 (November 19): 20-24.

DAHRENDORF, RALF
1959 *Class and Class Conflict in Industrial Society.* Stanford: Stanford University Press.

1967 *Society and Democracy in Germany.* Garden City, New York: Doubleday Anchor.

DANIELSON, JAMES L.
1974 "The Classical Model of Democratic Political Participation." Paper delivered at the annual meeting of the Southwestern Political Science Association, Dallas, Texas (March 28).

DAVIES, THOMAS M., JR.
1971 "The Indigenismo of the Peruvian Aprista Party: A Reinterpretation." *Hispanic American Historical Review* 51 (November): 626-645.

DAVIS, TOM E.
1964 "Dualism, Stagnation, and Inequality: The Impact of Pension Legislation in the Chilean Labor Market." *Industrial and Labor Relations Review* 17 (April): 380-398.

DEALY, GLEN
1974 "The Tradition of Monistic Democracy in Latin America." In Howard J. Wiarda, ed., *Politics and Social Change in Latin America: The Distinct Tradition.* Amherst, Mass.: University of Massachusetts Press.

DE LAS CASAS GRIEVE, ANGEL
1975 *Propiedad social: La empresa de la Revolución.* Lima: Ediciones CONAPS.

DELGADO OLIVERA, CARLOS
1973 *Testimonio de Lucha.* Lima: Ediciones PEISA.

DENNIS, JACK
1970 "Support for the Institution of Elections by the Mass Public." *American Political Science Review* 64 (September): 819-835.

DENTON, CHARLES F.
1971 *Patterns of Costa Rican Politics.* Boston: Allyn and Bacon.

DENTON, CHARLES F., AND PRESTON L. LAWRENCE
1972 *Latin American Politics: A Functional Approach.* San Francisco: Chandler.

DEWEY, JOHN
1927 *The Public and Its Problems.* Denver: Swallow.

DIÉGUEZ, HÉCTOR, AND ALBERTO PETRECOLLA
1974 "La distribución funcional del ingreso y el sistema previsional en la Argentina, 1950-1972." *Desarrollo Económico* 55 (December): 423-440.

DIETZ, HENRY A.
1974 "Becoming a Poblador: Political Adjustment to the Urban Environment in Lima, Peru." Stanford, California: Ph.D. dissertation, Stanford University.

1977a "Bureaucratic Demand-Making and Clientelistic Participation in Peru." In James Malloy, ed., *Authoritarianism and Corporatism in Latin America.* Pittsburgh, Pa.: University of Pittsburgh Press.

1977b "Some Modes of Participation in an Authoritarian Regime: The Case of Lima, Peru." *Journal of Political and Military Sociology* 5 (spring): 63-77.

DIETZ, HENRY A., AND RICHARD J. MOORE
1977 "Some Modes of Participation in a Non-Electoral Setting: The Poblador in Lima, Peru." Paper presented to the Conference on the Political Economy of Sun Belt Cities, Austin, Texas (January).

DIPALMA, GIUSEPPE
1970 *Apathy and Participation: Mass Politics in Western Societies.* New York: The Free Press.

DIRECCIÓN DE CAPACITACIÓN
1974 "Rol y ubicación de las unidades de capacitación en el SINAMOS," Lima: SINAMOS, mimeographed.

DIRECCIÓN DE ESTADÍSTICA Y CENSOS (CHILE)
1964 *Censo de Población, 1960.* Santiago de Chile.

DIRECCIÓN DEL REGISTRO ELECTORAL
1958   *Resultado elección presidencial, 4 de sept. de 1958.* Santiago de Chile: mimeographed.
1964   *Elección presidencial, 4 de sept. 1964.* Santiago de Chile: mimeographed.
1965   *Elección ordinaria de diputados: varones y mujeres, 7 de marzo de 1965.* Santiago de Chile: mimeographed.
1969   *Elección ordinaria de Congreso Nacional (domingo 2 de marzo de 1969).* Santiago de Chile: mimeographed.
1970   *Elección ordinaria de presidente de la república (viernes 4 de septiembre de 1970).* Santiago de Chile: mimeographed.

DIRECCIÓN GENERAL DE ESTADÍSTICA Y CENSO (URUGUAY)
1969   *IV Censo de población y II de vivienda, datos definitivos, cifras principales.* Montevideo.

DIRECCIÓN GENERAL DE ESTADÍSTICA Y CENSOS (COSTA RICA)
1975   *Censos nacionales del 1973: Población.* San José, Costa Rica.

DI TELLA, TORCUATO
1965   "Populism and Reform in Latin America." In Claudio Veliz, ed., *Obstacles to Change in Latin America.* New York: Oxford University Press.

DOBYNS, HENRY F.
1964   *The Social Matrix of Peruvian Indigenous Communities.* Ithaca, New York: Cornell Peru Project Monograph, Department of Anthropology, Cornell University.

DOUGHTY, PAUL L.
1968   *Huaylas: An Andean District in Search of Progress.* Ithaca, New York: Cornell University Press.

DOWNS, ANTHONY
1957   *An Economic Theory of Democracy.* New York: Harper and Row.

DOWSE, ROBERT E., AND JOHN A. HUGHES
1971   "Girls, Boys, and Politics." *British Journal of Sociology* 22 (March): 53-67.

DUFF, ERNEST A., AND JOHN F. MCCAMANT (WITH WALTRAUD Q. MORALES)
1976   *Violence and Repression in Latin America: A Quantitative and Historical Analysis.* New York: The Free Press.

DUNCAN, OTIS DUDLEY
1975   *Introduction to Structural Equation Models.* New York: Academic Press.

DUVERGER, MAURICE
1955   *The Political Role of Women.* Paris: United Nations Educational, Scientific and Cultural Organization.

ECLA (ECONOMIC COMMISSION FOR LATIN AMERICA)
1968   "Social Security and Development: The Latin American Experience." *Economic Bulletin for Latin America* 13 (November): 32-48.

EDELMANN, ALEXANDER T.
1969   *Latin American Government and Politics: The Dynamics of a Revolutionary Society.* Homewood, Ill.: Dorsey Press.

EINAUDI, LUIGI R.
1973   "Revolution From Within? Military Rule in Peru Since 1968." *Studies in Comparative International Development* 8 (spring): 71-87.

EINAUDI, LUIGI R., AND ALFRED C. STEPAN III
1971   *Latin American Institutional Development:Changing Military Perspectives in Peru and Brazil.* Santa Monica, Cal.: Rand Corporation.

EUBEN, J. PETER
1970   "Political Science and Political Silence." In P. Green and S. Levinson, eds., *Power and Community.* New York: Vintage Books.

FABREGAT, JULIO T.
1964   *Elecciones uruguayas: . . . 1962.* Montevideo: Cámara de Senadores.

1968   *Elecciones uruguayas: . . . 1966.* Montevideo: Cámara de Senadores.

1972   *Elecciones uruguayas: . . . 1971. Montevideo:* Cámara de Senadores.

FAGEN, RICHARD R.
1969   *The Transformation of Political Culture in Cuba.* Stanford: Stanford University Press.

1972   "Continuities in Cuban Revolutionary Politics." *Monthly Review* 23 (April): 24-48.

FAGEN, RICHARD R., AND WILLIAM S. TUOHY
1972   *Politics and Privilege in a Mexican City.* Stanford: Stanford University Press.

FEIERABEND, IVO K., AND ROSALIND L. FEIERABEND
1966   "Aggressive Behaviors within Polities, 1948-1962: A Cross National Study." *Journal of Conflict Resolution* 10 (September): 249-271.

FEIERABEND, IVO K., ROSALIND L. FEIERABEND AND BETTY A. NESVOLD
1969   "Social Change and Political Violence: Cross-National Patterns." In H. D. Graham and T. R. Gurr, eds., *Violence in America: Historical and Comparative Perspectives.* Washington, D.C.: National Commission on the Causes and Prevention of Violence.

FENNESSEY, JAMES
1968   "The General Linear Model: A New Perspective on Some Familiar Topics." *American Journal of Sociology* 74 (July): 1-27.

FIGUEROA, ADOLFO, AND RICHARD WEBB
1975   *Distribución del ingreso en el Perú.* Lima: Instituto de Estudios Peruanos.

FISHEL, JOHN T.
1976   "Modes of Participation in a Limited Democracy: A Highland District in Peru." Paper presented to the Seminar on the Faces of

Participation in Latin America: A New Look at Citizen Action in Society, San Antonio, Texas (November 12-13).

forth-
coming
"Communal Participation in a Highland Peruvian District." In Mitchell A. Seligson and John A. Booth, eds., *Political Participation in Latin America,* volume 2: *Politics and the Poor.* New York: Holmes & Meier Publishers.

FITZGERALD E. V. K.
1976   *The State and Economic Development: Peru Since 1968.* London: Cambridge University Press.

FITZGIBBON, RUSSELL H.
1957   "The Party Potpourri in Latin America." *Western Political Quarterly* 10 (March): 3-22.

1971   *Latin America: A Panorama of Contemporary Politics.* New York: Appleton-Century-Crofts.

FLANIGAN, WILLIAM H., AND NANCY H. ZINGALE
1975   *Political Behavior of the American Electorate.* 3rd edition. Boston: Allyn and Bacon.

FLORES OLEA, VICTOR
1967   "On Political Science in Latin America: Viewpoints." In Manuel Diegues Júnior and Bryce Wood, eds., *Social Science in Latin America.* New York: Columbia University Press.

FORMAN, SHEPARD
1976   "The Extent and Significance of Peasant Political Participation in Brazil." Paper presented at the Seminar on the Faces of Participation in Latin America: A New Look at Citizen Action in Society, San Antonio, Texas (November 12–13).

forth-
coming
"The Significance of Participation: Peasants in the Politics of Brazil." In Mitchell A. Seligson and John A. Booth, eds., *Political Participation in Latin America,* volume 2: *Politics and the Poor.* New York: Holmes & Meier Publishers.

FREE, LLOYD
1960   *Attitudes of the Cuban People Toward the Castro Regime.* Institute for International Social Research.

FRIEDRICH, PAUL
1962   "Assumptions Underlying Tarascan Political Homicide." *Psychiatry* 25 (November): 315-327.

1970   *Agrarian Revolt in a Mexican Village.* Englewood Cliffs, N. J.: Prentice-Hall.

FROHLICH, NORMAN A., JOE A. OPPENHEIMER, JEFFREY A. SMITH AND ORAN R. YOUNG
1974   "A Test of Downsian Voter Rationality: 1964 Presidential Voting." Paper presented at the annual meeting of the American Political Science Association, Chicago (September).

FURTADO, CELSO
1970   *Obstacles to Development in Latin America.* Garden City, New York: Doubleday and Co.

GAETE BERRIOS, ALFREDO
1952   *El Seguro Social y el Servicio Nacional de Salud.* Santiago: Editorial Juridica.

GALLUP URUGUAY
1962a   *Sondeo político del Departamento de Montevideo.* Reference 222/61, Montevideo (February).

1962b   *Sondeo político del Departamento de Paysandú.* Reference 250/62, Montevideo (June).

1965   "Image, Attitudes and Media Study." Montevideo.

1966a   *Encuesta de opinión pública: Departamento de Canelones.* Montevideo (May).

1966b   *Encuesta: opinión política e imagen de candidatos y partidos.* Reference 569/66, Montevideo (September).

1966c   *Indice Gallup de opinión pública.* Number 68-70, Montevideo (November 30-December 30).

1968a   *Indice Gallup de opinión pública.* Number 96-97, Montevideo (May).

1968b   *Investigación de opinion pública sobre gobierno y problemática nacional.* Reference 669/12/68, Montevideo.

1968c   *Investigación sobre la problemática nacional.* Reference 642/2/68. Montevideo.

1971   *Indice Gallup de opinión pública.* Number 180-181, Montevideo (November).

GAMSON, WILLIAM A.
1968   *Power and Discontent.* Homewood, Ill.: Dorsey Press.

GARCÍA, JOSE Z.
1974   "The 1968 Velasco Coup in Peru: Causes and Policy Consequences." Albuquerque: Ph.D. dissertation, University of New Mexico.

GARCÍA CRUZ, MIGUEL
1972   *Le seguridad social en México, Tomo I (1906-1958).* Mexico: B. Costa Amic.

GARRETT-SCHESCH, PAT
1975   "The Mobilization of Women during the Popular Unity Government." *Latin American Perspectives* 2 (spring): 101-103.

GERMANI, GINO
1972   "Stages of Modernization in Latin America." In S. A. Halper and J. R. Sterling, eds., *Latin America: The Dynamics of Social Change.* New York: St. Martin's Press.

GIL, FEDERICO
1966   *The Political System of Chile.* Boston: Houghton Mifflin.

GIL, FEDERICO, AND CHARLES PARRISH
1965   *The Chilean Presidential Election of September 4, 1964.* Washington, D.C.: Institute for the Comparative Study of Political Systems.

GISSI, JORGE BUSTOS
    1976   "Mythology about Women, with Special Reference to Chile." In June Nash and Helen Icken Safa, eds., *Sex and Class in Latin America.* New York: Praeger.

GOLDRICH, DANIEL
    1965   "Toward the Comparative Study of Politicization in Latin America." In D. B. Heath and R. N. Adams, eds., *Contemporary Cultures and Societies in Latin America.* New York: Random House.

GONZÁLEZ, EDWARD
    1974   *Cuba under Castro: The Limits of Charisma.* Boston: Houghton-Mifflin.

GONZÁLEZ, MIKE
    1976   "Ideology and Culture under Popular Unity." In Philip O'Brian, ed., *Allende's Chile.* New York: Praeger.

GRANMA WEEKLY REVIEW
    1966   *Granma Weekly Review.* (August 28).
    1968a   *Granma Weekly Review.* (September 22).
    1968b   *Granma Weekly Review.* (October 6).
    1970   *Granma Weekly Review.* (October 4).
    1974a   *Granma Weekly Review.* (October 20).
    1974b   *Granma Weekly Review.* (December 1).
    1975   *Granma Weekly Review.* (August 31).
    1976a   *Granma Weekly Review.* (October 10).
    1976b   *Granma Weekly Review.* (October 17).
    1976c   *Granma Weekly Review.* (October 31).

GREAVES, THOMAS C., AND JAVIER ALBÓ
    forth-   "An Anatomy of Dependency: A Bolivian Tin Miner's Strike." In
    coming   Mitchell A. Seligson and John A. Booth, eds., *Political Participation in Latin America,* volume 2: *Politics and the Poor.* New York: Holmes and Meier Publishers.

GREEN, GIL
    1970   *Revolution Cuban Style: Impressions of a Recent Visit.* New York: International Publishers.

GREENBERG, EDWARD S.
    1975   "The Consequences of Worker Participation: A Clarification of the Theoretical Literature." *Social Science Quarterly* 56 (September): 191-209.

HALPER, STEFAN A., AND JOHN R. STERLING
    1972   "Introduction." In S. A. Halper and J. R. Sterling, eds., *Latin America: The Dynamics of Social Change.* New York: St. Martin's Press.

HAMILTON, ALEXANDER
    1961   *Federalist Papers No. 6.* New York: Mentor.

HAMMOND, PAUL, AND SIDNEY ALEXANDER
1972   *Political Dynamics in the Middle East.* New York: American
            Elsevier.

HANDELMAN, HOWARD
1975a   "The Political Mobilization of Urban Squatter Settlements." *Latin
            American Research Review* 10 (summer): 35-72.

1975b   *Struggle in the Andes: Peasant Political Mobilization in Peru.*
            Austin: University of Texas Press.

forth-   "Unionization, Ideology, and Political Participation within the
coming   Mexican Working Class." In Mitchell A. Seligson and John A.
            Booth, eds., *Political Participation in Latin America,* volume 2:
            Politics and the Poor. New York: Holmes and Meier Publishers.

HARKNESS, SHIRLEY, AND PATRICIA PINZÓN DE LEWIN
1975   "Women, the Vote, and the Party in the Politics of the Colombian
            National Front." *Journal of Inter-American Studies and World
            Affairs* 17 (November): 439-464.

HAUSER, ROBERT H.
1970   "Context and Consex: A Cautionary Tale." *American Journal of
            Sociology* 75 (January): 645-664.

HECLO, HUGH
1974   *Modern Social Politics in Britain and Sweden.* New Haven: Yale
            University Press.

HEISKANEN, VERONICA STOLTE
1971   "Sex Roles, Social Class and Political Consciousness." *Acta
            Sociologica* 14 (nos. 1-2): 83-95.

HENDERSON, JAMES D.
1976   "Citizen Interaction with National Government in Colombia since
            1957: The Case of Tolima." Paper presented at the Seminar on the
            Faces of Participation in Latin America: A New Look at Citizen
            Action in Society, San Antonio, Texas (November 12-13).

HINTON, WILLIAM
1973   "Reflections on China." *Monthly Review* 25 (June): 30-43.

HIRSCHMAN, ALBERT O.
1971   *A Bias for Hope: Essays on Development and Latin America.*
            New Haven: Yale University Press.

HOBSBAWM, ERIC J.
1967   "Peasants and Rural Migrants in Politics." In Claudio Veliz, ed.,
            Obstacles to Change in Latin America. London: Oxford Univer-
            sity Press.

1971   "Peru: The Peculiar Revolution." *New York Review of Books* 17
            (December 16): 29-36.

HOROWITZ, IRVING LOUIS
1965   "Carisma del partido: Un análisis comparativo de las prácticas y
            principios políticos de las naciones del Tercer Mundo." *América
            Latina* 8 (January-March): 77-100.

1972   "The Norm of Illigitimacy: Toward a General Theory of Latin
            American Political Development." In S. A. Halper and J. R.

Sterling, eds., *Latin America: The Dynamics of Social Change.*
New York: St. Martin's Press.

HORTON, DOUGLAS E.

1974   *Land Reform and Reform Enterprises in Peru.* Report submitted
to the Land Tenure Center and the International Bank for Recon-
struction and Development (June).

HOUGH, JERRY F.

1975   "The Soviet Experience and the Measurement of Power." *Journal
of Politics* 37 (August): 685-710.

1976   "Political Participation in the Soviet Union." *Soviet Studies* 28
(January): 3-20.

HUNNIUS, GERRY

1973   "Workers' Self-Management in Yugoslavia." In G. Hunnius, G.
David Garson, and John Case, eds., *Workers' Control.* New York:
Vintage.

HUNTINGTON, SAMUEL P.

1968   *Political Order in Changing Societies.* New Haven: Yale University Press.

HUNTINGTON, SAMUEL, P., AND JOAN M. NELSON

1976   *No Easy Choice: Political Participation in Developing Countries.*
Cambridge: Harvard University Press.

ILO (INTERNATIONAL LABOR ORGANIZATION)

1936   *The ILO and Social Insurance.* Geneva: International Labor
Organization.

1942   *Approaches to Social Security: An International Survey.* Montreal:
International Labor Organization.

1944   *Social Security: Principles and Problems Arising out of the War.*
Montreal: International Labor Organization.

1945   *Social Insurance.* Montreal: International Labor Organization.

1972   "Social Security in Latin America: Evolution and Perspectives."
International Social Security Review 25 (no. 4): 305-356.

1976   *Social Policy in a Changing World.* Geneva: International Labor
Organization.

INKELES, ALEX, AND DAVID H. SMITH

1974   *Becoming Modern: Individual Change in Six Developing Countries.* Cambridge: Harvard University Press.

INSTITUTE FOR THE COMPARATIVE STUDY OF POLITICAL SYSTEMS

1963   *Chile Election Factbook: September 4, 1964.* Washington: Operations and Policy Research, Inc.

INTERNATIONAL SOCIAL SECURITY REVIEW

1973   "Peru." Vol. 26 (no. 4).

1974   "Argentina." Vol. 27 (nos. 2-3).

ISUANI, ERNESTO ALDO, AND RUBÉN ALBERTO CERVINI

1975   "Análisis del voto de izquierda en Santiago de Chile: Un modelo
causal." *Latin American Research Review* 10 (fall): 103-120.

JACKMAN, ROBERT, W.
1976   "Politicians in Uniform: Military Governments and Social Change in the Third World." *American Political Science Review* 70 (December): 1078-1097.

JAGUARIBE, HELIO
1973   *Political Development: A General Theory and A Latin American Case Study.* New York: Harper and Row.

JAQUETTE, JANE S.
1971   "The Politics of Development in Peru." Ithaca, N.Y.: Ph.D. dissertation, Cornell University.

1976   "Female Political Participation in Latin America." In June Nash and Helen Icken Safa, eds., *Sex and Class in Latin America.* New York: Praeger.

JAWORSKI, HELAN
1975   "La planificación participante y la planificación de base en el Perú." *Revista Interamericana de Planificación* No. 9, 34 (June): 5-15.

JEFFERSON, THOMAS
1935   Letter to John Taylor (May 28, 1816). In Charles M. Wiltse, *The Jeffersonian Tradition in American Democracy.* Chapel Hill: The University of North Carolina Press.

JENKINS, DAVID
1973   *Job Power, Blue and White Collar Democracy.* New York: Doubleday and Co.

JOHNSON, JOHN, J.
1958   *Political Change in Latin America: The Emergence of the Middle Sectors.* Stanford: Stanford University Press.

1964   *The Military and Society in Latin America.* Stanford: Stanford University Press.

JOHNSTON, GEORGE ALEXANDER
1970   *The International Labor Organisation: Its Work for Social and Economic Progress.* London: Europa.

JOURNAL OF INTER-AMERICAN STUDIES AND WORLD AFFAIRS
1972   "Military and Reform Governments in Latin America," special issue (November), vol. 14.

JOWITT, KENNETH
1975   "Inclusion and Mobilization in European Leninist Regimes." *World Politics* 28 (October): 69-96.

JUDA, LAWRENCE
1977   "A Note on Bureaucratic Politics and Transgovernmental Relations." *International Studies Notes* 4 (summer): 1-3.

KAHL, JOSEPH A.
1968   *The Measurement of Modernism: A Study of Values in Brazil and Mexico.* Austin: University of Texas Press.

KANDELL, JONATHAN
1975   "Famed Novelist Clashes with Peru's Military Rulers." *New York Times* (February 21): 7.

KARIEL, HENRY S., ED.
    1970   *Frontiers of Democratic Theory.* New York: Random House.

KASFIR, NELSON
    1974   "Departicipation and Political Development in Black African Politics." *Studies in Comparative International Development* 9 (fall): 3-25.

KENWORTHY, ELDON
    1970   "Coalitions in the Political Development of Latin America." In Sven Groennings, et al., eds., *The Study of Coalitional Behavior: Theoretical Perspectives from Four Continents.* New York: Holt, Rinehart and Winston.

KESSELMAN, MARK
    1973   "Order or Movement? The Literature of Political Development as Ideology." *World Politics* 26 (October): 139-154.

KEY, V. O.
    1966   *The Responsible Electorate: Rationality in Presidential Voting, 1936-60.* Cambridge: Belknap Press of Harvard University Press.

KIM, JAE-ON, NORMAN H. NIE AND SIDNEY VERBA
    1974   "The Amount and Concentration of Political Participation." *Political Methodology* 1 (spring): 105–132.

KISH, LESLIE
    1967   *Survey Sampling.* New York: John Wiley.

KLIMPEL, FELICITAS ALVARADO
    1962   *La mujer chilena: El aporte feminino al progreso de Chile. 1910-1960.* Santiago: Editorial Andrés Bello.

KLING, MERLE
    1964   "The State of Research on Latin America: Political Science." In Charles Wagley, ed., *Social Science Research on Latin America.* New York: Columbia University Press.

KNIGHT, PETER T.
    1975   "New Forms of Economic Organization in Peru: Toward Workers' Self-Management." In A. Lowenthal, ed., *The Peruvian Experiment: Change Under Military Rule.* Princeton, N.J.: Princeton University Press.

KOHL, JAMES, AND JOHN LITT
    1974   *Urban Guerrilla Warfare in Latin America.* Cambridge, Massachusetts: M.I.T. Press.

KUITENBROUWER, JOOST
    1973   "The Function of Social Mobilization in the Process towards a New Society in Peru." The Hague, Netherlands: Occasional paper no. 36, Institute of Social Studies.

LAMBERT, JACQUES
    1967   *Latin America: Social Structure and Political Institutions.* Berkeley: University of California Press.

LANDSBERGER, HENRY A., AND BOBBY M. GIERISCH
    forth-   "Political and Economic Activism: Peasant Participation in the
    coming   Ejidos of the Comarca Lagunera of Mexico." In Mitchell A.

Seligson and John A. Booth, eds., *Political Participation in Latin America,* volume 2: *Politics and the Poor.* New York: Holmes and Meier Publishers.

LANDSBERGER, HENRY A., AND CYNTHIA N. HEWITT
1970   "Ten Sources of Weakness and Cleavage in Latin American Peasant Movements." In Rodolfo Stavenhagen, ed., *Agrarian Problems and Peasant Movements in Latin America.* Garden City, N.Y.: Doubleday.

LANE, ROBERT E.
1959   *Political Life.* Glencoe, Ill.: The Free Press.

LANGTON, KENNETH P., AND RONALD RAPOPORT
1976   "Religion and Leftist Mobilization in Chile." *Comparative Political Studies* 9 (October): 277-308.

LAPORTE, ROBERT, JR., AND JAMES PETRAS
1971   *Perú: Transformación revolucionaria o modernización?* Buenos Aires: Amorrortu.

LARRAÍN ACUÑA, HERNÁN
1973a   "Tendencias electorales para marzo según Eduardo Hamuy." *Mensaje* 22 (January-February): 44-46.

1973b   "Eduardo Hamuy y las elecciones de marzo." *Mensaje* 22 (March-April): 131-132.

LATIN AMERICA
1975   Report of September 12.
1976   Report of June 6.

LEAL DE ARAUJO, LUCILA
1973   "Extension of Social Security to Rural Workers in Mexico." *International Labor Review* 108 (October): 295-312.

LEOGRANDE, WILLIAM M.
1976   "Cuban Democracy in Theory and Practice since 1959: Mechanisms of Elite Accountability." Paper presented at the annual meeting of the New York State Political Science Association, Albany, New York.

LERNER, DANIEL
1958   *The Passing of Traditional Society: Modernizing the Middle East.* Glencoe, Ill.: The Free Press.

LETTS COLMENARES, RICARDO
1971   *Perú: Mito de la revolución militar.* Lima: Cuadernos de Rebelión no. 15, Frente Revolucionario de Estudiantes Socialistas.

LEWIS, OSCAR
1959   *Five Families: Mexican Case Studies in the Culture of Poverty.* New York: Basic Books.

1966   *La Vida; A Puerto Rican Family in the Culture of Poverty: San Juan and New York.* New York: Random House.

LIEUWEN, EDWIN
1961   *Arms and Politics in Latin America.* New York: Praeger.
1964   *Generals vs. Presidents: Neomilitarism in Latin America.* New York: Praeger.

LIPSET, SEYMOUR MARTIN
1963   *Political Man: The Social Bases of Politics.* Garden City, N.Y.: Anchor Books
1967   "Values, Education and Entrepreneurship." In S. M. Lipset and A. Solari, eds., *Elites in Latin America.* New York: Oxford University Press.

LIPSET, SEYMOUR MARTIN, AND STEIN ROKKAN
1967   *Party Systems and Voter Alignments, Cross-National Perspectives.* New York: The Free Press.

LIPSITZ, LEWIS
1970   "On Political Belief: The Grievances of the Poor." In Philip Green and Sanford Levinson, eds., *Power and Community.* New York: Vintage Books.

LITTLE, D. RICHARD
1976   "Mass Political Participation in the U.S. and U.S.S.R.: A Conceptual Analysis." *Comparative Political Studies* 8 (January): 437-460.

LÓPEZ MÉNDEZ, SINECIO
1974   "Hueyapán: Un pueblo de la tierra fria." In L. Huelguera, et al., *Los campesinos de la tierra de Zapata, I: Adaptación, cambio y rebelión.* México: Centro de Investigaciones Superiores, Instituto National de Antropologia e Historia.

LÓPEZ PINTOR, RAFAEL
1969   *Algunos aspectos de la participación politica en Chile.* Santiago: Instituto de Administración.

LOTT, LEO B.
1957   "The 1952 Venezuelan Elections: A Lesson for 1957." *Western Political Quarterly* 10 (September): 541-558.

LOVEMAN, BRIAN
forth-   "Political Participation and Rural Labor in Chile." In Mitchell A.
coming   Seligson and John A. Booth, eds., *Political Participation in Latin America,* volume 2: *Politics and the Poor.* New York: Holmes and Meier Publishers.

LOWENTHAL, ABRAHAM F., ED.
1975   *The Peruvian Experiment: Continuity and Change under Military Rule.* Princeton: Princeton University Press.
1976   *Armies and Politics in Latin America.* New York: Holmes and Meier Publishers.

LUBOVE, ROY
1968   *The Struggle for Social Security, 1900-1935.* Cambridge: Harvard University Press.

LUDZ, PETER CHRISTIAN
1973   "Widerspruchstheorie und entwickelte sozialistische Gesellschaft." *Deutschland Archiv* 6 (May): 506-518.

MABRY, DONALD J.
1973   *Mexico's Acción Nacional: A Catholic Alternative to Revolution.* Syracuse: Syracuse University Press.

McCLINTOCK, CYNTHIA
 1976a "Self-Management and Political Participation in Peru, 1969-1975: The Corporatist Illusion." Ph.D. dissertation, Cambridge: Massachusetts Institute of Technology.
 1976b "Socioeconomic Status and Political Participation in Peru: The Impact of Agrarian Cooperatives, 1969-1975." Paper presented to the Seminar on the Faces of Participation in Latin America: A New Look at Citizen Action in Society, San Antonio, Texas (November 12-13).

McCLOSKY, HERBERT, PAUL J. HOFFMAN AND ROSEMARY O'HARA
 1960 "Issue Conflict and Consensus among Party Leaders and Followers." *American Political Science Review* 54 (June): 406-427.

McDONALD, RONALD H.
 1971 *Party Systems and Elections in Latin America.* Chicago: Markham.
 1972a "Electoral Fraud and Regime Control in Latin America." *Western Political Quarterly* 25 (March): 81-93.
 1972b "Electoral Politics and Uruguayan Political Decay," *Inter-American Economic Affairs* 26 (spring): 25-45.
 1975 "The Rise of Military Politics in Uruguay." *Inter-American Economic Affairs* 28 (spring): 25-43.

McEWEN, WILLIAM J.
 1975 *Changing Rural Society: A Study of Communities in Bolivia.* New York: Oxford University Press.

MACEOIN, GARY
 1974 *No Peaceful Way: Chile's Struggle for Dignity.* New York: Sheed and Ward, Inc.

MALLET, ALFREDO
 1970 "Diversification or Standardization: Two Trends in Latin American Social Security." *International Labor Review* 101 (January): 49-84.

MALLOY, JAMES M.
 1970a *Bolivia: The Uncompleted Revolution.* Pittsburgh: University of Pittsburgh Press.
 1970b "El MNR boliviano: Estudio de un movimiento popular nacionalista en América Latina." *Estudios Andinos* 1 (no. 1): 57-92.
 1976 "Social Insurance Policy in Brazil: A Study in the Politics of Inequality." *Inter-American Economic Affairs* 30 (no. 3): 41-67.
 1977b "Social Security Policy and the Working Class in Twentieth Century Brazil." *Journal of Inter-American Studies and World Affairs* 19 (February): 35-60.

MALLOY, JAMES M., ED.
 1977a *Authoritarianism and Corporatism in Latin America.* Pittsburgh: University of Pittsburgh Press.

MARTZ, JOHN D.
 1964 "Dilemmas in the Study of Latin American Political Parties." *Journal of Politics* 26 (August): 509-531.

1967   "Costa Rican Electoral Trends, 1953-1966." *Western Political Quarterly* 20 (December): 888-909.

1971   "Political Science and Latin American Studies: A Discipline in Search of a Region." *Latin American Research Review* 6 (spring): 73-100.

1972   *Ecuador: Conflicting Political Culture and the Quest for Progress.* Boston: Allyn and Bacon.

MARTZ, JOHN D., AND ENRIQUE A. BALOYRA
1976   *Electoral Mobilization and Public Opinion, The Venezuelan Campaign of 1973.* Chapel Hill, N.C.: University of North Carolina Press.

MASON, WARREN L.
1973   "Cognitive Patterns among British Labor Party Regulars." *Comparative Politics* 6 (October): 147-155.

MATHIASON, JOHN R.
1972   "Patterns of Powerlessness among the Urban Poor: Toward the Use of Mass Communications for Rapid Social Change." *Studies in Comparative International Development* 7 (spring): 64-88.

MATTELART, ARMAND
1965   *Atlas social de las comunas de Chile.* Santiago de Chile: Editorial del Pacifico.

MATTELART, ARMAND, AND MICHELE MATTELART
1968   *La mujer chilena en una sociedad nueva.* Santiago: Editorial del Pacifico.

MATTELART, MICHELE
1976   "Chile: The Feminine Version of the Coup de'Etat." In June Nash and Helen Icken Safa, eds., *Sex and Class in Latin America.* New York: Praeger.

MATTHEWS, DONALD R., AND JAMES W. PROTHRO
1966   *Negroes and the New Southern Politics.* New York: Harcourt, Brace and World.

MESA-LAGO, CARMELO
1974   *Cuba in the 1970's: Pragmatism and Institutionalization.* Albuquerque: University of New Mexico Press.

1976   "Farm Payment Systems in Socialist Cuba." *Studies in Comparative Communism* 9 (autumn): 275-284.

forth-   *Social Security in Latin America: Pressure Groups, Stratifica-*
coming   *tion, and Inequality.* Pittsburgh: The University of Pittsburgh Press.

MILBRATH, LESTER W.
1965   *Political Participation: How and Why Do People Get Involved in Politics?* Chicago: Rand McNally.

MILBRATH, LESTER W., AND M. L. GOEL
1977   *Political Participation: How and Why Do People Get Involved in Politics?* (Second ed., revised). Chicago: Rand McNally.

MISHRA, RAMESH
    1973   "Welfare and Industrial Man: A Study of Welfare in Western Societies in Relation to a Hypothesis of Convergence." *Sociological Review* 21 (new series, November): 535-560.

MOORE, RICHARD J.
    1977   "Assimilation and Political Organization among the Urban Poor: The Case of Guayaquil." Austin: Ph.D. dissertation, The University of Texas at Austin.

MORENO, FRANCISCO JOSÉ, AND BARBARA MITRANI, EDS.
    1971   *Conflict and Violence in Latin American Politics.* New York: Thos. Y. Crowell.

MORRIS, DAVID J.
    1973   *We Must Make Haste—Slowly: The Process of Revolution in Chile.* New York: Random House.

MOSS, ROBERT
    1973   *Chile's Marxist Experiment.* New York: John Wiley and Sons.

MYERS, DAVID J.
    1975   "Urban Voting, Structural Cleavages and Party System Evolution, The Case of Venezuela." *Comparative Politics* 8 (October): 119-151.

NASH, JUNE
    1967   "Death as a Way of Life: The Increasing Resort to Homicide in a Maya Indian Community." *American Anthropolgist* 69 (October): 455-470.

    1976   "A Critique of Social Science Roles in Latin America." In June Nash and Helen Icken Safa, eds., *Sex and Class in Latin America.* New York: Praeger Publishers.

NEEDLER, MARTIN C.
    1968a   *Latin American Politics in Perspective.* New York: Van Nostrand Reinhold.

    1968b   *Political Development in L.A.: Instability, Violence and Evolutionary Change.* New York: Random House.

NELSON, JOAN M.
    1969   *Migrants, Urban Poverty and Instability in Developing Nations.* Cambridge: Center for International Affairs, Harvard University, Occasional Papers in International Affairs, No. 22

NIE, NORMAN H., AND KRISTI ANDERSEN
    1974   "Mass Belief Systems Revisited: Political Change and Attitude Structure." *Journal of Politics* 36 (August): 540-591.

NORTH, LIISA
    1966   *Civil-Military Relations in Argentina, Chile, and Peru.* Berkeley: Institute of International Studies, Politics of Modernization Series No. 2.

    1975   "The Peruvian Aprista Party and Haya de la Torre: Myths and Realities." *Journal of Inter-American Studies and World Affairs* 17 (May): 245-253.

NUN, JOSÉ
　1967　　"The Middle-Class Military Coup." In Claudio Veliz, ed., *The Politics of Conformity in Latin America*. New York: Oxford University Press.

NYERERE, JULIUS K.
　1968　　*Ujamaa: Essays on Socialism*. New York: Oxford University Press.

OBLER, JEFFREY, AND JURG STEINER
　1977　　*The 'Burden' of Consociationalism, A Review Essay on Austria, Belgium, The Netherlands, and Switzerland*. Beverly Hills, California: Sage Publications.

O'DONNELL, GUILLERMO
　1973　　*Modernization and Bureaucratic Authoritarianism: Studies in South American Politics*. Berkeley: Institute of International Studies.

OFICINA NACIONAL DE APOYO A LA MOVILIZACIÓN SOCIAL (ONAMS)
　1973　　"Plan de capacitación ideo-política para el personal de la ONAMS." Lima: Comisión Nacional de Capacitacion, Direccion de Capacitacion, mimeographed.

OLSON, MANCUR, JR.
　1968　　*The Logic of Collective Action: Public Goods and the Theory of Groups*. New York: Shocken Books.

PAIGE, JEFFREY M.
　1971　　"Political Orientation and Riot Participation." *American Sociological Review* 36 (October): 810-820.

PALMER, DAVID SCOTT
　1973　　*"Revolution from Above": Military Government and Popular Participation in Peru, 1968-1972*. Ithaca, New York: Cornell University Latin American Dissertation Series No. 47.

　1974a　"Authoritarian Regimes and Reform: Military Government in Peru." Paper presented at the Annual Meeting of the American Political Science Association, Chicago.

　1974b　"Social Mobilization in Peru." In Leila Radfield, ed., *Chile and Peru: Two Paths to Social Justice*. Kalamazoo, Mich.: Institute of International and Area Studies, Western Michigan University.

PALMER, DAVID SCOTT, AND KEVIN JAY MIDDLEBROOK
　1976　　"Corporatist Participation under Military Rule in Peru since 1968." In David Chaplin, ed. *Peruvian Nationalism: A Corporatist Revolution*. New Brunswick, N.J.: Transaction Books.

PALMER, DAVID SCOTT, AND JORGE RODRÍGUEZ BERUFF
　1972　　"The Peruvian Military Government: The Problems of Popular Participation." In *BULLETIN: Institute of Development Studies, Military Regimes* 4 (September): 4-15.

PARRISH, CHARLES J., AND JORGE TAPIA VIDELA
　1970　　"Welfare Policy and Administration in Chile." *Journal of Comparative Administration* 1 (February): 455-476.

PARRISH, CHARLES J., ARPAD J. VON LAZAR AND JORGE TAPIA VIDELA
  1967   The Chilean Congressional Election of March 7, 1965. Washington, D.C.: Institute for the Comparative Study of Political Systems.

PARRY, GERAINT
  1972   "The Idea of Political Participation." In Geraint Parry, ed., Participation in Politics. Manchester: Manchester University Press.

PATEMAN, CAROLE
  1970   Participation and Democratic Theory. Cambridge: Cambridge University Press.

PAYNE, JAMES L.
  1965   Labor and Politics in Peru: The System of Political Bargaining. New Haven: Yale University Press.

  1968   Patterns of Conflict in Colombia. New York: Oxford University Press.

PEASE GARCÍA, HENRY, AND OLGA VERME INSÚA
  1974   Peru: 1968-1973 Cronología política. 2 vols. Lima: DESCO, Centro de Estudios y Promocion del Desarrollo.

PEATTIE, LISA R.
  1968   The View from the Barrio. Ann Arbor: University of Michigan Press.

PEQUEÑO VALDIVIA, OSCAR, AND ABRAHAM FUDRINI SALES
  1973   "Transferencia de poder o manipulación de los sectores populares: SINAMOS: Contribucíon a su estudio." Lima: Thesis, Universidad Nacional Mayor de San Marcos.

PÉREZ-STABLE, MARIFELI
  1976   "Institutionalization and Workers' Responses." Cuban Studies/ Estudios Cubanos 6 (May): 323–341.

PERLMUTTER, AMOS
  1974   Egypt: The Praetorian State. New Brunswick, N.J.: Transaction Books.

PETRAS, JAMES
  1970   Politics and Social Forces in Chilean Development. Berkeley: University of California Press.

  1973   "The Working Class and Chilean Socialism." In Dale Johnson, ed., The Chilean Road to Socialism. Garden City: Anchor Press.

PIKE, FREDERICK, B.
  1963   "Aspects of Class Relations in Chile, 1850-1960." Hispanic American Historical Review 43 (February): 14-33.

PLAN INCA
  1974   Plan Inca: Plan del Gobierno Revolucionario. Lima, Peru.

PORTES, ALEJANDRO
  1971   "Political Primitivism, Differential Socialization and Lower-Class Leftist Radicalism." American Sociological Review 36 (October): 820-835.

1972   "Rationality in the Slum: An Essay on Interpretive Sociology."
        Comparative Studies in Society and History 14 (June): 268-286.

1973   "The Factorial Structure of Modernity: Empirical Replications and
        a Critique." *American Journal of Sociology* 79 (July): 15-43.

1974   "Modernity and Development: A Critique." *Studies in Compara-
        tive International Development* 9 (spring): 247–279.

POWELL, JOHN DUNCAN
1970   "Peasant Society and Clientelist Politics." *American Political
        Science Review* 64 (June): 411-425.

PREBISCH, RAUL
1971   *Change and Development—Latin America's Great Task.* New
        York: Praeger.

PROTHRO, JAMES W., AND PATRICIO CHAPARRO
1975   "Public Opinion and the Movement of the Chilean Government to
        the Left, 1952-1970." In Arturo Valenzuela and Samuel Valen-
        zuela, eds., *Chile: Politics and Society.* New Brunswick, N.J.:
        Transaction Books.

PROTHRO, JAMES W., AND CHARLES M. GRIGG
1960   "Fundamental Principles of Democracy: Bases of Agreement and
        Disagreement." *Journal of Politics* 22 (May): 276-294.

QUIJANO, ANÍBAL
1971   *Nationalism and Capitalism in Peru: A Study in Neo-Imperi-
        alism.* New York: Monthly Review Press.

1972   "Imperialismo y capitalismo del estado." *Sociedad y Política*
        (Lima) 1:1 (June): 5-18.

RAMOS, SAMUEL
1962   *Profile of Man and Culture in Mexico.* Austin: University of Texas
        Press.

RANIS, PETER
1968a   "Trends in Research on Latin American Politics: 1961-1967."
        Latin American Research Review 3 (summer): 71-78.

1968b   "A Two-Dimensional Typology of Latin American Political
        Parties." *Journal of Politics* 30 (August): 798-832.

1971   *Five Latin American Nations: A Comparative Political Study.*
        New York: Macmillan.

RAWLS, JOHN
1971   *A Theory of Justice.* Cambridge: Belknap Press of Harvard Uni-
        versity Press.

RAY, TALTON F.
1969   *The Politics of the Barrios of Venezuela.* Berkeley: University of
        California Press.

REPASS, DAVID E.
1971   "Issue Salience and Party Choice." *American Political Science
        Review* 65 (June): 389-400.

RICHARDSON, MILES
    1970   *San Pedro, Colombia: Small Town in a Developing Society.* New
                York: Holt, Rinehart and Winston.

RIMLINGER, GASTON
    1971   *Welfare Policy and Industrialization in Europe, America, and
                Russia.* New York: Wiley.

RISQUET, JORGE
    1963   "El PURS en las montañas de Oriente." *Cuba Socialista* 24
                (August): 115-119.

ROBERTS, BRYAN R.
    1973   *Organizing Strangers: Poor Families in Guatemala City.* Austin:
                University of Texas Press.

    1975   "Center and Periphery in the Development Process: The Case of
                Peru." *Latin American Urban Research: Urbanization and In-
                equality: The Political Economy of Urban and Rural Develop-
                ment in Latin America.* Beverly Hills: Sage Publications.

ROBINSON, JOHN P., ET AL.
    1969   *Measures of Political Attitudes.* Ann Arbor: Institute of Social
                Research.

ROCA, SANTIAGO
    1975   "The Peruvian Sugar Cooperatives: Some Fundamental Economic
                Problems, 1968-1972." Ithaca, New York: Cornell University,
                Program on Participation and Labor-Managed Systems: Self-
                Management in Peru No. 10.

RODDICK, JACQUELINE F.
    1976   "Class Structure and Class Politics in Chile." In Philip O'Brian,
                ed., *Allende's Chile.* New York: Praeger.

ROEMER, MILTON I.
    1964   "Medical Care and Social Class in Latin America." *The Milbank
                Memorial Fund Quarterly* 42 (July): 54-64.

    1973   "Development of Medical Services under Social Security in Latin
                America." *International Labor Review* 108 (July): 1-23.

ROMANUCCI-ROSS, LOLA
    1973   *Conflict, Violence and Morality in a Mexican Village.* Palo Alto:
                National Press Books.

ROSENBERG, MARK B.
    forth-   "Social Security Policy Making in Costa Rica: A Research Re-
    coming   port." *Latin American Research Review.*

ROSENBERG, MARK B., AND JAMES M. MALLOY
    1976   "Politics, Participation and Social Security in Latin America."
                Paper presented to the Seminar on the Faces of Participation in
                Latin America: A New Look at Citizen Action in Society, San
                Antonio, Texas (November 12-13).

ROSTOW, W. W.
    1962   *The Stages of Economic Growth: A Non-Communist Manifesto.*
                Cambridge: Cambridge University Press.

ROUSSEAU, JEAN JACQUES
    1962   *The Social Contract.* Excerpted in Carl Cohen, ed., *Communism, Fascism and Democracy.* New York: Random House.

RUSSELL, CHARLES A., JAMES A. MILLER AND ROBERT E. HILDNER
    1974   "The Urban Guerrilla in Latin America: A Select Bibliography." *Latin American Research Review* 9 (spring): 37-79.

RUSSETT, BRUCE M., ET AL.
    1964   *World Handbook of Political and Social Indicators.* First edition. New Haven: Yale University Press.

RUSTOW, DANKWART
    1963   "Turkey's Second Try at Democracy." *Yale Review* 52 (summer): 518-538.

RYS, VLADIMIR
    1966   "Comparative Studies of Social Security: Problems and Perspectives." *International Social Security Review* 19 (July-August): 242-268.

SALISBURY, ROBERT H.
    1975   "Research on Political Participation." *American Journal of Political Science* 19 (May): 323-341.

SANTA LUCIA, PATRICIA
    1976   "The Industrial Working Class and the Struggle for Power in Chile." In Philip O'Brian, ed., *Allende's Chile.* New York: Praeger.

SANTISTEBAN, JORGE
    1975   "Industrial Communities: Achievements and Problems." Paper presented at the Second International Conference on Self-Management. Ithaca, New York (June 6-8).

SAYEED, KHALID B.
    1967   *The Political System of Pakistan.* Boston: Houghton-Mifflin.

SCAFF, LAWRENCE A.
    1975   "Two Concepts of Political Participation." *Western Political Quarterly* 28 (September): 447-462.

SCHMIDT, STEFFEN W.
    1974   "*La Violencia* Revisited: The Clientelist Basis of Political Violence in Colombia." *Journal of Latin American Studies* 6 (May): 97-111.

SCHMITT, KARL M.
    1969   "Congressional Campaigning in Mexico: A View from the Provinces." *Journal of Inter-American Studies and World Affairs* 11 (January): 93-110.

SCHMITTER, PHILIPPE C.
    1972   "Paths to Political Development in Latin America." *Proceedings of the Academy of Political Science* 30:83-105.

SCHMITTER, PHILIPPE, ED.
    1973   *Military Rule in Latin America.* Beverly Hills, California: Sage.

SCHUESSLER, KARL
    1969   "Covariance Analysis in Sociological Research." In Edgar F. Borgatta, ed., *Sociological Methodology.* San Francisco: Jossey-Bass.

SCHUMPETER, JOSEPH A.
    1950   *Capitalism, Socialism and Democracy.* Third ed., New York: Harper and Row.

SCOTT, ROBERT
    1959   *Mexican Government in Transition.* Urbana: University of Illinois Press.

    1965   "Mexico: The Established Revolution." In Lucian Pye and Sidney Verba, eds., *Political Culture and Political Development.* Princeton: Princeton University Press.

    1967   "Political Elites and Political Modernization: The Crises of Transition." In S. M. Lipset and A. Solari, eds., *Elites in Latin America.* New York: Oxford University Press.

SELBOURNE, DAVID
    1976   "A Chorus of Sycophants." *Harpers* (June).

SELIGSON, MITCHELL A.
    1972a   "Old Wine in New Bottles: The Utility of Data Reanalysis in the Social Sciences." *Historical Methods Newsletter* 5 (June): 101-107.

    1972b   "The 'Dual Society' Thesis in Latin America: A Reexamination of the Costa Rican Case." *Social Forces* 51 (September): 91-98.

    1973   "Transactions and Community Formation: Fifteen Years of Growth and Stagnation in Central America." *Journal of Common Market Studies* 11 (March): 173-190.

    1974   "The Peasant and Agrarian Capitalism in Costa Rica." Pittsburgh: Ph.D. dissertation, University of Pittsburgh.

    1975   *Agrarian Capitalism and the Transformation of Peasant Society: Coffee in Costa Rica.* Buffalo: State University of New York Special Studies Series, No. 69.

    1977a   "Agrarian Policy in Dependent Societies: Costa Rica." *Journal of Inter-American Studies and World Affairs* 19 (May): 201-232.

    1977b   "Prestige among Peasants: A Multidimensional Analysis of Preference Data." *American Journal of Sociology* 83 (November): 632–652.

    1977c   "Trust, Efficacy and Modes of Political Participation." Paper presented to the Southwestern Political Science Meeting, Dallas, Texas (April).

    forthcoming-a   *The Demise of the Yeoman: Agrarian Capitalism and the Transformation of Costa Rica.* Madison: University of Wisconsin Press.

    forthcoming-b   "Unconventional Political Participation: Cynicism, Powerlessness, and the Latin American Peasant." In Mitchell A. Seligson and John A. Booth, eds., *Political Participation in Latin America,* volume 2: *Politics and the Poor.* New York: Holmes and Meier Publishers.

SELIGSON, MITCHELL A., AND JOHN A. BOOTH
1976   "Political Participation in Latin America: An Agenda for Research." *Latin American Research Review* 11 (fall): 95-119.

forth-   "Development, Political Participation, and the Poor in Latin
coming-a   America." In Mitchell A. Seligson and John A. Booth, eds.,
          Political Participation in Latin America, volume 2: *Politics and the
          Poor.* New York: Holmes and Meier Publishers.

forth-   "Structure and Levels of Political Participation in Costa Rica:
coming-c   Comparing Peasants to City Dwellers." In Mitchell A. Seligson and
          John A. Booth, eds., *Political Participation in Latin America,*
          volume 2: *Politics and the Poor.* New York: Holmes and Meier
          Publishers.

SELIGSON, MITCHELL A., AND JOHN A. BOOTH, EDS.
forth-   *Political Participation in Latin America,* volume 2: *Politics and the*
coming-b *Poor.* New York: Holmes and Meier Publishers.

SELIGSON, MITCHELL A., AND JOSÉ ML. SALAZAR X.
1978   "Political and Interpersonal Trust among Peasants: A Reevaluation." Paper presented to the Conference on Attitudinal and
        Behavioral Change in Rural Life. University of Nebraska,
        April 13-15.

SHARKANSKY, IRA, AND DONALD VAN METER
1975   *Policy and Politics in American Governments.* New York:
        McGraw-Hill.

SILVERT, KALMAN, AND GINO GERMANI
1961   "Politics, Social Structure and Military Intervention in Latin
        America." *European Journal of Sociology* 2:62-81.

SINAMOS
1974   "Reunión de trabajo de las unidades de capacitación del Sistema."
        Cienaguilla, Peru (August 13-17), mimeographed, no pagination.

SINDING, STEVEN
1972   "The Evolution of Chilean Voting Patterns: A Reexamination of
        Some Old Assumptions." *Journal of Politics* 34 (August): 774-
        796.

SMITH, PETER H.
1974   *Argentina and the Failure of Democracy: Conflict among Political
        Elites, 1904-1955.* Madison: University of Wisconsin Press.

SOARES, GLAUCIO A. D.
1967   "Intellectual Identity and Political Ideology among University
        Students". In S. M. Lipset and A. Solari, eds., *Elites in Latin
        America.* New York: Oxford University Press.

1969   "Desarrollo económico y estructura de clase: Nota para teoría."
        Revista Paraguaya de Sociología 6 (no. 15).

SOLARI, ALDO E.
1967   *El desarrollo social del Uruguay en la postguerra.* Montevideo:
        Editorial Alfa.

SOLARI, ALDO E., ET AL.
1966   *Uruguay en cifras.* Montevideo: Universidad de la República.

SPALDING, ROSE J.
1977   "Theories of Social Welfare Policy Development: A Case Study of
            the Mexican Social Security System." Chapel Hill: University of
            North Carolina, unpublished manuscript.

STOKES, WILLIAM S.
1952   "Violence as a Power Factor in Latin American Politics." *Western
            Political Quarterly* 5 (September): 445-469.

STONE, CARL
1975   "Political Determinants of Social Policy Allocations in Latin
            America." *Comparative Studies in Society and History* 17 (July):
            286-308.

STRICKON, ARNOLD, AND SIDNEY M. GREENFIELD, EDS.
1972   *Structure and Process in L. A.: Patronage, Clientage and Power
            Systems.* Albuquerque, University of New Mexico Press.

SUÁREZ, ANDRÉS
1972   "The Cuban Revolution: The Road to Power." *Latin American
            Research Review* 7 (fall): 5-30.

TALLET, JORGE
1969   "Understanding Latin America." *South Atlantic Quarterly* 68
            (summer): 285-294.

TANNENBAUM, FRANK
1974   "Politics and Government in Latin America." In Frank Tannen-
            baum, *The Future of Democracy in Latin America.* New York:
            Alfred A. Knopf.

TAYLOR, CHARLES L., AND MICHAEL C. HUDSON
1972   *World Handbook of Political and Social Indicators.* Second
            edition. New Haven: Yale University Press.

TAYLOR, PHILIP B., JR.
1954   "Interparty Cooperation and Uruguay's 1952 Constitution." *Wes-
            tern Political Quarterly* 7 (September): 391-400.

1960a   *Government and Politics of Uruguay.* New Orleans: Tulane
            University.

1960b   "The Mexican Elections of 1958: Affirmation of Authoritarian-
            ism?" *Western Political Quarterly* 13 (September): 722-744.

TELLER, CHARLES
1972   "Internal Migration, Socio-Economic Status and Health: Access to
            Medical Care in a Honduran City." Ithaca, New York: Ph.D. dis-
            sertation, Cornell University.

THOMAS, HUGH
1971   *Cuba: The Pursuit of Freedom.* New York: Harper and Row.

THOMPSON, DENNIS F.
1970   *The Democratic Citizen, Social Science and Democratic Theory
            in the 20th Century.* Cambridge: Cambridge University Press.

THRELFALL, MONICA
1976   "Shantytown Dwellers and People's Power." In Philip O'Brian,
            Allende's Chile. New York: Praeger.

THUCYDIDES
 1962   "The Funeral Oration of Pericles." Excerpted in Carl Cohen, ed.,
          Communism, Fascism, and Democracy. New York: Random
          House.

TINGSTEN, HERBERT
 1963   *Political Behavior: Studies in Election Statistics.* Totowa, N.J.:
          Bedminster Press.

TOURAINE, ALAIN, AND DANIEL PÉCAUT
 1970   "Working Class Consciousness and Economic Development in
          Latin America." In Irving Louis Horowitz, ed., *Masses in Latin
          America.* New York: Oxford University Press.

TOWNSEND, JAMES R.
 1969   *Political Participation in Communist China.* Berkeley and Los
          Angeles: University of California Press.

TRABAJO POPULAR UNIVERSITARIO (TPU)
 1974   "Transcrito para reunión de evaluacion del T.P.," Ancón, Peru:
          (June). Mimeographed.

TSURUTANI, TAKETSUGU
 1976   "Japan as a Postindustrial Society." In Leon Lindberg, ed., *Politics
          and the Future of Industrial Society.* New York: David McKay.

TUGWELL, FRANKLIN
 1965   "The Christian Democrats of Venezuela." *Journal of Inter-
          American Studies and World Affairs* 7 (April): 245-267.

TULLIS, F. LAMOND
 1970   *Lord and Peasant in Peru: A Paradigm of Political and Social
          Change.* Cambridge: Harvard University Press.

TULLOCK, GORDON
 1968   *Toward a Mathematics of Politics.* Ann Arbor: University of
          Michigan Press.

URBANSKI, EDMUND STEPHEN
 1966   "Tres revoluciones de Hispanoamérica: México, Bolivia y Cuba."
          Journal of Inter-American Studies and World Affairs 8 (July): 419-
          436.

UZCATEGUI, RAFAEL
 1966   *Seguro Social Obligatorio.* Caracas: Universidad Central de
          Venezuela.

VALDEZ PALLETE, LUIS
 1971   "Antecedents de la nueva orientación de las Fuerzas Armadas en
          el Perú." *Aportes* 19 (January): 163–181.

VALENZUELA, ARTURO
 1977   "Political Participation, Agriculture, and Literacy: Communal
          versus Provincial Voting Patterns in Chile." *Latin American Re-
          search Review* 12 (no. 1): 105-114.

VANGER, MILTON I.
 1969   "Politics and Class in Twentieth Century Latin America." *His-
          panic American Historical Review* 49 (February): 80-93.

VERBA, SIDNEY
1967   "Democratic Participation." In B. Gross, ed., "Social Goals and Indicators for American Society, Vol. II," *The Annals of the American Academy of Political and Social Science* 373 (September): 53-78.

VERBA, SIDNEY, AND NORMAN H. NIE
1972   *Participation in America; Political Democracy and Social Equality.* New York: Harper & Row.

VERBA, SIDNEY, NORMAN H. NIE, ANA BARBIC, GALEN IRWIN, HENK MOLLEMAN AND GOLDIE SHABAD
1973   "The Modes of Participation: Continuities in Research." *Comparative Political Studies* 6 (July): 235-250.

VERBA, SIDNEY, NORMAN H. NIE AND JAE-ON KIM
1971   *The Modes of Democratic Participation: A Cross-National Comparison.* Beverly Hills: Sage Publications.

VERBA, SIDNEY, AND GOLDIE SHABAD
1975   "Workers' Councils and Political Stratification: The Yugoslav Experience". Paper delivered at the annual meeting of the American Political Science Association, San Francisco (September).

VILLANUEVA, VICTOR
1969   *Nueva Mentalidad Militar en el Perú?* Lima: Librería-Editorial Juan Mejía Baca.
1972   *EL CAEM y la revolución de la fuerza armada.* Lima: Campodonico.

VON LAZAR, ARPAD
1971   *Latin American Politics: A Primer.* Boston: Allyn and Bacon.

VON LAZAR, ARPAD, AND ROBERT R. KAUFMAN, EDS.
1969   *Reform and Revolution: Readings in Latin American Politics.* Boston: Allyn and Bacon.

WALKER, JACK
1966   "A Critique of the Elitist Theory of Democracy." *American Political Science Review* 60 (June): 285-305.

WEBB, RICHARD, AND ADOLFO FIGUEROA
1975   *Distribución del ingreso en el Perú.* Lima: Instituto de Estudios Peruanos, Perú Problema No. 14.

WEBER, MAX
1968   *Economy and Society: An Outline of Interpretive Sociology.* G. Roth and C. Wittich, eds. New York: Bedminster.

WEINER, MYRON
1971   "Political Participation: Crisis of the Political Process." In Leonard Binder, et al., *Crises and Sequences in Political Development.* Princeton: Princeton University Press.

WEINSTEIN, MARTIN
1975   *Uruguay: The Politics of Failure.* Westport, Conn.: Greenwood Press.

WELLHOFER, E. SPENCER
  1975   "Political Party Development in Argentina: The Emergence of Socialist Party Parliamentarianism." *Journal of Inter-American Studies and World Affairs* 17 (May): 153-174.

WERTHEIMER, ALAN
  1975   "In Defense of Compulsory Voting." In J. Roland Pennock and John W. Chapman, eds., *Participation in Politics.* New York: Lieber-Atherton.

WILKIE, JAMES W.
  1970   *The Mexican Revolution: Federal Expenditure and Social Change since 1910.* Berkeley: University of California Press.

  1974   *Statistics and National Policy.* Los Angeles: UCLA Latin American Center.

WILLEMS, EMILIO
  1975   *Latin American Culture: An Anthropological Synthesis.* New York: Harper and Row.

WILLIAMS, EDWARD J.
  1967   *Latin American Christian Democratic Parties.* Knoxville, Tenn.: University of Tennessee Press.

  1973   "Secularization, Integration and Rationalization: Some Perspectives from Latin American Thought." *Journal of Latin American Studies* 5 (November): 199-216.

WISEMAN, VICTOR
  1969   *Politics: The Master Science.* New York: Pegasus.

WOLFE, MARSHALL
  1968   "Social Security and Development: The Latin American Experience." In Everett Hassalow, ed., *The Role of Social Security in Economic Development.* Washington: Government Printing Office.

WOODWARD, JULIAN, AND ELMO ROPER
  1950   "Political Activity of American Citizens." *American Political Science Review* 44 (December): 872-885.

YGLESIAS, JOSÉ
  1969   *In the Fist of the Revolution: Life in a Cuban Country Town.* New York: Vintage Books.

YOUSSEF, NADIA
  1973   "Cultural Ideals, Feminine Behavior and Family Control." *Comparative Studies in Society and History* 15 (June): 326-347.

ZEITLIN, MAURICE
  1970   *Revolutionary Politics and the Cuban Working Class.* New York: Harper and Row.

ZEITLIN, MAURICE, AND JAMES PETRAS
  1970   "The Working Class Vote in Chile: Christian Democracy versus Marxism." *British Journal of Sociology* 21 (March): 16-29.

ZIMBALIST, ANDREW
  1975   "The Development of Workers' Participation in Socialist Cuba." Paper prepared for presentation at the 2nd annual Conference on Workers' Self-Management, Ithaca, N.Y.: Cornell University.

ZIMBALIST, ANDREW, AND BARBARA STALLINGS
    1974   "Showdown in Chile." In Paul Sweezy and Harry Magdoff, eds., *Revolution and Counter-Revolution in Chile.* New York: Monthly Review Press.

ZOLBERG, ARISTIDE
    1968   "Military Intervention in the New States of Tropical Africa: Elements of Comparative Analysis." In Henry Bienen, ed., *The Military Intervenes.* New York: The Russell Sage Foundation.

ZUKIN, SHARON
    1975   *Beyond Marx and Tito: Theory and Practice in Yugoslav Socialism.* Cambridge: Cambridge University Press.

Notes on Contributors

ENRIQUE A. BALOYRA is associate professor of political science at the University of North Carolina at Chapel Hill. He has recently published *Electoral Mobilization and Public Opinion: The Venezuelan Campaign of 1973* with John D. Martz. He is author of a number of articles on Latin American politics and is completing a second book on Venezuela.

THOMAS A. BAYLIS is associate professor of political science at The University of Texas at San Antonio. He is the author of *The Technical Intelligentsia and the East German Elite* and of several articles dealing with participation in Eastern Europe.

ROBERT E. BILES is assistant professor of political science at Sam Houston State University. He has written numerous articles on political attitudes and participation in Uruguay.

JOHN A. BOOTH is assistant professor of political science at The University of Texas at San Antonio. He has published articles and monographs on community development in Costa Rica and on political participation in Latin America. With Mitchell A. Seligson he co-organized the recent Seminar on the Faces of Participation in Latin America: A New Look at Citizen Action in Society, and is co-editor of *Political Participation in Latin America,* volume 2: *Politics and the Poor* (forthcoming).

HENRY A. DIETZ is assistant professor of government at The University of Texas at Austin. He has published articles on and has just finished a forthcoming book on Peruvian politics and the urban poor of Lima.

WILLIAM M. LEOGRANDE is assistant professor of government at Hamilton College. He is the author of several articles and papers on Cuban politics. His current research focuses on comparative political elites and civil-military relations in communist political systems.

JAMES M. MALLOY is professor of political science at the University of Pittsburgh. He is the author of *Bolivia: The Uncompleted Revolution,* co-editor of *Beyond the Revolution: Bolivia Since 1952,* editor of *Authoritarianism and Corporatism in Latin America,* and is currently completing a book on social security policy in Brazil.

JOHN D. MARTZ is professor of political science at the University of North Carolina at Chapel Hill and Editor of the *Latin American Research Review.* He is author of many articles and several books, the most recent of which is *Electoral Mobilization and Public Opinion: The Venezuelan Campaign of 1973,* written with Enrique Baloyra.

STEVEN M. NEUSE is assistant professor of political science at The University of Texas at El Paso. He has published articles on state employees and public responsibility norms, and on women in the public service. His research focuses on professionalization in the public sector and international intergovernmental organizations.

DAVID SCOTT PALMER is chairman of Latin American Studies at the Foreign Service Institute and professorial lecturer at the School of Advanced International Studies, The Johns Hopkins University. He has published numerous articles on Peruvian politics.

MARK B. ROSENBERG is assistant professor of political science at Florida International University. His present research and publications concern social security policy and systems in Costa Rica and Latin America in general.

LAWRENCE A. SCAFF, associate professor of political science, University of Arizona, has published articles on political theory in several journals. In addition to the theory of participation, his current research interests include the philosophy of social science and Max Weber's political thought.

MITCHELL A. SELIGSON, assistant professor of political science at the University of Arizona, has published several articles on Costa Rican peasants, and is the author of *The Demise of the Yeoman: Agrarian Capitalism and the Transformation of Costa Rica.* With John A. Booth he co-organized the Seminar on the Faces of Participation in Latin America: A New Look at Citizen Action in Society, and is co-editor of *Political Participation in Latin America,* volume 2: *Politics and the Poor* (forthcoming).

EDWARD J. WILLIAMS is professor of political science at the University of Arizona. His work has appeared in numerous professional journals and he is author of *Latin American Christian Democratic Parties, The Political Themes of Inter-American Relations,* and *Latin American Politics: A Developmental Approach.* He is presently engaged in research on Mexican-United States relations.

SANDRA L. WOY is a Ph.D. candidate at the University of Virginia. Formerly acting assistant professor of political science at California State College at Bakersfield, she is now associated with the University of North Dakota, where she continues her research on social mobilization in post-1968 Peru.

Index

Index